gryphon house inc.

July 7, 2000

Ellen Gannett
Assoc. Director
Nat.'l Inst. On Out-of-School Time
Wellesley College
Wellesley, MA 02124

Dear Ms. Gannett,

We've been publishing books that promote early childhood education
for over 25 years – but this season something very special happened.
We've published a unique book by Nancy P. Alexander, **Early
Childhood Workshops That Work!** – a groundbreaking,
comprehensive guide that illustrates how to design, organize, conduct
and evaluate early childhood workshops and training seminars. It
gives me great pleasure to share this incredible resource with you. As
a recognized expert in the field, I know you'll find it of interest.

At Gryphon House we are very excited about **Early Childhood
Workshops That Work!** As we all know, an effective early
childhood workshop or in-service training session doesn't just happen.
Good training results from the instructor's skill, knowledge, and
ability to plan a session based on what participants need and want.
Nobody is better at capturing the art of workshops than Nancy
Alexander. She is Executive Director of Northwestern State
University's Child and Family Network, and President of the
American Society for Training and Development (ASTD).

Your copy of the book is enclosed with my compliments. I would love
to hear your thoughts on the book when you have a free moment. As
an authority in the field, I really value your input. Please feel free to
email me at leah@ghbooks.com or call me at your convenience at 800-
638-0928. I'd love to know what you think of **Early Childhood
Workshops That Work!**

Thanks in advance for your time.

Sincerely,

Leah Curry-Rood
Vice President

P.O. Box 207
Beltsville, MD 20704-0207 USA

10726 Tucker Street
Beltsville, MD 20705 USA
(301) 595-9500
FAX (301) 595-0051
800-638-0928

E-mail: info@ghbooks.com
http://www.ghbooks.com

Early Childhood Workshops That Work!

EARLY CHILDHOOD

Workshops
that Work!

The Essential
Guide to
Successful
Training and
Workshops

Nancy P. Alexander

Ilustrations by Katheryn Davis
Photographs by Nancy P. Alexander

gryphon house
Beltsville, Maryland

Acknowledgments

Throughout my career, there have been numerous individuals who have inspired me, motivated me, and challenged me—many from whom I have learned and from whom I continue to learn. Just as I have benefited from the experience and expertise of others, I hope that many will benefit from my work and effort in completing this book.

As I made a career transition from focusing on how children grow and learn to how adults learn about children, I became increasingly aware of the many similar, yet significant differences in teaching adults and children. Relationships and interactions, appropriate environments, using all the senses, and learning by doing, are all just as important for adults as they are for children. A major difference, however, is that adults have many life experiences to build upon and to share. This book is based on those insights and premises.

As the idea for a book about training adults to work with children grew, the challenge became one of choices—what to include of the thousands of possibilities, and what should be omitted. My effort focused on having a significant amount of information that is useful to everyone—from ideas to activities to the logistics of training to the pitfalls to avoid. With the help and support of many, I think anyone who conducts training can find new ideas and useful information herein.

At the conclusion of any large project, there are always many persons to thank, and this book is certainly no exception. There are some special people who must be acknowledged and thanked for their help—especially my husband, Charles, who tolerated my late night and early morning immersion in the project for months, Dr. Janie Humphries and Bryan Sullivan who thoroughly read the draft manuscript and offered many suggestions. Thanks, too, to all the other trainers from whom I have learned and to my students who make all the effort worthwhile.

During the time this book was being written, my formerly independent nonprofit program became a part of Northwestern State University, opening opportunities for strengthening and expanding the training we offer. My thanks to all those responsible for sharing the vision of what can be accomplished for young children by linking informal and noncredit early childhood training into the university system. Dr. Austin Temple, Pat Pierson, and Cheryl McBride were instrumental in making the link happen and in providing on-going support and encouragement.

Training is one of the ways we pass on our skills and knowledge of what works with young children and what they need. I hope that this book will be helpful in improving the capabilities of those who care for and about our most important resources—our children.

© Copyright 2000, Nancy P. Alexander

Published by Gryphon House, Inc.
10726 Tucker Street, Beltsville, MD 20705

World Wide Web; www.gryphonhouse.com

Text Illustration: Katheryn Davis

Library of Congress Cataloging-in-Publication Data

Alexander, Nancy, 1941-
    Early childhood workshops that work! : our threaten planet / Nancy Alexander ; illustrations by Katheryn Davis,
p.cm.
    Includes bibliographical references (p.) and index.
    ISBN 0-87659-215-9
    1. Teachers' workshops--Planning. 2. Teachers--In-service training. 3, Early childhood education--Activity programs. I. Title.

LB1743 .A44 2000
372'.071'55--dc21   00-035367

CHAPTER 1
DESIGNING TRAINING 11

Chapter 2

Activities for Individuals, Partners, Small Groups and Whole Groups 33

Chapter 3

Demonstrations, Learning Games, and Other Learning Experiences 71

Chapter 4
Making and Using Effective
Workshop Materials 141

CHAPTER 5
COMPONENTS OF EFFECTIVE TRAINING....181

CHAPTER 6
TROUBLE SHOOTING 207

Designing Training

Workshop and Training Design

An effective workshop or training session does not just happen. Good training results from the instructor's skill, knowledge, and ability to plan based on what participants need and want. At its basic level, training design requires finding out what participants need and want, selecting or creating activities that will help them learn what they need to know, and arranging the training. How do you design and conduct effective training?

Conducting Needs Assessments

The first step in training design is to determine the goals for the training event through a needs assessment. A needs assessment can take many forms. It may be as simple as a conversation with a director about the purpose of the training. It may be as detailed as a thorough analysis of the skills required for a specific job. However the needs assessment is conducted, for training to be effective, it must be designed around the expectations and needs of supervisors and trainees. Both stakeholders must be involved at this level and be committed to change.

Ideas for conducting needs assessments:

- Use questionnaires, interviews, or telephone surveys.
- Establish a representative committee to determine training goals.
- Hold focus groups or brainstorming sessions.
- Use an assessment tool such as a rating scale or classroom observation form.
- Evaluate requests for help or document problems.
- Use an outside consultant to suggest areas needing improvement.

Those who have a say in the training program are more likely to benefit from it and to implement changes in the workplace. Those who have training done "to" them will often be resistant to change. On page 261 in the Appendix is a sample questionnaire for a needs assessment. The same form could be the basis of an interview or a starting point for developing a guide for focus groups or brainstorming sessions.

Guidelines for Questionnaires

To receive maximum response from a questionnaire, use these guidelines:

1. Keep it short enough that it can be completed quickly.
2. Make the layout attractive.
3. Use the format to aid understanding.
4. Be sure the language is clear and easy to understand.
5. Include the purpose for gathering the information and what will be done with it.
6. Include a deadline and instructions on what to do with the questionnaire when completed.
7. Test the questionnaire with several people before distributing it widely to determine areas that may be unclear.

Analyzing Training Needs

Find out why the training is required and what needs to be changed. What is not being done or should be done differently? What problems have occurred or what new skills are needed? What do the trainees recognize as needs, and what do supervisors see as needs? Identify the new or changed behaviors that are desired based on the information you have gathered. The more specific you can be, the better you will be able to target needs and to support improvement.

Setting Realistic Goals

A common mistake in training design, especially in one-shot workshops, is to try to accomplish too much in too short a time. Doing so sets one up for failure. Select the most important skills that trainees need to acquire or the most urgent information they need to learn, and focus on those. Trying to cover too much content is the downfall of many training events.

Trainees want to incorporate changes a little at a time. They need time to implement new strategies and get feedback to feel a sense of mastery before going on to the next step. Cover a complex task in several training sessions rather than trying to put too much new information into a single session.

Writing Learning Objectives

Once you determine goals, the next step is to write learning objectives for a session. Objectives must be specific, measurable, and stated in outcome form. For example, "demonstrate how to ..." or "name four reasons for..." are good, measurable objectives. An easy test is to see if each objective is something that the participants can do before they leave the session. If they cannot, then the objectives may be unrealistic.

Written objectives have many benefits. They help trainers focus on outcomes and guide the trainer in selecting appropriate activities to develop the needed skills and concepts. Written objectives also help learners have a clear understanding of what they will be able to do at the completion of the training.

Writing good objectives takes experience and practice. Here are some examples of realistic and appropriate objectives for a three-hour workshop on working with parents.

At the conclusion of the training, the learner will be able to:

1. List and describe at least four ways to communicate with parents.
2. Demonstrate how to greet both parents and children when they arrive.
3. Explain in his or her own words the importance of working with parents.
4. Write a one-paragraph summary of classroom activities for a parent newsletter.

An objective describes what the leaner will do to demonstrate achievement and mastery. Generally, an objective must be something that can be seen or heard. The box at the right shows some comparisons of words that are appropriate and inappropriate to use in writing training objectives.

An objective tells what the learner will be able to do at the end of the training. It does not address what the instructor will do. An objective describes the behavior or performance of the learners, not what the learner is expected to know, think, feel, or understand. If one begins an objective with a general statement such as, "The learner will understand the importance of play," explain what "understanding" means. Tell how the learner will demonstrate understanding. Perhaps you expect learners to answer questions, to solve problems, to describe, to explain, or to demonstrate a procedure. Whatever you mean by understanding should be defined and described following a general statement.

An objective is about the end rather than the means, and describes a product rather than a process. It talks about learner performance rather than course content. It describes the conditions under which the learner will be performing the behavior. Do you expect the learner to perform with or without assistance? For example, an infant caregiver may be expected to follow procedures for diaper changing with a chart for reference, or without the chart.

Appropriate	Inappropriate
Calculate	Recall
Prepare	Remember
Choose	Understand
Construct	Realize
Complete	Conclude
Name	Recognize
Describe	Grasp
Demonstrate	Value
Explain	Appreciate
List	Believe
Operate	Be familiar with
Define	Consider
Produce	Accept
Make	Be aware of
Select	Comprehend
Apply	Know
Write	Recollect
Classify	Conclude

An instructional objective often includes information about the level of performance that will be considered acceptable. If a learner should be able to perform a task within five minutes or without errors, indicate these expectations. Usually, the decision about acceptable performance is arbitrary. The experience and knowledge of the instructor are important in determining satisfactory performance.

Be SMART

SMART is a good way to remember the criteria for writing objectives. Objectives for training should be:

S pecific
M easurable
A ttainable
R elevant
T rackable

Answering "What's in It for Me?"

For trainees to fully commit to training and be motivated to change, they must see a purpose in the training. Trainers frequently call this the "What's in it for me?" need. Look at a session from the participants' viewpoint. If they do not see some immediate benefit to what they will learn, they may not put forth the effort to change what they do. As a result, you may teach, but they may not learn. Long-term goals such as getting a promotion will motivate some, but most will work best if they see that changing the way they are working will make their jobs easier or more satisfying. Plan activities to demonstrate the value of improving and changing to help trainees see that it is to their advantage to learn new procedures and skills.

Include activities in the plan that trainees can implement right away to help them recognize the value of training. Include ways to help them overcome barriers. Help them see that change is possible, and that they can influence what happens at their work site. The more they see that they can be successful, the more they will be motivated to venture into other changes.

Help them see that their job is easier when they provide a good program. Connect activities to happier children and parents when possible. Show discipline issues such as how a well-arranged classroom reduces discipline problems, or how preparing and planning keeps children interested and involved rather than misbehaving.

Consider trainees' self-concepts, and help them appreciate and value the positive feelings from doing a good job. Use activities that support feelings of success. Encourage systems of recognition and reward for their efforts. Emphasize the professionalism and respect that comes from knowledge and skills.

Planning

Careful planning is essential for training to have the desired results. Although a good trainer may seem natural and appear to operate spontaneously with a group, her easy manner is the result of careful planning and experience. She plans everything from objectives and activities to questions and review techniques. A good trainer decides ahead of time how she will move participants from activity to activity. She will plan how to pair up partners and divide into small groups. She will decide how to ensure that the session stays on schedule, and she will evaluate the effectiveness of the training throughout the workshop and afterward. A good trainer will have several additional activities should she have extra time. She is prepared to shorten the time allowed for an activity if necessary. She will be so familiar with her materials that she can maintain eye contact and be responsive to participants. Here are some considerations for planning effective training:

Components of Quality Planning

Preparation

Preparation means having well-thought-out activities and materials that are relevant to participants' needs. A good training event will appear to flow—with the facilitator moving the group through activities in a smooth, seemingly effortless manner. Preparation means that the trainer:

- Assessed the needs of the participants.
- Identified activities and experiences to address those needs.
- Planned a variety of activities that allow for interaction, movement, hands-on experiences, and review.
- Is very familiar with the activities and materials.
- Has more activities than she expects to use.
- Has a plan for adapting activities if necessary.
- Checked the room arrangement and the housekeeping details.
- Checked all audiovisual equipment to ensure that it operates properly before the session.
- Has enough handouts and supplies for the number of participants.
- Planned a means of evaluating learning.
- Is relaxed and ready to greet participants.

Relevance

Effective training is relevant to the particular needs of trainees. Trainees often come to a training situation with questions that they need answered or they seek specific information. Consequently, trainees must see the activities as something useful to them now or in the near future. How does the trainer ensure that training is relevant? Needs assessment and surveys are a good beginning. Asking at the start of a session what participants want to learn will provide additional on-the-spot information. If the trainer is very experienced and able to adapt quickly to expressed needs, she can further individualize training even as it is under way. Plan some open-ended experiences to allow trainees to participate in activities and relate them to their work situation. Give trainees actual case situations to discuss to help make the training relevant to each individual's needs. Use realistic examples as a basis for activities to make it more likely that trainees will recognize and appreciate the relevance.

Adaptability

Adaptability means that the trainer has considered several ways to conduct the activities she has planned. For example, an activity may be intended for small groups but can be quickly adapted to become a partner or whole-group activity. Changing an activity to another format is a useful adaptation when the room is too small to move around in or the chairs are fixed in place. The trainer who finds a group not understanding or responding to a particular activity must quickly revise the instructions or substitute another experience. If time is cut short because someone else went overtime, shorten an activity or omit it all together.

Individualized

In any group training setting, there will be individuals with diverse needs. Some individuals will need more repetition than others. Most groups will include a variety of learning styles and personalities. Some people in a session may be beginners and some may be veterans with much experience. Individualizing to meet these different needs is a challenge for even a highly skilled trainer. One effective way to individualize is to offer choices. Allow participants to select a topic or an issue to explore. Offer several possibilities and let them select according to their job responsibilities and needs. Plan for a variety of topics that small groups may address. Offering choices gives the trainees some control over their learning and helps them feel that their needs are recognized and valued. Other ways to individualize are:

- Plan some activities that each individual does alone.
- Plan open-ended activities.
- Offer options based on the ages of the children with whom trainees work.
- Suggest possibilities for completing tasks based on job responsibilities.
- Plan time for independent exploration of chosen topics.
- Offer choices for small group activities or projects.
- Suggest a variety of ways to complete assignments.
- Plan follow-up activities for trainees to use resources available at their work site.

Guidelines for Planning

While there are many approaches to planning, some important common factors include involving the various learning styles, having a balance of types of activities, and offering a variety of activities to hold interest.

Involving All Learning Styles

Individuals will prefer learning in different ways. They may learn easiest when information is presented in particular ways. Some will want to see what you are talking about, and some will prefer hearing information. Ensuring that you include opportunities for each participant's learning style is essential to effective training. Here are some ways to meet the needs of learners who prefer one learning style over the others:

Visual Learners—Show them what you mean and give them something to look at as much as possible. Use posters, slides, overhead transparencies, props, and other visual materials to help trainees focus their attention. Use videos to help them see exactly what is meant and how to perform. Visual learners will want their information in writing for reference and as handouts to take with them.

Auditory Learners—Some adults learn primarily through auditory channels. They will need to hear the instructor and others discuss ideas and situations. Include opportunities for them to listen and to summarize what others have to say. These folks will like the small group reports, and they will want to have charts, forms, and procedures explained to them. Do not just give them information to read—they will want you to discuss and review printed material.

Kinesthetic Learners—Many adults need hands-on activities and will want opportunities to actually do what they want to learn. These learners will benefit greatly from supervised practice. Guidance and coaching while doing the tasks will help them feel successful and competent. Kinesthetic learners will like role play, games, and learning stations. They will want to actually do art, music, and science activities, not just hear about the activities or see examples of completed products.

Providing Balance

Plan a balance of whole group, small group, partner, and individual activities. Sitting in a large group for long periods will be tiring for many. Individual activities allow for those who may not wish to participate in groups. Participants need a combination of serious and light activities, known and unknown material to keep their attention and maintain involvement. Participants will want familiarity and novelty. They will want time to work alone and time to work with others, time to work with old friends and meet new people. Balance helps keep participants from feeling frustrated with interactions or information that makes them uncomfortable.

Varying activities between the whole group, small groups, partners, and individuals helps hold interest. The very act of moving around to form small groups or partners helps maintain participants' attention. Changing the types of activities will facilitate interactions with a variety of people in the room and the sharing of ideas. The change will create a sense of "something new" that rekindles interest in the training topic.

Including Variety

Include a variety of activities to keep participants attentive and alert. A trainer will need to present a skill or cover information several times. Approaching the concept or skill in a different way each time will help keep the repetition interesting. Covering material in a variety of ways allows for review without monotony. Variety helps you provide for participants with different learning styles. It helps keep participants from feeling like "I've heard all this before" and "it's just the same old thing."

Outlining Training Content

Creating an outline of the content for training is a good way to begin to organize material once you determine the objectives. Outlines help the trainer to identify, select, organize, and sequence content to aid understanding. An outline can serve as a reference for the trainer while conducting training.

To outline training content, identify these entities for each objective and activity:

1. **Actions**—What the learner will do to meet the objectives. List the actions that the learner will take to accomplish this objective.
2. **Knowledge**—What the learner needs to know to do this activity. Identify the information the learner must know to be able to take the action.
3. **Sequence**—The order in which the content is to be presented. Sequence the knowledge and the actions in the order they will logically occur in the training. Consider that the knowledge will often need to precede actions. One must first know and understand certain information before taking action related to that information.

Sequence of Content

Sometimes the order in which one presents information will not matter. However, many times new skills and information will be learned more readily if the presentation of information and skills follows a particular sequence. Here are suggestions for ordering the content of your session:

Simple to Complex

When presenting information that is new, help trainees feel successful by starting with easy steps or concepts before moving into more complicated skills or ideas. Following a progression from easy to more difficult helps you lead the participants into complex tasks without overwhelming them.

Familiar to Unfamiliar

When participants have some experience or prior training, a quick review of what they know will help tie the new skills they must learn to what they already know. By presenting information early that they recognize, you will help trainees feel successful and capable. Trainees want a balance of things they know along with opportunities to learn the unknown. When learners feel secure by recognizing they already have certain knowledge and skills, they will be more confident in the training situation, hence more willing to tackle new challenges.

Chronological Order

Cover content or skills in the order they will be used, particularly when the new skills include steps in a procedure. Plan in terms of first, second, next, and last. Chronological order is a logical way to present such skills as emergency evacuation, proper diapering, or procedures for Cardiopulmonary Resuscitation.

Relative Importance

When there is much new information or when a session is long, put the most important part first. Putting the most important part first allows the trainer to spend the necessary time on the main issues without fear of running over the allotted time. Also, trainees are sometimes more alert in the mornings or at the beginning of a session than they are toward the end. When you put the most important information first, do not forget to allow time for a review before the session ends.

Logical Grouping

Sometimes the training content will be more effectively presented when similar or related tasks or ideas are grouped together. For example, ways to interact with children during mealtime may relate to serving food or to talking to children. Therefore, the information could be included in a small group activity on supervising mealtime or on ways to support language development. Decide the logical relationship that works for the content.

Planning Aids

Use planning aids to help you get into the habit of logical, systematic training design. Here are several suggestions of ways to approach planning. Select or devise a system that works for you.

Be SMART

A good way to remember some of the components of training design is SMART. Remembering the word SMART can help you design training as well as objectives.

Be **S M A R T** about training.
S elect the curriculum and activities
M atch them to the trainees
A dapt to better meet trainees' needs
R elevant—make the activities relevant to individuals
T est for mastery

ORGANIZING LEARNING EXPERIENCES

Here is another way to structure learning activities:

Component	Purpose
Introduction	Gain the learners' attention. Provide an overview of the goals, objectives, and plans for the session. Review previously learned material.
Directions	Tell the learner how to do the activity. Describe any guidelines or requirements needed to complete the activity. Answer questions and clarify instructions.
Activity	Have the learners engage in the learning experience. Actively involve trainees. Include using several senses. Assess strengths and needs of the learners.
Practice and Feedback	Have the learners practice the skill, use the knowledge, or display the desired behaviors under supervision. Improve performance with coaching support. Demonstrate mastery.
Retention and Transfer	Have the learner plan for implementation. Overcome barriers to using the newly acquired skills and knowledge on the job. Reinforce learning. May include follow-up experiences.

HOW LONG?

Here is a guide to provide an idea of how much time to allow for each part of a workshop or training session. The example below is for three-hour sessions, but could be easily adapted to longer or shorter sessions.

SAMPLE WORKSHOP FORMAT

5-10 minutes	Welcome, overview, icebreaker
5-10 minutes	Opening activity, attention grabber, motivator
10-15 minutes	Content presentation
15-20 minutes	Activity, performing tasks, supervised practice
5-10 minutes	Summary and review
10-15 minutes	Break

10-15 minutes	Content presentation
15-20 minutes	Activity, performing tasks, supervised practice
5-10 minutes	Summary and review
10-15 minutes	Break (may include an activity, viewing displays, or resources)
10-15 minutes	Content presentation
15-20 minutes	Activity, performing task, supervised practice
5-10 minutes	Summary and review
5-10 minutes	Assignments, evaluation, next step

Checklist for Training Plan

Whichever system you use to organize your training, some common components are essential for training success. Here is a checklist to evaluate your training plan for completeness. Review any training plan you expect to use, asking yourself if the plan includes:

- Comments or activities to introduce the topic
- A motivational activity to help participants see the need for the new skills or information
- A way for learners to share what they know
- An overview of the training, including the objectives and their importance
- A schedule or timeline for activities
- A "tell" and "show" for the training content
- Specific questions related to the objectives
- An exercise or experience for hands-on involvement
- A summary of the key points
- References and resources for participants to get more information
- A transition to support implementation at the work site
- Plans for follow-up activities

Planning for Learning Transfer

Training experiences can be entertaining and a great hit with participants, but unless there is improvement on the job, it is all for naught. Always include activities and materials that assist with performance at the work site. Conducting a music workshop has little impact unless participants know the tunes or have access to them once they return to their work responsibilities. Post-training activities, self-assessments, and discussions that focus on how to implement new skills help trainees to carry skills over from the classroom to the job. Involving supervisors and co-workers is another key to ensuring that expectations are met. Follow-up activities such as refresher training and support group meetings help, too. More detailed information and suggested experiences for addressing transfer of learning is in Chapter Six: Troubleshooting, page 207.

Planning for Involvement

Involvement can take many forms. Small group assignments, finding a solution to a problem, and teaching a portion of the material to others are some of the ways to involve trainees. Locating information in guides or manuals, self-assessment forms and tests, handouts that require responses, and listing information learned are more ways to involve participants. Involvement means that learners will be doing something related to the content of the session, talking about something related to the goals of the training, or working on something related to the objectives. Without involvement, training will be much less effective if it has any effect at all. Numerous activities for active participation in learning are in Chapter Two: Activities for Individuals, Partners, Small Groups, and Whole Groups on page 33.

Planning for Movement

It is easy to become caught up in covering the content when you know how much trainees need to learn. Some trainers feel as if they want to condense a complete college course into a one-day workshop. However, trainees need to thoroughly master a few main ideas rather than to be exposed to hundreds that they will not remember or use. When caught up in the too-much-to-cover cycle, trainers may overlook the importance of movement and fall back on passive experiences. Why is movement important enough that plans must provide for it?

Mental involvement is often dependent on physical involvement. It is difficult for trainees to concentrate on learning if they are not engaged in using the information. When trainees sit for long periods, they will be more vulnerable to becoming mentally caught up in personal responsibilities and concerns. Moving around gives trainees an opportunity to interact with a variety of people and serves to stimulate renewed interest. Here are some other reasons to plan for movement:

Regroup Participants—Splitting up into small groups or partners requires movement and provides a break in the activity. A secondary benefit to dividing is that it allows you to separate trainees who may be distracting others with side conversations. Separating into groups or finding partners lets you put persons with those they may not know. Mixing up the partners or groups will stimulate the sharing of new ideas because persons often sit with co-workers with whom they came. Sometimes an individual may attend with colleagues with stronger personalities or with supervisors, and the situation may be intimidating. Dividing into small groups is a good way to get individuals separated and more involved.

Adapt to Short Attention Span—The very act of moving around helps participants refocus their attention. Movement may take a few minutes, but it pays off in closer attention afterward. Just getting up and moving around reduces fatigue and refreshes participants.

Stimulate Interest—Moving helps stimulate interest and a sense of expectation about what is going to happen next. Knowing that a change is about to happen helps learners anticipate new opportunities for learning.

ACTIVITIES

In addition to dividing into groups or changing partners, providing a quick break during times that participants must sit for a lengthy time is desirable. Here are some instant energizers to insert in whole group activities when you see fatigue setting in:

Air Writing—When participants need a quick energizer, have them "write" in the air with one arm using very wide motions. Then have them "write" with their other arm. Have them stand on one of their legs (caution them to hold on to their chair) and "write." Air writing is a good, quick break to insert when participants have been sitting a long time or have the after-lunch doldrums. They can write their name, a new term or process they are learning, or the name of a new friend they have made during the session.

Aerobics or Marching in Place—Some hopping and marching in place can relieve fatigue when participants have been sitting awhile. Keep a cassette tape or compact disc of active march music on hand for a quick pick-up.

Stretching in Place—Guide participants in some stretching exercises. Have them stand up at their seats and follow your directions for an easy, instant energizer. Try reaching for the ceiling, reaching up and leaning to the right, then left. Have them push their arms straight down without bending. You also might add some "tense and relax" movements.

Simon Says—Play a quick game of "Simon Says." Perform a movement yourself, stating the movement as you do it. Unless you say "Simon Says" before you describe the movement, participants should not do it. Work fast to make it more difficult and to add humor. The sillier the movement, the more fun the group will have.

Action Rhymes—Perform an action rhyme that participants can do with children. You not only get a quick change-of-pace break, but participants learn a new activity to do in their classroom.

Experience Counts!—Have everyone stand. Ask those who have one-year or less of experience in the field to sit. Then ask those with three or fewer years of experience to sit. Ask those who have five or fewer years to sit. Proceed to seven, then ten, continuing until the number left standing is about ten to twenty percent of the group. Call attention to those who remain standing as potential mentors from whom others can learn. Recognize the standing participants' experience and their knowledge. This activity not only provides an opportunity to move, but gives recognition to the veterans in the group and acknowledges their contributions to the field.

Popcorn—Have everyone pretend to be popcorn and "pop" in place. Play lively music. Start and stop the music several times to add interest.

Making Arrangements for Training

Preparation for training includes not only designing the content and activities, but making the logistic arrangements as well. Arranging training essentially involves three areas:

1. Selecting the topic, planning the agenda, activities, and content
2. Arranging the place—date, time, location
3. Publicizing and registering participants

Because the first two components are considered at length in other sections, this section will address publicizing the training. One of the most common means of informing possible participants of upcoming training is direct mail to programs. One-or two-page flyers are more likely to catch the attention of the director and to be read than a lengthy form letter will be.

Flyers

When designing flyers to promote training, remember the five Ws—who, what, when, where, why. Any training notice must answer these questions. A map or directions to the site, the location of the training room, and where to park are helpful to include.

Include information about how to register. It is helpful to arrange the flyer information to place the address label on the back of the registration form that will be mailed in to register. Putting the label on the back of the registration form tells where the registration is from in the event that the form is incomplete or difficult to read. Be sure to include how much the session will cost and how to make out checks. Include any policies about refunds, credits, or substitutions.

Ensure that all information needed by the participant, such as directions to the site, are not on the part that the participant will return to you. Because some participants will not have ready access to a copy machine, put all the information they need on the part they keep after sending in the registration form.

Generally, sending a flyer out about three weeks ahead of the event is good timing. Sending flyers too far ahead means that they may be lost or misplaced. Sending a flyer without enough notice may mean that people will have difficulty arranging to attend or will already have commitments.

Consider how you want to handle the registration of several persons from the same site. Do you just want a list of names, or do you want a separate form for each person? If you anticipate that participants may want to copy the flyer or fax it, use light colored paper. Dark paper makes it difficult to get a good copy or to fax.

Proof, Proof, Proof!

Always have at least two other persons proofread your flyer. It is easy to overlook one's own mistakes. Because you know the information, you may not see omissions or unclear wording. Proof for the five Ws and check everything, especially time, dates, and locations. In addition to the usual spelling, grammar, and accuracy, here are some important facts to check on a flyer promoting training:

Directions and Location

If you include directions, do you give them from each direction a person might come? Do you give exit numbers or street names? Is there more than one exit with the same street name? Do you identify landmarks? Actually driving and following your written directions will help you see if they are clear. Better yet, have someone else follow your directions. If you are mailing to persons in other towns, be sure you name the city where the training will be held. Many towns have similar street names that may cause confusion if there is no city listed on the flyer. If the training is not in your city, some recipients may assume it is because the mail comes from you.

Date and Time

Is the date right? Did you include the day of the week? It is helpful to the recipient to know the session is on a Saturday without having to refer to a calendar. Did you include the time for registration and the beginning of the session? What about ending time? Recipients may make decisions to attend or not based on whether a session is over in time for other commitments.

Credit

What about credit? Is credit given? Does the training meet regulations or count toward a credential? What and how much does it count? Is it clock hours or continuing education units?

Who Should Register?

Is it clear who will benefit from the session? For example, a session on nutrition may help food service employees or classroom teachers depending on the content. Is the training for persons who work with infants and toddlers, or for those who work with school-age children? Be sure the recipients know who will benefit from the training.

Logistics of a Training Session

Every session will have some common matters to address regardless of the training topic. Opening with a strong beginning sets the stage for a productive workshop and makes a good first impression. Taking care of housekeeping details immediately will prevent interruptions later. Ending on a strong note will help participants leave with a positive memory.

Even routine matters such as distributing door prizes or closure activities can reinforce the content of the session. They can add humor or they can support networking. Many of the activities to facilitate transfer of learning to the job make good closure activities.

Opening the Session

People like predictability. Trainees will want to know what is going to happen and when it will happen. Give trainees an overview of the goals and objectives at the beginning of the session. Tell them what to expect and about how much time each portion of the session will take. Review the participation expectations and any guidelines for behavior. Spend time at the beginning to help remove anxiety or apprehensions. Welcome the trainees and express appreciation to them for attending. Thank anyone who has contributed to the organization and to the preparation of the session. Let trainees know you are glad to be there and enjoy being with them.

Start on time. You establish credibility during the first few minutes. Do not undermine your own efforts by not being prompt. Even if there are latecomers, begin on time and let the latecomers ease into the room. For ongoing sessions, failing to start on time sets the stage for participants to come late to future sessions. Once they start coming late, it is difficult to start on time because they are not there!

Plan to keep on schedule to the extent possible and let participants know that you will. Participants will worry about other responsibilities if they perceive that they will not finish on time. They may even worry about ending early if they ride a bus or have arrangements for someone to come to get them. Generally, finishing five to ten minutes early will leave a good impression with trainees since they usually do not like to run over the stated ending time. It is better to schedule another session they will look forward to than to keep them well past the assigned ending time.

Housekeeping Details

Include time at the beginning of the session to give an overview of the day's schedule. Take time to address questions that participants likely want to know but may not have asked such as:

- Where are the restrooms?
- Where are the telephones?
- Where is a water fountain?
- When will there be a break?
- What about lunch or snacks?
- What time will the session end?
- What if one has to leave early?
- How do they get credit for the training?
- Where do personal items such as purses and coats go?

Ending the Session

Do not just quit when you have finished the activities. Provide a logical ending so participants will know when the session is finished. Closure to the event is important for them. Plan the ending carefully to leave a good impression and to serve as a transition activity. Ensure that you have a good conclusion by including the following components:

1. Summaries and review—What are the key points in the session? What did each person learn?
2. Planned implementation—How will the participants put into practice what they have learned? Where can they get more information and support? What do they do next? Will there be any follow-up?
3. Evaluations and certificates—How did they like the session, and what did they learn? How will you use the evaluation information? What type of record of their participation is kept?
4. Trainer follow-up—What are you going to do now? Are there unanswered questions you will respond to later? Will you schedule another session? Will you let them know about other training opportunities?
5. What now? —What do they do next? Should they enroll in another session? If so, what and when?

Closure Activities

Specific closure activities can offer a final positive experience. Closure activities can help secure friendships and connections among trainees and bring the session to a logical conclusion. Closure activities can contribute to trainees' remembering the training as a positive experience, and they can add humor.

Hand Squeeze—When participants are seated in a circle, a good way to end a session is the Hand Squeeze. Ask participants to hold hands with you. Squeeze the hand on the person on your right, who squeezes the hand of the person on her right, and so on. Continue around the circle until the "squeeze" reaches your left hand. Another version is to let each one tell something about what they like about their work or what they are going to do differently related to the training as they squeeze the next person's hand.

If participants are not seated in a circle, have them form a circle while standing and cross their arms before they take someone's hand. The squeeze also can be sent around a second time in reverse if desired.

Group Hug—The Group Hug is best to use when participants know each other either before the session or because they have been together in training for an extended period. Group Hug provides closure to the session and leaves everyone on a positive note. Have participants form a large circle. Ask them to lightly put their hands on their neighbors' shoulders. Then ask them to take three steps forward to form a giant, group hug.

Bye-bye—Announce that since the session is over, you want to give everyone a chance to say good-bye. Ask them to turn to the right and wave good-bye to their neighbor. If everyone follows the instructions, most will be waving to the back of their neighbors. This "mistake" usually generates a good laugh. Waving "hello" the same way at the beginning of a session can be an example that mistakes are OK. Give these instructions, then laugh with the audience at the mistake you made.

One Small Step—Remind trainees of the words of Neil Armstrong when he took the first step on the moon—"One small step for man, one giant leap for mankind." Ask them to think about the small steps they can take to make a difference with children. Ask them as they leave to think about all the small steps that together make a giant leap.

The Longest Journey—Reveal a banner with the saying, "The longest journey begins with the first step." Ask trainees to take the first step as they leave the training to implement what they have learned.

Distributing Door Prizes—Tired of drawing names out of a box? Even the closing act of selecting recipients of door prizes can be a learning experience and add fun and humor to the training session. Here are some out-of-the-ordinary ways to select winners for door prizes:

Clear Communication—Have the following statements on a poster or overhead transparency. Put one on each transparency or cover all but one on a poster. Have as many statements as you have prizes. The first person to come to the front and tell what a phrase means in simple words wins the prize. You also can use this activity as a demonstration of the importance of using plain, understandable language.

1. The obsessive affection for the medium of fiscal exchange is the foundation of the undiminished quantity of misery, adversity, and corruption.

The love of money is the root of all evil.

2. An individual human is incapable of being in possession of a circular baked item while at the same time consuming the object.

You can't have your cake and eat it too.

3. A feathered vertebrate enclosed in the grasping device has a higher estimated value than a pair encapsulated in the dwarf tree.

A bird in the hand is worth two in the bush.

4. A financial unit equal to one percent of a federal reserve note equal to one dollar that is stored is a monetary unit equal to one percent of that same federal reserve note brought in by way of return on services rendered.

A penny saved is a penny earned.

5. It is fittingly more satisfactory to bequeath than to come into custody of.

It is better to give than to receive.

6. Perform the actions directed toward beings of the same species in the same manner that you would desire to be the recipient thereof.

Do unto others as you would have them do unto you.

7. A movement using an implement of tailoring performed within short duration will produce a net return ninefold.

A stitch in time saves nine.

Scavenger Hunt—The first person who comes to the front with the item you name wins the prize. Start with difficult-to-find items, then lead up to easier ones until you have a winner. Trainees will scramble to search their purses, briefcases, and tote bags to find what you name.

An expired driver's license
A lucky rabbit's foot
A temporary driver's license
An unopened package of shoelaces
A holiday card addressed to you
An extra pair of panty hose (or socks)
A water bill
A postcard from another state
A $2 bill
A photo with two girls and one boy in it
A dry cleaning receipt
A receipt from a fast-food restaurant
An unopened package of gum
A coupon for something free
A postage stamp

Tough Questions—Ask the following questions until you have a winner. Many will think they know the answer until they realize the trick.

1. How long did the Hundred Years War last?
2. From which animal do we get catgut?
3. What animal gives us camel's hair brushes?
4. What color is the purple finch?
5. In which country are Panama hats made?
6. What animal was the inspiration for the name of the Canary Islands?
7. What was the first name of King George VI?
8. How long was the Thirty Years War?

Answers

1. 116 years, from 1337 to 1453
2. Sheep and horses
3. Squirrel fur
4. Crimson
5. Ecuador
6. Dogs, from the Latin name *Insularia Canaris* or Island of the Dogs
7. Albert. He dropped the name Albert at the request of Queen Victoria that no future king be called Albert.
8. Thirty years, from 1618 to 1648

Hot Potato—This game is a way to distribute door prizes when you have many prizes. Have participants sit in a circle and give everyone an item. If you do not have enough prizes for all, give some participants the door prizes and the others inexpensive trinkets. Play lively music and have participants pass the items around the circle until the music stops. Then everyone keeps the item they have. To make the activity more interesting, have several practice sessions before you give away the prizes. If you have time, reverse the direction of passing the items several times.

Mr. And Mrs. Wright—This game is another way to distribute door prizes when you have many. Give every person something—either a prize or a trinket. For this game, participants sit in a circle while you read the story of Mr. and Mrs. Wright. Every time they hear the words *right, Wright,* or *write,* they pass the items to the right. When they hear the word *left,* they pass their items to the left. Pause slightly after you say the words that require passing. At the end, everyone keeps what he or she has. This game is a good way to distribute holiday gifts for class exchanges as well.

Mr. and Mrs. Wright live on the left side of Rightway Street. The Wright's house is green with white trim (the word "white" may confuse some and add humor). They have lived there a long time, ever since they left New Orleans, which they left to get a job working at William Wright's Widget store. One day, Mr. Wright asked Mrs. Wright if they had any coffee left.

"No," said Mrs. Wright. "We have no coffee left at all. And I'm too busy writing this letter to the Leftus sisters who left White Plains to get some right now."

So Mr. Wright said he would go to the store right away, and he left the house. He left at four o'clock to go right to the store that sold good coffee. He walked down the street one block and turned to the right. He walked down another block and turned to the left. Then he came to a stoplight, and went right into the store that was on the left side of the street. Mr. Wright asked the clerk where the coffee was.

"Right over there on the left," said the clerk.

Mr. Wright looked at all the different kinds of coffee.

"Humm," he said to himself. "I wonder which is the right coffee that Mrs. Wright will want?" He looked to the right and he looked to the left. He saw many, many kinds of coffee. One coffee was called "Brew Right" and he decided to buy that. He saw there were only two cans left so he took them both. He went to the cashier to pay for his Brew Right coffee, but alas, he discovered that he could not find enough money. He looked in his left pocket and he looked in his right pocket. He found some money, but he did not have enough to buy both cans of coffee. He took one can right back and put it back on the shelf on the left side, which was right where he got it. Then he paid for his one can that he had left, and he left the store. He walked home, turning to the left, then the right, then the left again.

"Hello, Mrs. Wright," he said when he got home. "I just bought one can of Brew Right coffee and came right back from the store because I didn't have enough money left to buy anything else. Now, I have absolutely no money left."

"Is that right?" said Mrs. Wright. "Well, you did the right thing. I'll write a note that we need to go to the bank right away to get more money since you have none left."

"Sit right down, and I will make us a cup of Brew Right coffee." And she did.

Joke Prizes—Joke door prizes can add humor. Describe the door prizes with great enthusiasm.

Prize to Describe	What to Give
A Diamond Pin:	Dime and pin
The Whole Box:	Show a box of interesting or expensive items such as jewelry, watches or even dollar bills. Tell trainees that you are going to give away the whole box. Then give the box alone.
A Large, Colored TV:	Write the letters T and V very large on poster board. Color the letters in a variety of colors.

A Cell Phone with a
Lifetime of Free Calls:

Give a small toy telephone or two tin cans and a string. Tell the winner he can talk all he wants for free.

A Spaghetti Dinner for Two:

A can of spaghetti, with paper plates, napkins, and forks.

A Necklace of Pearls:

An inexpensive necklace with the name Pearl on it. Tell the winner that it belonged to Pearl.

An Evening at the Movies:

A coupon for a free video rental

CHAPTER 2

Activities for Individuals, Partners, Small Groups, and Whole Groups

Icebreakers and Opening Activities

You have five minutes to make a first impression. Participants will form an opinion of the instructor and the training event during the first few minutes of a session. Accordingly, the instructor must start out with an activity that will involve participants right away and help them view the session as fun, exciting, and worthwhile. Icebreakers and other opening activities will provide an opportunity to make a good first impression.

Why Icebreakers?

"We'll start out by each one telling who you are and where you are from." How many of us have sat through these openings and wished that we were somewhere else? When an instructor does not recognize the importance of these opening activities, commonly called icebreakers, opportunities for getting to know the participants and creating a desire to learn are lost. Icebreakers set the stage for training. Because they are at the beginning, they can motivate trainees to participate or make them want to tune out. When well chosen, icebreakers can be effective in getting a session off to a good start. If trite and routine, they can do just the opposite.

Icebreakers can serve a variety of purposes. They not only provide a transition, but they can be a source of information for the facilitator as well as the trainees. They can add humor and fun. They can promote interaction by helping participants become comfortable in the setting. Here are some reasons to employ good icebreakers:

Introduce Participants to Each Other—In many icebreakers, participants learn something about each other. This helps them see what they have in common. Giving them something to talk about during the session or at break helps overcome shyness. Promoting interaction with the others in the group helps to meet the social needs of the trainees.

Learning about Participants' Needs and Concerns—Often icebreakers require that participants tell something about their working situation, their training expectations, or their needs and concerns. With this information, the trainer can then adapt and individualize the training to meet those needs.

Build Rapport and Relax Participants—Many icebreaker activities help build a relationship between participants and help them feel comfortable with each other. Building relationships encourages interaction in the training session and helps the participants feel a part of the group. Icebreakers give recognition and attention to each participant, and they help facilitate networking.

Team-building—Some icebreakers can build a spirit of cooperation in a group. These icebreakers are especially useful if the group is going to be together for some time and do not know each other well. Team-building activities will often take more time than other activities. These activities are especially useful for retreats or when a group will be involved in on-going work where working closely together is essential.

As a Learning Activity—Some icebreakers require trainees to recall information or to share information with others. They can emphasize a point related to the training. They can serve as a review of previous training and help trainees relate prior information to current goals. Icebreakers that call for participants to share information offer an opportunity to recognize the experiences and knowledge of participants.

Demonstrate Interaction—Icebreakers get trainees involved from the beginning and let them know that the trainer cares about what they have to say. Good icebreakers create an atmosphere that trainees are to be active rather than passive learners.

Add Humor and Fun—Some icebreakers simply add an element of fun to the training session. Humorous activities help build a positive attitude about the training to come. Humorous and fun icebreakers reassure participants that the training is not going to be boring.

As a Transition Activity—Whatever specific purposes icebreakers serve, they are an important transition activity in adult training settings. Adults come to training with much baggage. They may be concerned about personal problems or responsibilities. They may be self-conscious around others or have had negative experiences in learning settings. Often they are preoccupied with family responsibilities. A major purpose of icebreakers is to break through this preoccupation so participants will focus on the present.

Consequently, icebreakers serve to help trainees put those distractions behind them and focus on the training session. Icebreakers provide a transition and starting point. They send a message that the training is under way.

Selecting the Right Icebreaker

Because the icebreaker sets the tone for your training, choosing one is an important decision. Select it carefully according to the following criteria. Consider the:

- Size of the group.
- Experience of the group.
- Goals of the session and the relevance of the icebreaker to the goals.
- Time you can devote to the activity.

- Length of the session—is it an ongoing class or a onetime event?
- How likely the group is to know each other, and how well they know each other.

Often, the trainer must consider all of these factors. When groups are large, consider breaking into smaller groups and using icebreaker activities in the separate small groups. Everyone does not have to meet everyone else. Small groups allow for everyone to take part in a shorter time.

Activities that require reading may not work if the literacy level of participants is low. If trainees are shy, icebreakers that allow them to do something while they talk will help overcome self-consciousness.

Choose or adapt an activity that limits the time someone can talk when you can allow only a few minutes for an icebreaker. Some of the activities have built-in controls that limit the time introductions will take. For example, in Wrapped Around My Finger (page 36), you can cut short pieces of yarn ahead of time if you need brief introductions. Others require participants to "Tell three things about . . ." to limit the time.

For a day-long session or training that extends over several days, select longer, team-building activities. When working cooperatively on tasks is required, spending the time to become acquainted and working together on an opening experience can help meet the teamwork goals. When a group will have an ongoing relationship such as committee work, team-building icebreakers can help develop a sense of team spirit quickly. Although they generally take longer than other icebreakers, the time is well spent when cooperation is integral to the success of the event.

Icebreakers that require participants to do something with their hands seem to be most effective in overcoming shyness or self-consciousness. When trainees focus on what they are doing, they appear to be less concerned about themselves. These icebreakers are a good springboard to becoming involved for those who might be reluctant to speak to a group.

Icebreakers that inject humor into the process are good to use with participants who are required to attend—especially if they are reluctant to be present. Humorous and fun ice-breakers can help participants see that a training session can be fun and does not have to be boring. Starting with humor early in the session helps participants have a positive attitude about the training.

If you want to know more about the needs of the group, pick an activity that calls for individuals to tell why they are attending the session. Ask them to tell what they want to get from the session or to relay something about their jobs or special skills. Information about hobbies and outside interests can be useful, too.

There is no rule that everyone must do the same thing. Try using several different activities as icebreakers. For example in a group of thirty, you might use three separate icebreakers—one for the first ten participants, a different one for the next ten, and another one for the remaining members of the group. Changing icebreakers helps sustain interest and reassures participants that the session will not be monotonous. Do not be afraid to change activities, too, if one is not working or not getting the response you want. If participants are taking too long in their responses and others are getting restless, switch to a different activity that restricts the time one can talk.

Whatever the specific purpose of the activity chosen, icebreakers play an important role in the training process. Select them carefully.

Introductory Icebreakers

Where Are You From?—Have trainees write on a laminated map with a dry-erase marker or affix a sticky note to show where they are from. Use a state map for a statewide training, a United States map for regional or national groups, or a world map for international sessions. This activity will help some trainees find something in common.

Personality Bags—Hand out small paper or plastic bags to the trainees. Ask them to put three items from their purse, wallet, or briefcase in the bag. As they introduce themselves, have them tell why they selected the items and how the items relate to their personalities and interests.

Circle Stickers—Give each person an index card and three one-inch circle stickers. Ask each person to write something she likes about working with children on each of her three stickers. Instruct her to circulate and meet at least three new people. Each person gives each person she meets one of her stickers and she gets one in return. Each participant puts the stickers on her index card and writes the names and places of work of her new acquaintances. The process continues until each person's stickers are gone. For variety, substitute die-cut note paper related to the training topic for the index cards.

Wrapped Around My Finger—Have participants cut a piece of yarn when they register. Do not tell them how much to take even though many will ask. Have each participant wrap the yarn around his finger while he introduces himself. He is to talk about himself until he runs out of yarn. He must stop when he runs out, even if he is in mid-sentence. Cut the yarn yourself if you want some control over how much time you wish to spend on this icebreaker. Cut short pieces if you have a large group or little time; longer pieces if you want to spend more time or if you conduct introductions in small groups. This icebreaker works very well because it gives people something to do with their hands while they talk.

Alike and Different—Have participants talk to someone they do not know. Tell them to find five things they have in common and five ways they are different. They can then introduce the other person to the group.

Toilet Paper Game—Pass around a roll of toilet paper and instruct the participants to "take how much you usually need." It works best for each participant to take at least four or five squares. If someone takes fewer, add, "No one uses just two squares!" For each square, each person is to tell one interesting fact about himself.

Riddle, Riddle—Make a list of riddles and a list of answers. Copy the riddles on one color of paper and the answers on another, then cut the paper into strips. Number the riddles and answers correspondingly; the numbers help you be sure you have an answer for each riddle that you hand out since you may not use them all at each session. Distribute riddles to half the participants and answers to the other half. Pass the strips of paper out randomly so the person with the riddle is not sitting by the person with the answer to that riddle. A person with a riddle introduces herself, reads her riddle, and the person who has the answer gives his answer, then introduces himself. Books of riddles for children can be found in libraries or purchased. Hint: Have an answer sheet for yourself.

Fortune Cookies—Prepare strips of paper so that each has a statement to finish such as "I was born in _____" or "My favorite leisure activity is _____." Each person draws a strip of paper, then introduces herself and finishes the statement on the paper. Then, ask the participant to tell if that was good fortune and why it was good for them. You can also use real fortune cookies and let the participants read their fortunes when they introduce themselves.

Adjective Introductions—Participants introduce themselves with an adjective that starts with the same letter as their first names and describes something about them. For example, Paula may be Prompt Paula, Gretchen may be Genuine Gretchen, or Sonja might be Serious Sonja. Using the adjectives adds humor and makes the names easier to remember.

Names, Names, Names—This activity will usually work best with smaller groups since it can take a while. Let the first person tell her name. Then the next person names the first person and adds her name. The third names the first, second, and then herself. Continue until the last person names all of the people in the group. This is especially good if the group is going to be together for several sessions and needs to know each other's names.

Hoops—This is a very active introduction and requires open space. Have participants make a circle holding hands. The goal of this activity is to pass a hoop around the circle without breaking the hand-holding. Trainees will soon figure out that they must put the hoop over their head and then step through it. When it is their turn, they introduce themselves before they pass the hoop over themselves. After the hoop has gone around once, try passing two hoops, each going in a different direction, this time without the introductions. This activity works well with groups of about fifteen to twenty-five.

Jelly Beans—Make a chart like the one below. Pass around a bowl of jelly beans or other colored candies and ask each participant to take only one. Then, to introduce himself, each participant should talk about the category that relates to the color of the jelly bean or candy that he chose. For example, if he selected red, he would talk about his family; if orange, he would tell about an exciting experience.

Red   Your family
Orange Your most exciting experience
Yellow Your employment
Green   What you want to do five years from now
Blue   What you want to do ten years from now
Purple Your pets or pets you would like to have
Black   The person you most admire
White   Your favorite foods

Other possibilities for topics to substitute are: your hobbies and interests, your home town, your best friend, a favorite teacher, a first job, or a favorite movie. Participants also may take several candies, then tell several things about themselves based on the colors they took.

Name Story—Read the story *Chrysanthemum* by Kevin Henkes to the group. Use the book to open a discussion about how each person got their name. Alternatively, tell how and why your parents selected your name for you.

Name Song—Sing a song such as "Skip along, Josie" or "Riding in a Buggy, Miss Mary Jane," using each participant's name. Have everyone join in. Because this introduction will take longer than some, it will work best with groups that are not too large.

Toothpicks—Give each person five to ten toothpicks. The larger the group, the more toothpicks each person will need. Participants in turn introduce themselves and tell something they have never done that they think most of the others have done. Each person who has done the thing stated will give the speaker a toothpick. Continue until one person has all the toothpicks. The trick is to find something unique that you have done that the others have not. Because this activity can take some time, it is best used with groups that will be together for a long time.

Shoebox Autobiographies—Each person puts together small items that will fit in a shoebox. These items should represent interests, hobbies, and cultural background. Share the shoeboxes in small groups to become acquainted. This is a good technique for a group that is going to be together for several sessions or for a class.

Similarities—Make a grid similar to a mileage chart between cities. Write each person's name at the top and also down the left side. In this way, all names intersect all other names. Each participant is responsible for finding something she has in common with every other person. Write the characteristic or interest that is shared in the block where the names intersect. As each person completes her row, give her a star to put in the square where her own name intersects. This is a great way to help a class get acquainted since everyone meets everyone else.

Interview—Pass out interview sheets (see Appendix page 270). Participants complete the sheets by interviewing someone next to them. Then, they introduce the person they interviewed to the group. For variation, they could move around and meet someone new to interview.

People Bingo—This activity can include general items that will work for almost any group. Or, it can be customized with some unique characteristics or experiences of the trainees when the instructor knows the participants or can get information before the session. Give participants grids that have a category in each box. Let the participants move around and ask others about the categories or descriptions on the grid until they find a box that describes each of the participants, recording the appropriate name in each box. When they use every name, they are finished. For a sample grid, see page 94 in chapter 3.

> **Note**: If making a generic chart, make more boxes than you have participants. This will help avoid participants finding that the last person does not fit in the last box! If making a chart specific to the group, make sure to use unique facts that are unlikely to fit more than one person. To get unusual information ahead of time, ask for "The most unusual thing you have ever done," or "Your most outstanding accomplishment," or "What interest do you have that you consider unique?"

Scavenger Hunt—Ask participants to indicate where they would find the following items. Have each person who finds one of the items introduce herself and then introduce one person who did not find an item. If participants do not catch on to where these items could be found, give hints until they do so. If the group is too large, divide into small groups, use an additional icebreaker with this one, or add to the list. Suggestions for a list:

- A screw shorter than 1/4 inch (6 mm) (on eyeglasses)
- A picture of Andrew Jackson (on a $20 bill)
- An outline of a state (often on driver's license)
- A picture of Abraham Lincoln (on a penny)
- A toll-free telephone number (on telephone cards, insurance cards, etc.)
- A small brush (on mascara)
- A picture of a pyramid (on a $1 bill)

Rhymes and Rhythms—Ask participants to introduce themselves by giving their first names and rhyming them with things they want. Start them off with an example: "My name is Sandy, I want some candy." If a participant cannot think of a rhyme, let the group suggest one, or let him clap the rhythm of his name. Encourage participants to use their imaginations. Let them know that they can exaggerate to make the rhymes.

Photo—For an ongoing class or a full-day session, photos help participants get to know each other more quickly. With one-hour photo processors easily available, even regular cameras can produce quick pictures. The photos can be placed on a bulletin board or be used to make "Wanted" posters. They can identify projects that individuals complete or be given as keepsakes to remind participants of the training.

Mirror, Mirror—Pass around a hand mirror. Let participants introduce themselves by talking to the mirror. They should tell the mirror something about themselves. They also may tell what they wish they would see when they look at themselves.

Icebreakers Related to Training Content

Measure Up—Ask participants to tell something good about themselves as they pass a ruler around. They should tell how they "measure up" in the training topic. For example, in a session on language development, one might say, "I measure up by reading at least two books a day to my class." This activity is effective also when participants form small groups to share ideas.

Magic Wand—Pass around a magic wand with the instructions "If you could change anything about your program, what would it be?" Participants pass the wand around, introduce themselves, and tell what they would like to change with a wave of the magic wand. Make a wand by attaching a star to a dowel or purchase one inexpensively. To relate the activity to a specific topic, ask trainees to tell what they would change in relation to their ability to do some task. Make the task related to the training content such as communicating better with parents, working effectively with challenging children, or having more science activities.

Name That Tune (or Book)—The leader gives one of the following words or writes them on a flip chart or overhead transparency. Participants try to see who can be the first to think of and sing a children's song or say an action rhyme that has one of the words in it. Then they introduce themselves. Continue until everyone has been introduced. As it gets more difficult, let them help each other. For a session on children's literature, change the instructions to naming or finding a children's story or book title they remember that includes each word. This activity helps participants share songs or books they remember, and helps them relate music and books to language and vocabulary development. The same activity can be done in teams or conducted as a scavenger hunt where participants find books or rhymes.

Five	Spider	Bird	Kittens
Puppy	Bumblebee	Orange	Water
House	Round	Frog	School
Ten	White	Rainbow	Rain
Butterfly	House	Chicken	Duck
Car	Boy	Snow	Robin
Girl	Square	Cow	Bus
Truck	Red	Train	Farm

Memory—Have participants face someone they do not know. For one minute, they study each other, trying to remember as much as possible about the other person. Then, they turn their backs to each other and change three things about themselves. When they turn around, they try to guess what three things are different. Let each person introduce his partner and tell what his partner changed and how many of the changes he was able to recognize. This activity can relate to observing children. It can also remind participants that it is difficult for children to remember everything they are expected to do.

Tip Bag—Have trainees write a tip or suggestion to put in a party bag. Select a bag related to the topic of the session or relate it to the instructions: For example, a bag with a happy face can be used for "It makes me happy when... ." A bag decorated with a telephone can be "Something I want to communicate is..." or "I want to ask about... ." Bags that have "Congratulations" or party designs on them can be used for "I want to congratulate myself for..." or "I want to celebrate that I... ."

Twenty Questions—Put an object related to children in a paper bag. Prepare one bag for each small group in your session, and tell the group leader or one participant what is in the bag. Participants in the group each take a turn asking questions about what is in the bag until a total of twenty questions are asked. A simple variation is to let someone in the group write down an item related to the training topic, and let the others have twenty questions to guess what it is.

Starting with a Bang—Write the goals and objectives of the training session on small strips of paper. Put the strips inside balloons before you blow up the balloons. At the beginning of the session, ask volunteers to pop the balloons and read the goals and objectives to the group.

Another version could be to insert the following questions in balloons to help participants remember what their own childhood was like. As the volunteer pops the balloon, she reads the questions and responds. For variation, she might ask someone else to answer. Here are some possible questions:

- What was the most discouraging experience you had as a child?
- Who were you always happy to be with when you were a child and why?

- What were some favorite experiences with brothers or sisters or cousins?
- What brought you the most recognition or reward as a child?
- How did you like school as a child?
- What do you remember about your favorite teacher?
- What do you remember learning in school first?
- Who was your best friend as a child?
- What was your favorite book as a child?
- What do you remember about learning to read?
- What were some favorite activities for you as a child?
- Who read stories to you when you were a child?

Icebreakers Just for Fun

Paddle Ball—Pass around a paddle ball and ask participants to introduce themselves while keeping the ball moving. Most people will try to bounce the ball as intended and will wind the ball around the paddle or swing it like a pendulum. Some will eventually realize that the instructions call only for moving the ball. They will take hold of the ball and simply move it with their hand. If participants do not realize they can do it that way, repeat and emphasize the directions until they do. This activity also works as a review with participants summarizing key points as they pass around the paddle.

Childhood Metaphors—Ask participants to choose one of the following terms and relate it to their early experiences when they introduce themselves.

As a child, my preschool years were like:
a quilt
a zoo
a flower garden
a shopping mall
a roller coaster

As a child, my early school years were like:
an orchestra
a train station
a rural town
a department store
a circus

Sing, Sing a Song—Divide into small groups and give each group a prop that will remind them of a song. After participants in each group get to know each other, they sing the song waving the prop. A frog puppet might generate "Five Little Speckled Frogs" or a farmer's hat might stimulate a rousing chorus of "Old MacDonald Had a Farm."

Individual Activities

Individual activities are those training experiences where participants complete a task alone without interacting with others. Answering questions in writing, thinking about a concept or idea, and reading and summarizing information are all examples of individual activities. Often these individual activities can be the basis for other activities or serve as a catalyst for discussion. Writing down ideas and information is helpful to those persons who primarily learn kinesthetically, and it reinforces learning for many others. It also requires trainees to think about a topic when preparing to participate in partner or small group activities.

Completing any task alone is an individual activity, but the same task may be adapted for small groups or for partners. For example, if participants each make a poster for parents describing the value of dramatic play, it is an individual activity; participants also could complete the task with a partner or with others in a small group. However, some activities are best done individually. Here are some common individual activities:

Reflective Thinking—Participants are engaging in reflective thinking when they are asked to identify what they learned in a session or what they will do differently now that they have attended training. Handouts or worksheets can include questions that require reflective thinking. Asking trainees to think about their childhood or past experiences are other examples. Thinking about their experiences with teaching, with guidance strategies, or in implementing activities is a good way to help them recognize the need for improvement. "Why?" questions often call for reflective thinking.

Note-taking—Facilitate note-taking by giving participants paper and pencils at the beginning of a session. Use handouts or worksheets with a lot of white space or places specifically for notes to encourage writing. Interactive handouts also promote note-taking. Note-taking requires participants to select key elements to record, and it requires them to summarize information. Writing notes allows trainees to put information in a form that is meaningful to them. It also reinforces learning and helps them remember information.

Interactive Handouts—Interactive handouts are handouts that call for participants to write in additional information or to take action. For example, a sheet may list three ways to communicate with parents and leave space for trainees to write in several more that they use or learn from the discussion. A handout may give the steps in performing a task, then ask trainees to write down information about the steps. These handouts are sometimes called worksheets to distinguish them from handouts that are intended primarily for reading. Self-evaluations and simple quizzes are also interactive handouts. Interactive handouts are effective because they call for participants to think, write, or take action, and thus reinforce learning.

Self-evaluation—Self-evaluation is a good tool for identifying areas that need improvement as well as personal strengths. Checklists and rating scales are some ways to evaluate one's self. When worksheets call for reflective thinking, they are requiring trainees to examine how and why they do things. They are an excellent tool for helping trainees pinpoint the areas that need changing and thus begin effecting change.

Case Studies—Case studies allow learners to come to a decision or solve a problem concerning a situation. Case studies are most useful when a topic is complex and there are many possible solutions or points of view. Case studies should be realistic and have enough detail to allow for the development of relevant solutions. They can be completed individually, but it is often helpful to discuss the solutions in order for participants to recognize the diverse viewpoints. Case studies are very valuable learning tools, but can be time-consuming to develop and conduct.

Reading Assignments—Reading assignments may be outside assignments that will be the basis of discussion, or, if they are short, they can be completed during a session. Reading assignments save time since most learners can read faster than an instructor usually talks. It is a fast way of building a foundation of information and provides a common experience and reference for participants. The disadvantages of reading assignments are that learners read at different speeds or may feel embarrassed if they are poor readers. If the material is too long, or the reading level is too hard, participants may become bored. It is also difficult to know if participants are understanding and learning without an additional activity to follow the assignment.

JOURNALING

Journaling is the process of writing down thoughts and recording activities over a period of time. A journal is similar to a diary, with the exception that an assigned journal usually has specific issues or topics to address. For journaling to be effective, it must include reflective thinking and some self-evaluation. When journals are assigned as a class requirement, participants should receive guidance about their writing or questions they should answer, especially in the early stages. Journals have the side benefit of developing skills in writing and self-expression. They can also serve as a report on outside-assigned experiences, providing the instructor feedback and insight from trainees. An example of a sample journal assignment can be found on page 266 of the Appendix.

WORD GAMES

Crossword Puzzles—Doing crossword puzzles is a good way to learn or review definitions or examples of principles. Participants may discuss their answers with a partner after they complete the puzzle independently. Give participants the words from which to choose if they have little familiarity with the terminology. See page 267 in the Appendix for an example of a simple crossword puzzle to review the components of anecdotal records.

Word Find—Another way to become familiar with terminology and to learn vocabulary is a Word Find. Make a Word Find form including the new vocabulary that you want to teach or review. This can be an individual or a partner activity. When a training program contains many concepts, techniques, terminology, or buzzwords, this is a useful review and reinforcement technique. While software programs are available to create word puzzles, you can just follow these steps.

1. Make a list of the words or key phrases you want to include.
2. Rewrite the list, starting with the longest word and ending with the shortest.
3. Using a sheet of graph paper, create the Word Find grid by transferring the words from your list onto the graph paper.
4. Write the longest word first, in any direction. Continue adding words working from the longest to the shortest. This will help ensure that the longer words will fit on the paper.
5. As you write each word, alternate between writing left to right, right to left, top to bottom, bottom to top, left diagonal up or down, and right diagonal up or down. Diagonals can be forward or backward.
6. Photocopy your Word Find puzzle, saving the original to use as an answer key.
7. On the photocopy, fill in the blank spaces with random letters. Then write the list of words to find at the bottom of the page. This will be the completed puzzle that you will distribute to participants.

Have participants work individually to find the words. After they find the words, ask them to think about how each word, concept, or principle was covered in the course and how it relates to their work. Ask them to share their ideas with a partner. See pages 297-299 in the Appendix for a Word Find on "Equipment for Toddlers" and a Word Find on "Scheduling."

Word Scramble—To teach new vocabulary or to review terminology, scramble the letters in words and let participants unscramble them. Simply make a list of the words, phrases, or even sentences, then rewrite the letters in a different order. For fun, offer a prize to the first one finished. See page 268 in the Appendix for a Word Scramble on "Props for the Housekeeping Center."

Word Jumbles—In word jumbles, the participant reads the questions and writes the answers on spaced lines. One or more of the letters in the answer words are written inside circles. After all the questions have been answered, the participant unscrambles the circled letters to make a word or phrase that answers a final question. See page 269 in the Appendix for a Word Jumble on "Interest Centers."

Letter Cross-out—In Letter Cross-out, trainees must uncover a hidden word or phrase by crossing out letters that are not in the word or phrase. To make Letter Cross-outs, simply add random letters to the word or phrase with which you want them to be familiar. Keep the letters of the word or phrase in the correct order. Provide a clue to the hidden word or phrase. See sample below.

What all early childhood educators should be:

T P T M R O D S E F O L E S R S I S X O E E N T A L

answer: PROFESSIONAL

Partner Activities

Working with another person helps participants think through and express their ideas. The act of communicating ideas to someone else increases understanding. Selecting a partner is also a useful way to involve reluctant participants or to break up groups that may be engaging in side conversations. When participants interact with someone outside their own work site, they are more apt to get new ideas and thus have a better experience.

Partner activities can provide interaction in a room where the setup does not easily lend itself to dividing into small groups. Participants can simply turn to someone near them. To pair up persons who are less likely to know each other, have odd number rows talk to the persons behind them and even numbered rows talk to the persons in front of them. This technique will create pairs who are not sitting together.

Interviews and debates are useful activities for partners and work with almost any training topic. These activities give everyone a chance to talk and to share their ideas and opinions. Interviews are especially good for those who may not be comfortable sharing ideas in a group. Debates are good for seeing several points of view.

Some of the benefits of using interviews and debates are:

Candor—participants will often be more open and honest when working in pairs than in small groups. They will worry less about what others think of them because they are with only one other person.

Active involvement—all persons are involved in asking and answering questions.

Self-expression—everyone has an opportunity to talk.

Analysis—participants see that opinions can be diverse and get to examine other points of view.

Articulation—participants have an opportunity to rehearse ways to express their views.

Because partners may spend too much time on one or two questions and not get to all of them, give them an approximate time they should spend on each question. Announce periodically when they should be proceeding to the next question during the interview or debate.

INTERVIEWS

Interviewing someone is helpful for both the questioner and the interviewee. Interviewing helps the questioner, who obtains new information or ideas; it helps the person being interviewed by giving her an opportunity to express her ideas or experiences. Participants feel an ownership in the learning process because they are involved in gathering the information. Generally, one partner will interview the other, then the roles are reversed, with the interviewer becoming the interviewee.

Partners often find a written guide to be helpful in an interview. The guide may serve as a place to write answers before the interview to allow time to think about what to say, or it can include space to write the responses of the interviewee. It may include space for both notes of what one wants to say and the responses given by the partner. A written guide helps partners remember the questions and the answers. You may also use overhead transparencies or flip charts to post the questions and have the partners use blank paper for notes.

Questions for interviews should be open-ended so they encourage a wide variety of responses. Interviewing is usually conducted with all questions asked of the same partner. However, you may use a rotation system to give participants a chance to talk to more than one person.

DEBATES

In debates, individuals take a position and find or state information to support their position. A debate helps trainees see several sides of an issue. Debates also give them experience in supporting their beliefs and arguing both sides of an issue. They can help participants see that few positions are entirely right or wrong. Debates give trainees opportunities for self-expression and evaluation.

Questions for debates should be those that are complex or where the action required is dependent on the situation. This will encourage partners to express different points of view. Debates call for participants to support a specific stand or course of action that they agree with or that is assigned to them.

If participants do not have experience with debates, ask for volunteers to debate some irrelevant issues to demonstrate the technique to the whole group. Here are some fun topics for debate that can add humor as well as warm up participants to debate procedures.

- The best ice cream flavor is chocolate or vanilla.
- Toothpaste should be squeezed from the bottom or the middle.
- The best combination for a sandwich is peanut butter and jelly or peanut butter and banana.
- Dogs or cats make the best pets.
- The best food for a cookout is hamburgers or hot dogs.
- Toilet paper should be hung with the loose end over or under the roll.
- The best sport is baseball or football.

Have a person take each side and argue the reasons why her way is better. Use props to add a little extra humor. You can even make it a three-way debate if you add a third option such as strawberry ice cream in addition to vanilla and chocolate, or soccer in addition to baseball and football.

Partner Worksheets

Worksheets can be designed specifically for use by partners. Such worksheets allow a pair of participants to work together and are especially useful when small groups are not possible. In designing partner activities and worksheets, consider the following:

1. Be sure participants have some experience or a foundation of knowledge to share about the topic. Participants who have worked only with infants may not have information to share about working with school-age children. They will, however, be able to relay ideas from their own childhood that will apply to working with school-age children.
2. Make the procedures clear and give them in writing to minimize the need for oral instructions.
3. Give clear instructions about who does what part, when, and for how long.
4. Consider the noise factor. Many people will be talking at once in the same room.
5. Too many steps in the activity may cause confusion. Clarifying information is difficult once partners start working.
6. Feedback is difficult for you to give with partner activities in large groups.

Although it is common to have a spokesperson report for small groups, time and attention spans seldom allow for reports from partners. In a group of only twenty participants, adults would have to listen to ten reports, and most adults will not want to sit that long.

Consequently, the instructor has little opportunity to clarify information or to address misunderstandings. Here are some ways to provide for reports when there are too many to have every pair report:

1. A few partners can report to provide a sampling of the ideas.
2. Reports can be given in small groups to reduce the number of reports that any one person will hear.
3. After the first few reports, ask for new information that does not repeat anything already stated.

Sample Partner Worksheets are on pages 272-274 of the Appendix.

Other Partner Activities

Pair and Share—Participants turn to a person near them for a brief sharing of ideas or suggestions or to work on a short task. Pair and Share is similar to partner worksheets, but generally is for a shorter time and does not require written guidance. Pair and Share requires that participants find someone sitting near them so a minimum amount of time is spent selecting a partner or moving around. If several Pair and Share experiences are held during a session, ask trainees to find different partners near them each time rather than staying with the same one. Having different partners will mean trainees interact with more people.

Memory—Participants review developmental milestones of infants through preschoolers by playing Memory. Make cards with pictures and developmental milestones on them. The cards are placed face-down, and participants play Memory. When they match the word with a picture, they discuss what they can do to support children's development as they approach that particular stage. For example, if participants match a card that reads "pulling up" with a picture of a child who has pulled himself up to a standing position, participants may discuss the importance of providing sturdy furniture and letting children move around freely on the floor, providing them opportunities to pull up.

Another way to use the cards is to stack the word cards or the picture cards between two partners. Each partner draws a card in turn and the partners discuss the milestone on the card. They discuss what they can do to support children's development as in the procedure above.

Carousel—Put half of the group in a center circle facing outward. This group forms the carousel. Put the other half of the group in an outer circle facing inward. They are the riders. Provide questions for partners to answer. After they have answered their question, have the carousel (the inner circle) move one person to the left and invite the new partners to answer another question. Continue as long as you have questions. Carousel also is a good way for memberss of a group to get to know each other.

Selecting Partners

Pairing up a participant with another can be as easy as asking each person to work with the person beside him. However, since participants often sit with people they know, it is often preferable to find another way to match participants in pairs. When the group needs to move around or you want participants to interact with people other than their work colleagues, use one of these suggestions to have participants select a partner. Often, the activity can provide an opportunity for participants to meet someone they did not know before they came. Here are some easy ideas for choosing partners:

Ticket to Ride—Using duplicate sets of numbered tickets, give each person one ticket. Ensure that persons who came together or who are sitting together do not get the same ticket number. Then, at the appropriate time, ask participants to find the person who holds the same number. A roll of tickets is inexpensive to purchase and will last through many sessions; alternatively, you can make your own tickets.

Tag, You're It!—Color code name tags and give them out in a way that persons who walk in together do not get the same color. Then at the appropriate time, ask participants to find a partner with the same color name tag. This system gives participants some choice in selecting a partner since several people may have the same color tag.

Let's Play Cards—A deck of cards can be used to pair partners. Distribute the cards, then ask participants to find someone with the same number as the card they hold. Depending on the time available and the number of participants, you may ask them to find a person with the same number and the same color. If the group is large, use several decks and instruct participants to match the number and the suit.

Match Game—This activity uses some typical early childhood materials. Give half of the participants a part of a toy and ask them to find someone with the other part. For example, give half of the group plastic bolts and give the remaining half the nuts that match. Two-piece puzzles work well, too. Match Game can have a seasonal theme; for example, you can match one-half of a plastic egg with the other half. Or the activity may relate to the training, such as matching a word with a definition. Two-piece puzzles can be matched, too.

Related Word Match—When participants enter, give each one a card with a word on it. Shuffle and distribute the cards so people coming in together will not receive corresponding cards. For example, when you give someone the card that reads "fork," wait until more people come in before you give someone the card that reads "spoon." When you are ready, have participants find partners by looking for someone with a word that corresponds to their word.

Some words to match are:

fork and spoon

brush and comb

pen and pencil

macaroni and cheese

cup and saucer

socks and shoes

flower and vase

rice and gravy

cow and milk

bacon and eggs

dog and bone

peanut butter and jelly

bread and butter

hammer and nails

soup and crackers

lettuce and tomato

table and chair

moon and stars

sing and dance

cake and ice cream

Cake Bake—Hand out cards that have one of the following cake varieties or the corresponding name on them. Then ask participants to find their partner at the break. Give them a few examples to get them started. This activity adds humor and matches participants. If time is limited, or the group is large, number the matching pairs to make the process move more quickly. Another way to speed up the process is to provide an answer chart.

for Gabriel	angel food cake
for John Chapman	apple cake (Johnny Appleseed)
for a monkey	banana cake
for the new baby	birthday cake
for the lumberjack	black forest cake
for the baseball batter	bundt cake
for the jeweler	carrot (caret) cake
for a mouse	cheesecake
for the Mad Hatter and the White Rabbit	cup cake
for a grocer	fruit cake
for the candyman	fudge cake
for Hansel, who loves chocolate	German chocolate cake
for Virginia	gingerbread
for a geologist	layer cake
for a sculptor	marble cake
for an elephant (or squirrel)	nut cake
for the painter or artist	orange cake
for the prospector	pancake
for Little Jack Horner	plum cake
for someone wanting to lose weight	pound cake
for someone who is not tall	shortcake
for a gossip	spice cake
for someone who takes advantage of someone else	sponge cake
for the bride and groom	wedding cake
for a gymnist	upside-down cake
for the baby	pat-a-cake
for an expresso lover	coffee cake

Paper Plate Puzzles—Ask early arrivals to decorate paper plates with markers. Have them cut each plate in two pieces. You will need enough plates for each attendee to get one-half of a plate. To be sure you have enough, come with a few already made. Pass out the pieces randomly. Have attendees find the person with the matching piece for a partner. You also can cut plates into three or more pieces if you want to divide the group into triads or small groups.

Favorite Foods—Have participants list items such as a favorite food or birthday month. You may need to limit foods to a category such as favorite vegetable or fruit to create more matches. Then, ask participants to circulate around the room until they find someone else who has listed the same favorite and introduce themselves. Have those who do not find anyone after an allotted time pair with someone else who did not find a match.

Small Group Activities

Small group activities are excellent learning opportunities for adults. Since adult learners need to express themselves, small group experiences are desirable because they give learners more chances to talk. Some participants may be reluctant to speak up in a large group and will be more at ease in a small group. Generally, training evaluation comments indicate that adult learners prefer small group activities. Adults bring many experiences to the training setting, and small group activities make use of that experience. The small groups also provide a forum for participants to express other concerns and to be recognized.

Disadvantages and Cautions

- Sometimes the learning environment does not allow for easy movement into groups. Large lecture auditoriums or rooms with fixed seating are difficult to use for small group activities.
- Trainers express concern that misinformation may be passed on to other trainees. Small groups may be led by a volunteer or someone less experienced than the instructor. As a result, there is sometimes a concern that participants will suggest or recommend inappropriate or outmoded methods, and the other participants may leave with wrong information.
- Problem participants may interfere with the group process and, consequently, the learning.
- It may be difficult to accurately estimate the time needed because the groups' experiences and interests will vary and may be unknown to the trainer.
- Learning points may be lost, and the groups may lose the focus of the activity.

Dealing with These Concerns

When possible, select a facility that does not have fixed seating and where chairs are easily moved. When fixed seating is unavoidable, try adapting activities to triads and let groups of three persons sitting nearby work together.

Be sure that someone knowledgeable is in each small group or appoint leaders. Usually, if anyone makes an inappropriate suggestion, another person in the group will counteract it. If the trainer or her assistant circulates among the groups, she can suggest an alternative to the suggestion. Later, the trainer can give correct information at a time when they will not embarrass anyone. The following statements are helpful in reacting to incorrect information given in a small group setting:

- "Many people once thought that, too, but current research tells us that ..."
- "Under some circumstances that might be so, but usually we find that..."
- "What are some alternative ways to..?"
- "Can anyone suggest another way to..?"

Circulate among the groups. Listen to the comments of each group and, when appropriate, offer a comment or ask a question to stimulate ideas. Small group discussion time is not a signal for the trainer to take a break. The trainer is an important part of the activity. Offer frequent summaries of what the group is discussing to help keep them focused. Monitor the groups and intercede to deal with problem participants if the need arises. Ask open-ended questions to keep the groups on task if they wander from the topic. You may even sit down for a short time in each group and offer comments as a participant.

Have a reporting period to summarize key points. Reporting time will give you another chance to address incorrect information and to clarify misunderstandings.

Guidelines for Working with Small Groups

- Give instructions orally before dividing the group. Provide written directions if the instructions are complex or if there is an activity to complete.
- Be clear about the time limits. State the time the group activity will end.
- Have a recorder keep a record of the group's work. Use small dry-erase white boards when flip charts are not convenient.
- Offer a button to the spokesperson. The button not only serves as an incentive to volunteer, but helps you quickly identify the person who will be reporting when they rejoin the large group.
- Move to each small group in turn until each group settles into the task. Use the time to clarify and further explain the assignment and expectations.
- Continue to circulate among the groups to answer questions or add pertinent information to the discussion. Ask questions to keep the groups focused and be available as a resource for information.
- Announce when the groups have about five minutes left, so they can wrap up their discussions.
- Allow time for a report from each group to the whole group. Reporting provides a chance to summarize and select key points.

Group Leader Tasks

When you choose group leaders, select those who can keep the discussion moving and streamline the reporting process. Effective group leaders will:

- Lead the activity according to the verbal or written instructions given by the instructor.
- Keep track of time so that as much of the activity as possible is covered in the allotted time.
- Help keep the group focused on the task at hand.
- Take notes or have a recorder take notes of important ideas suggested or conclusions that the group reaches.
- Summarize the conclusions of the group at the end of the activity.

Novel Ways to Select Group Leaders

When you wish to provide participants an opportunity to gain experience as a leader, use some of these methods to choose the group leader. These novel ways to select leaders are also useful when there is no one who volunteers quickly.

- On the count of three, everyone points to a group member they want to speak for the group. The one who gets the most "points" is the spokesperson.

- Ask for the total number of feet in each participant's household—(a cat = 4, a bird = 2, people = 2 each). The person with the highest number is the leader in the group.
- Find out who has the earliest or latest birthday during the year.
- Ask participants to write their middle names on a sheet of paper. The person with the longest middle name is the leader.
- Choose the person who has worked in the same job the longest.
- Ask the person who came the longest distance.
- Pick the person who has worked in the field the longest.
- Select the person who is newest in the field.
- Ask for the mother's first name. The first or last alphabetically becomes the leader.

Dividing into Groups

Encourage trainees to meet people and work in groups that are not made up of their friends and co-workers. Meeting others is one of the benefits of a training session. Furthermore, dividing into small groups gives the instructor an opportunity to change the dynamics of the training and to vary the interaction. Of course, one can simply have the group count off according to the number of groups you want. However, there are many more interesting ways to divide into small groups.

- **Birthdays**—separate into the months of birthdays. For four groups, January, February, and March will comprise one group, April, May, and June will comprise another, and so on. You can easily divide into three, four, or six groups by the number of months you assign to each group.
- **Playing cards**—pass out playing cards, one to each participant. If you need two groups, divide by color; if you need four groups, divide by suits; if you need five groups, divide by suits and face cards.
- **Name tags**—color code name tags and give them out randomly. Have everyone with the same color go to the same group.
- **Stickers**—put a variety of stickers on name tags depending on the number of groups you want. The stickers can have a seasonal theme or tie into the training topic.
- **Social Security Numbers**—have persons gather with others who have the same last digit. Or total the last four digits and find others with the same or similar total. Divide by odd or even numbers. Telephone numbers will work as well.
- **Division by Candy Bar**—Place a bowl of small candy bars on each table and invite each attendee to take one. Have as many varieties of candy as the number of groups you want. If you want to divide into six groups, put six different varieties in the bowl. After everyone has chosen one, ask participants to divide into groups according to the candy they have chosen.
- **Division by Puzzles**—Use the same number of puzzles as the number of groups you want. Pass out a piece of puzzle to each person. Have participants form groups according to the puzzle where their piece belongs. To make the

activity go more smoothly, use puzzles that have different-colored back-grounds.

- **Favorite Pets**—Ask for a show of hands about favorite pets—dogs, cats, birds, or fish. You can expect that more will select dogs and cats. If you want groups about even in size, combine birds and fish or use categories such as large dogs and small dogs, short-haired or long-haired dogs, and solid color or mixed cats. Then divide into groups according to the participants' favorites.

Facilitating Group Reporting

Keep track of time when leaders are reporting their groups' conclusions to the larger group. State the time limits up front and limit reporting to a few minutes each. Even if each reporter takes ten minutes, most of the participants spend forty minutes listening if there are four groups! Use a kitchen timer, stop watch, or ask a volunteer to call time.

Ensure that each group has a chance to share its most important ideas by asking the leaders to state those ideas first. It is often helpful to ask groups to select their top three to five issues or suggestions for the report. Selecting the top ones requires that the groups prioritize, which is an important facet of their learning.

If there are more than four groups, have each leader give one- or two-minute summaries. The summaries can build on one another so that every group has the opportunity to contribute something new. For example, after the first group leader reports, the second group leader might state that his group concurs with the first group's conclusions and only add new information.

If reports are running too long, bring them to a conclusion by waiting for a pause and politely saying, "Thank you very much." Smile so it is clear your comment is not meant to cut them off, but is simply to remind them that there are time limits . A suggestion that participants share more information with each other at the break or after the session can also be helpful.

Typically, trainers will select the group to report first, often a group identified as Group one, or they will ask a group to volunteer. For variation, have the group with the highest number report first. Or, try rolling a die to see which group goes first. Roll again to see who will go second, third, and so on.

SMALL GROUP DISCUSSION IDEAS

Here are examples of directions for several small group discussion activities:

Planning

As a group, choose a theme that you might use with preschoolers. Then answer the following questions based on the theme you have selected. Chose someone to keep a record of your ideas.

1. How is this theme relevant to the children in your classroom?
2. What are some age-appropriate activities that you would conduct?
3. How can you help parents understand the value of this theme?
4. What are some ways to evaluate the success of the activities?

Values

Discuss each of the following topics in your group. Be prepared to summarize your discussion with the whole group.

1. You wish to help a child develop an understanding of what it means to be honest. What are some ways you can do it?
2. You wish to help children develop an appreciation for beauty. How can you do that?
3. You want children to experience success and achievement. How will you provide for it?

Teacher-made Materials

In your group, discuss the following situation. Be as creative as you like. Be prepared to share your three best ideas for each curriculum area with the whole class.

A parent has donated 500 small plastic containers in assorted sizes, shapes, and colors. Design an activity for each of the following curricular areas:

1. Math
2. Science
3. Motor development
4. Art
5. Language and emerging literacy
6. Dramatic play
7. Health

Team Games

Teams may be established for a specific activity or for the duration of a training session or series of sessions. Many of the same guidelines for small groups are applicable to teams. Small group activities and team activities are often interchangeable. Usually there will be a spirit of competition in team games. Small group activities can be translated into team activities simply by adding the competitive element.

Alphabet Search—Alphabet Search helps trainees become familiar with early childhood materials. Divide into teams. Ask each team to fill a bucket with objects from a classroom (or a catalog if the training is not in or near a classroom). They must find one object for each letter of the alphabet: "A" might be alphabet blocks, "B" might be a stuffed bear, "C" might be crayons, and so on. A recorder lists items as they are put in the bucket. The first team to come up with twenty-six items "wins." Teams continue to search until all teams finish. The teams then exchange buckets and discuss how they might use the items with children.

Countdown—Ask teams to list as many ways to work math concepts into the curriculum in a meaningful way as they can. Be sure they include many different math concepts, not just counting. Some possibilities are passing out napkins, using blocks, making graphs, charting attendance, or using peg boards. Give teams a time limit and count backward aloud as the time comes to an end. Usually about two or three minutes is enough, with the countdown starting at ten seconds from the end.

Knowing Colors—Have teams list as many words as they can for shades of red, blue, and green. After about five to ten minutes, the team with the most names will be the winner. Help participants to recognize the variety in our language and how there are levels of knowledge; although children may recognize basic colors, there is still much more to learn.

Jigsaw—Jigsaw helps participants be responsible for their learning by making each one an "expert" in one aspect of the topic. The "expert" then teaches his part to the others on his team. For example, participants on heterogeneous teams may be assigned reading or reference materials. Each person receives an "expert sheet" that contains a different subtopic to research. After each one has completed the task, the "experts" meet together to discuss their subtopic in an "expert" group. Then the "experts" return to their original teams and teach their teammates about their topics. To culminate the activity, each person may take a brief quiz about the content of the subtopics. Jigsaw supports interdependency since each participant depends on his teammates to provide information.

For example, if the topic is unit blocks, the subtopics to research might be:

1. How to set up a block area
2. Appropriate accessories to use with blocks
3. How to guide children in the block area
4. What children learn from blocks

Expert Sheet
How to Set Up a Block Area

Read the reprint of the article that you receive on this topic. Summarize below the areas to consider when setting up a block area:

1. Location in relation to other interest areas
2. Defining the area
3. Storage of blocks and accessories
4. Equipment and items needed

For a group of twelve trainees, divide into three teams with four members each. After completing the activities and the "expert sheets," each team will have an "expert" in each of the four subtopics who will teach the others on the team about his subtopic.

One member of each team completes the "expert sheet" on how to set up a block area, another completes a similar sheet on appropriate accessories. A third completes a sheet on guiding children, and the last completes a sheet on what children learn. Then all the experts on setting up a block center meet together; all the experts on appropriate accessories meet; all the experts on guiding children meet, etc. Each expert then returns to his team and teaches what he knows to the other team members. Then each person on each team is knowledgeable in all aspects of the topic.

Round Robin—Round Robin is an interactive version of brainstorming. It provides a structured system for all to participate and to share ideas and information with everyone in the group. The instructions for Round Robin are:

1. Write questions on pieces of poster board, one question to a poster. Have enough posters and questions for the number of small groups you will have.
2. Place the posters around the room.
3. Divide into groups of five to seven people each.
4. Assign (or have each group select) a poster with which to start.
5. Each group chooses a leader to lead the discussion and to record responses on the posters.
6. Groups begin by asking one person for his response to the question.
7. The leader writes the response.
8. The leader asks another person for a response and writes her response.
9. The groups continue until each person has given one response.
10. The groups spend five to seven minutes at each poster.
11. Participants do not discuss or evaluate the ideas at this step.
12. The groups move around the room to another poster with another question when instructed and repeat the process until they have been to every poster.
13. When each group returns to its original poster, it will find ideas and responses to the question contributed by the other groups.
14. The groups now discusses the ideas and, as a group, selects five that they want to share with everyone.

In a simpler version of Round Robin, each person in a group is given a few minutes to speak. The key element in Round Robin is that each person gets a chance to speak in turn.

Other Activities for Small Groups

Dramatic Play—This activity can be varied in many ways. Give groups the following directions and the materials they will need to complete the activity.

1. Choose a theme for a dramatic play area.
2. Look through the early childhood equipment catalogs for items that will stimulate dramatic play centered on the theme you have selected. List the items.
3. List additional items that you can collect or purchase inexpensively.
4. Be prepared to discuss the items your group selects with the whole group.

How Old Is This Child?—The goal of this activity is to learn to use resources such as development charts and screening instruments. Pass out descriptions of children at different developmental stages. Give enough information that trainees can use the resources to estimate the children's ages. Working in small groups, have trainees use development charts, screening instruments, and the like to estimate the age of the children based on the descriptions of what the children are doing. As the trainees discuss the information about the children, they become more familiar with developmental milestones and the associated ages. Be sure the trainees understand that development is individual.

Zip-closure Bag—Place a variety of items in a zip-closure bag. Select everyday items such as rubber bands, paper clips, crayons, peanuts, coins, or small trinkets. Let each group tell how the items in the bag relate to the subjects under discussion. For example, the rubber band may represent being stretched to the limit or stretching to improve one's skills; the coin may represent the need to manage money or to be cost-effective; the crayons may remind them of art activities, etc.

In a slightly different version, let each person contribute an idea that links the item and the topic being discussed. For instance, if the topic is how to get parents involved, and someone has a paper clip, she might say, "Parents can help with paperwork." If someone has a rubber band, she might say, "We must reach out (stretch) to parents to help them do the best they can."

Items to include in zip-closure bags:

Q-tip	Pencil	Eraser
Marble	Paper clip	Candy
Candle	Small magnifying glass	Coupon
Notepad	Toy car	Play money or coin
Rubber band	Block	Key
Small whistle	Balloon	Bandage strip
Safety pin	Business card	Piece of jewelry

Scavenger Hunt—Give each group a list of items, some that are rather common and some that are more difficult to find. The items listed under the zip-closure bag activity can be used here, too. Each group tries to find the items in purses, wallets, or briefcases. The first group to find all of them, or the group that finds the most, gets a small prize. Then each person relates his items to his work or the training topic and shares a tip or idea. A program director who finds the money, for example, might share a cost-cutting idea.

Dramatic Dolls—Enlarge the pattern of the doll on page 275 in the Appendix. Let trainees make their own doll from butcher paper or construction paper. Then have them write the characteristics they value in children on the dolls. Use the dolls as a springboard to a discussion of how to develop the characteristics they value. This is a good activity for a session on discipline and guidance.

In another version, ask participants to give the dolls names that characterize a child's behavior, then write down the circumstances that factor into that kind of behavior. Here are some examples:

Grouchy Gwen	Did not eat breakfast, had a disappointment on the way to school, was criticized this morning.
Curious Cassandra	Allowed to follow her own interests, given freedom within limits, exploration not squelched.

Impatient Ima	Bossy Bea
Happy Heather	Responsible Regina
Resilient Rachel	Disastrous Demetria
Critical Catherine	Energetic Evan
Aggressive Arthur	Friendly Freda

For other versions of this activity, write on the doll figures any of the following:

- Negative characteristics that will begin a discussion of what causes negative behavior.
- One's own strengths as a teacher.
- Skills you want to work on as a teacher.
- Characteristics important to getting along in the workplace.
- Ways to respect cultural differences.
- Characteristics that help communication with parents.

You're Singing My Song—Choose a song that best describes your role as director, caregiver, or trainer. Use the choice as a basis for group discussion. Participants may also select their own songs.

Heartbreak Hotel

Nobody Knows the Trouble I've Seen

What I Did for Love

Send in the Clowns

Climb Every Mountain

Simple Gifts

Day by Day

If We Make It Through December

The Impossible Dream

Searchin'

I'm Just a Girl Who Can't Say No

Money Makes the World Go Round

I Never Promised You a Rose Garden

If I Had a Hammer

My Way

The More We Get Together

Tomorrow

I've Got the World on a String

Whole Group Activities

Lectures

In spite of the generally negative reaction of trainers and participants to lectures, lectures can be effective and should be a part of a trainer's repertoire. There are many instances when information must be conveyed quickly. Lectures may be the best means of communicating the most up-to-date information when participants are well versed in an issue. Lectures are useful when many people must be informed of changes in procedures or given an overview of steps in a process.

When are lectures appropriate?
- When much information must be conveyed quickly such as describing a new procedure or instructions for completing a new form.
- When the information is so new that listeners may have little experience upon which to draw.
- As a keynote speech with a large group.
- For motivational or inspirational talks.

How do we make lectures interesting and effective?
- Do not read information aloud.
- Summarize, then give detailed information to participants as a handout.
- Maintain eye contact as much as possible.
- Talk to the participants, not at them.
- Make lectures interactive.
- Ask questions and invite comments.
- Use illustrations whenever possible.
- Illustrations help maintain attention and help visual learners focus on the information. Illustrations may be overhead transparencies, flip charts, props, or pictures that show what you are describing. Illustrations are useful even when the information is in a handout. They keep the group's attention on the speaker rather than dividing attention between the speaker and the handout.

- Allow time for questions and make it comfortable for participants to ask questions.
- Let the audience know that you will be around after the session to answer individual questions.
- Limit the time.
- Keep lectures as short as possible. Sitting and listening too long will cause participants to "tune out" and daydream.

Panel Presentations and Discussions

A panel in its simplest form is a lecture. Generally, a panel consists of people with different expertise, but who share a common interest in an issue. For example, a panel on child abuse recognition and prevention might include a child protection worker, a police officer, a social worker, a parent education specialist, and a family violence counselor. Usually, each person on a panel will have an allotted time to present information, then they may answer questions directed to a specific panel member or the group as a whole. Often they will react to each other's comments, adding information or even asking questions. This interchange with each other is the main difference between a panel and a series of short lectures by different speakers. Another difference is that a panel often speaks from a seated position. All guidelines that apply to a lecture readily apply to panels.

Facilitator-led Discussions

Frequently it is necessary to provide a foundation of information for participants. Sometimes a trainer will want to find out what a group already knows. Also, a trainer may want to solicit ideas from the group. A whole-group discussion can serve to review content, summarize information, and provide a framework from which participants may work. Facilitator-led discussions are also a way to find out what participants already know and what they want to get from the training.

A facilitator may have in mind several key points he wishes the group to identify. After the group has identified some key points, he can add any that they have omitted. Here are some tips for facilitator-led discussion:

- Write (or have someone write) the group's comments on a flip chart, overhead transparency, or a dry-erase board. Writing the comments helps focus attention, serves as a reminder of what was said, and provides a record of the group's thoughts. If you do the recording, try not to turn your back to the audience. Stand beside the flip chart or white board so your side, rather than your back, is toward the audience. Having another person to record information is preferable since it frees you to keep eye contact with the audience and to focus on the discussion.
- Ask open-ended questions. "What are some ways to communicate with parents?" will get a variety of responses. "Should you communicate with parents?" will not generate much discussion since it calls for a "yes" or "no" answer. If some key points are missed, the facilitator can ask leading questions to try to help participants think of them.

- Seek responses from many people, not just one or two. Ideas for how to structure a discussion to get responses from many people and how to handle monopolizers are in Chapter 6: Troubleshooting, on page 207.

Interactive Whole Group Experiences

Inner Circle—Inner Circle is a way to solicit involvement from quieter members of a group. Inner Circle also lets the instructor create an interactive setting in a large group. For Inner Circle, arrange chairs for about one-fourth to one-half of the trainees in a circle. The others will sit around the circle. Trainees in the inner circle are the only ones who will participate in the discussion. The others will be observers and can complete a worksheet that offers their reaction to the discussion. Then the observers will describe their reaction to the discussion or may rotate into the inner circle.

Attitudes about Children—Pass out pads of sticky notes and have each person take three sheets. Ask each person to write a behavior, characteristic, or trait of children on each sheet. Give them a few examples, identifying some that are positive as well as negative. Some examples might be: dependent, hitting, growing, noisy, learning.

After they finish, put the sheets on the wall or on charts that you have labeled "desirable" and "undesirable." Depending on the size of the group, you might need several pairs of charts or need to conduct the activity at a break to prevent crowding around the charts. Then have each person walk around the room and write on an index card what he considers the five most desirable and five most undesirable traits. When they are finished, have participants return to their seats and follow up with a discussion. Generally, the desirable behaviors will be those we value and like; the undesirable ones will be those we have difficulty handling or that especially irritate us. Prompt participants to suggest some ways to separate the behavior from the child. Discuss how labeling children affects their behavior and how we can react to children without showing favoritism.

Setting Priorities—To identify priorities in a large group when there are many suggestions, list all ideas on the pages of a flip chart. Then ask each person to vote for ten, listing the number of votes for each idea. After selecting the top ten, ask for everyone to vote for the top five. Continue until you have successfully narrowed down the number of priorities.

Attention-grabbers and Motivators

Props can support whole group discussion. Many Hats is a good technique for helping early childhood personnel and trainers think about the various important roles that they play in the lives of families and children. Often, the whole group can be involved in an activity such as Many Hats, Building Children's Self-Esteem, or Attitudes.

The Many Hats We Wear—Have an assortment of hats placed at various places when trainees arrive. If the group is too large, or you do not have enough hats, ask for volunteers to sit at the seats where you have placed hats. Wear a hat yourself to demonstrate what you want participants to do. Encourage everyone who has a hat to put it on and wear it. Ask them to use their imagination and think about how the hat relates to

their jobs. Some trainees will give humorous suggestions. Some possible answers follow, but participants will come up with many, many more.

The Many Hats of Directors and Caregivers

- Construction Hat—building child care; building families
- Graduation Cap—providing accurate, up-to-date information about children; having knowledge and skills
- Sailor Hat—helping parents navigate the sea of subsidies; weathering rough water; running a tight ship
- Air Force, Army, or Marine Hat—consulting with military families; drills; leading the way
- Business Hats (male, female)—networking with business; having business skills
- Baseball Helmet—hitting a home run; success; striking out; sometimes failing
- Hunting Hat—finding your target population; hunting for money
- Old-fashioned Hat—know the history of the field; old-fashioned values; remembering traditions
- Cowboy Hat, Sombreros, Turbans, or other ethnic headgear—respecting and responding to cultural differences
- Firefighter Helmet—keeping children safe; conducting fire drills; meeting regulations; being prepared; assisting with natural disasters
- Rain Hat—Surviving rainy days; being prepared; saving for a rainy day
- Nurses Cap—nurturing children; keeping them healthy; examining sick children; developing health policies
- Feather-decorated Hat—smoothing the ruffled feathers of unhappy parents or dissatisfied staff
- Football or other helmet—to protect you when you feel you are hitting your

head against the wall
- New Year's Eve Hat—making resolutions; getting a fresh start; celebrating
- Holiday Hats—recognizing cultural traditions; celebrating; having fun
- Magician or Leprechaun—trying to get money out of a hat; looking for the pot of gold
- Gardener's Straw Hat— nurturing children and families and helping them grow
- Wedding Veil or Hat—helping parents make the right match with children's needs
- Sherlock Holmes Hat—detecting what children need; finding the right activity; looking for clues to children's behavior

The Many Hats of Trainers
- Dr. Seuss Hat—we must be versatile and creative
- Very small hat—we all wear many "mini" hats
- Construction Hat—building better programs through training
- Graduation Cap—providing accurate, up-to-date information based on research
- Sailor Hat—helping trainees navigate the sea of scholar"ships"
- Air Force, Army, or Marine Hat—working with military child care centers
- Train Engineer Hat—being a leader in "train"ing
- Business Hats (male, female)—networking with businesses
- Baseball Helmet—for a Family Day Care "Home" run
- Hunting Hat—finding the target population
- Old-fashioned Hat—knowing the history of child care and building on it
- Cowboy Hat, Sombreros, Turbans, or other ethnic headgear—respecting and responding to cultural differences and learning styles of participants
- Firefighter—helping employees put out fires
- Rain Hat—being prepared
- Nurses Cap—nurturing new employees and keeping them healthy
- Feather-decorated Hat—smoothing the ruffled feathers of complainants and dissatisfied personnel
- Football or other helmet—to protect you when you feel you are hitting your head against the wall
- Magician or Leprechaun—helping employees use available resources; having a hat full of tricks; looking for the pot of gold
- Gardener's Straw Hat—nurturing young trainees and helping them grow
- Wedding Veil or Hat—making the right match between training and providers
- Sherlock Holmes Hat—detecting training needs; finding clues to doing a better job

Building Children's Self-Esteem—This activity is a very effective way to demonstrate how our words and actions affect children. By combining visual imagery with actions and words, the message hits home with trainees in a dramatic and memorable way.

As the participants read positive comments, a child figure is unfolded. As they read negative comments, the shape is destroyed.

Prepare ahead of time:

1. Make a large paper shape of a child by tracing around a child, then draw features and clothes on the figure.
2. Display the figure folded. Make about ten folds so that participants cannot tell it is a child until it is time for the activity.
3. Write negative and positive comments on strips of paper or index cards. Put one comment on each strip or index card; use one color of paper or index card for the positive comments and another color for negative ones. This will allow you to call on participants to read the comments by the color of the paper or card they hold.
4. Distribute the positive and negative comments to participants.

Conducting the activity:

5. Ask participants to select a name for the child. Refer to the child by name frequently to personalize the activity.
6. Have the participants read aloud positive phrases.
7. As the participants read their positive phrases, unfold the child figure until it is completely unfolded and visible.
8. Solicit comments about how the child feels when someone makes these positive comments.
9. Next, have the participants read negative phrases as you cut up the figure. Repeat the negative phrases with emphasis as you slice the figure.
10. Solicit comments about how the child feels when negative comments are made.

Positive Statements

1. "Thanks for remembering to feed our fish."
2. "Please remember that loud voices are for outside."
3. "That's a tough problem, but you figured it out by yourself."
4. "I enjoy having you in my class."
5. "You worked the puzzle all by yourself."
6. "Please use your walking feet inside."
7. "I am really happy that you are well and back at school."
8. "I really miss you when you are not here."
9. "I'm so glad your mother is coming to our parent night."
10. "Would you like to sit beside me at lunch?"
11. "I know you feel sad when your mother leaves."
12. "Thanks for helping to get the snack ready."
13. "I know you are angry, Michael. I like it when you use your words."
14. "You really helped Quinton a lot today."
15. "Thank you for being so nice to our new student."
16. "You can climb all the way to the top!"
17. "Which paint color would you like? "
18. "You laced your shoes all by yourself."
19. "The square blocks go here by this shape."
20. "Wow! You carried that heavy chair all by yourself."

Negative Statements
1. "You are so clumsy!"
2. "I just cannot trust you to do anything right."
3. "You never watch where you are going."
4. "He was really bad again today."
5. "Stop gobbling up your food and eat slowly."
6. "Get that thumb out of your mouth. You're much too old for that."
7. "You know you are just the slowest one in the class."
8. "Let me help you up the steps. You might fall."
9. "How did you get so dirty!"
10. "Why can't you be good like your sister."
11. "How many times do I have to tell you not to do that?"
12. "Quit pestering me."
13. "That's easy. Anyone could do it. I don't know why you can't."
14. "He's lazy, just like his father."
15. "Sit still and be quiet. No talking during group time."
16. "Can't you do anything right?"
17. "That is too heavy for you to carry. I know you'll just drop it."
18. "You can't even color in the lines."
19. "Stop crying and don't be such a baby."
20. "You just always have to be mean, don't you?"

Positive Feelings

Safe	Encouraged	Smart	Happy
Capable	Guided	Important	Decisive
Responsible	Appreciated	Loved	Smart
Independent	Proud	Understood	Loved
Values	Respected	Touched	Powerful

Negative Feelings
Professional Development Living Pie Chart—Discuss the stages of professional growth

Hurt	Disliked	Discouraged	Unappreciated
Dumb	Upset	Unhappy	No good
Embarrassed	Angry	Incapable	Insignificant
Incompetent	Ridiculed	Unsafe	Sad
Unloved	Humiliated	Threatened	Unwanted

listed below. Then have participants line up by the stage in which they fit, with Survival first, Consolidation next, Renewal next, and Maturity last. Have the line move to form a circle. Stand in the center with a ball of yarn. Hand the end of the yarn to the first person in Survival. Have her throw it back to you. Throw it to the first person in Consolidation and have her throw it back to you. Then do the same with the first person in Renewal and again with the first person in Maturity. Your circle will be a demonstration of a pie chart that represents the group's professional growth stages. You can also have the lines stand side by side and make a bar graph.

Stages of Professional Growth

Survival	1-2 years of experience or new job
Consolidation	2-4 years of experience
Renewal	3-5 years of experience
Maturity	6+ years of experience

Here's another version of a living pie chart or graph.

Phases of a Career

Dues-paying	Entry or beginning level
Mainstreaming	Secure about our job choice
Excelling	Satisfaction in our career and competency
Re-assessing	Considering or making a change
Peaking	Contentment and confident with ourselves and our career
Transitioning	Creating a bridge to the future, making decisions about the next step

More Living Pie Charts—The living pie chart activity works with any question with four to six possible answers. For example, if your question is "What is your favorite flavor of ice cream?" have all the people who choose vanilla stand together, all those who choose chocolate stand together, etc. Then have participants form a circle with all the ones who chose the same flavor together. Hand the end of the yarn to the first person who said vanilla and ask her to return it to the center. Find the last person who said vanilla and throw the yarn ball to her as you hold on to the yarn. Have her hold on and throw the ball back to you. If the next choice is chocolate, find the last person who said chocolate and throw the ball to her, letting her hold on and throw it back to you. Continue around the circle until you have completed your human pie chart.

Vision of Childhood—Have statistics about children printed on labels or index cards. Good sources for the statistics are *The Kids Count Data Book* and the *Children's Defense Fund Annual Report*. Have participants make a poster or mural showing their vision of how they will change these statistics.

Demonstrations, Learning Games, and Other Learning Experiences

Demonstrations

Demonstrations may be classified in two general categories. Demonstrations can emphasize a point in a dramatic way or illustrate a concept. These types of demonstrations can grab participants' attention and show trainees the importance of personal attributes and characteristics.

Another type of demonstration provides learners with an example of the correct steps to complete a task. This second type gives learners a model to aid understanding and retention. Both types of demonstrations help participants understand exactly what you mean.

Demonstrations aid retention because they often involve analogies and the use of several senses. This section includes a collection of the first type of demonstrations to emphasize important factors in working for and with young children. Typically, the instructor conducts a demonstration, although it may require participation by the trainees. The following guidelines apply to both types of demonstrations:

Guidelines for Effective Demonstrations

- Be sure everyone can see and hear what you are doing. If they cannot, they will not understand the point you are making or know how to complete the task. A wonderful science activity may be useless in an auditorium with one hundred people if it is conducted on a table in the front.

- Explain what you are doing while you conduct the activity. Help trainees discover and understand what point you are making and why you are doing that specific activity. Telling the learners why you are doing what you are doing helps them understand the rationale behind the activity. Explanations assist those who need auditory reinforcement.

- Jumping around in the sequence of an activity will only confuse the audience. For demonstrations of activities, conduct activities in the same order in which you want trainees to do them.

- If the demonstration requires many steps or is a difficult procedure, do it several times. Give instructions in writing for trainees to take with them.

- Remember that a procedure that seems very simple to you may not make sense to trainees when they get back on the job.

- Demonstrations used to illustrate a point effectively or to help participants remember key ideas often involve analogies or use examples. Here are some demonstration ideas that are useful for helping early childhood personnel understand work-related issues.

COPING WITH CHANGE

Change Is Hard—To demonstrate that change is difficult and that old habits are hard to break, have everyone cross their arms. Then have each one reverse and put the other arm on top. Discuss the awkward feeling that results. Relate the activity to being comfortable with existing habits. Discuss the difficulty of learning to do something differently. Ask participants to think about how the awkwardness will eventually go away if they repeat the procedure hundreds of times and become used to the new way. Ask if anyone had to learn to write with the other hand because of an injury and if this change became easier over time. Lead the group to understand that learning new ways may be hard at first, but can be done.

For variation or as additional examples, have everyone clap several times. Then have them clap again with the other hand on top. Add humor by joking about appreciating the applause! Discuss how difficult and awkward clapping in a new way seems. Or, have participants clasp their hands in their laps and notice which thumb is on top. Then ask them to clasp their hands again, this time placing the opposite thumb on top. Ask them to describe how this action feels. Help them identify that they can become comfortable in their ability to accomplish new tasks. Another way to show that people like to do things the way they have always done them is to require participants to change seats at a break. Discuss how all of us are creatures of habit and like our familiar ways of doing things. Lead participants to recognize that while change is difficult at first, they can become used to it as the new techniques become more familiar.

River Rocks—Pass around a water-smoothed pebble. Discuss how this was once a much larger, jagged rock but now it is smooth and rounded because of many years of moving water wearing it away. Relate this to how trainees can make change, often not in any one big event, but slowly, with consistency, over time just as the river changed the rock.

Honey, Not Vinegar—Everyone has heard, "You catch more flies with honey than vinegar." Help participants recognize that force is not a good way to change behavior. Pair up participants and have them face each other. Ask one person in each pair to clench his hand and hold it in front of the other. Then tell the second person to open the hand of the first person. After a short time, ask them to stop. Most participants will try to pry open their partner's fists. Ask if anyone was able to open her partner's hands without using force. Usually, someone recognizes a solution that is simply asking the partner to open his hand. Lead the group in a discussion about effective techniques to facilitate change without using force. This activity can initiate a discussion about regulations compared to voluntary standards for programs.

IMPORTANCE of WORKING TOGETHER

The Chain—To demonstrate the importance of working together, pass out paper strips (about one by ten inches or three by twenty-five centimeters), markers, and crayons. Give each person a strip of paper to decorate. Ask what participants, as individuals, can do with their decorated paper strip. Usually only a few suggestions will be given. Pass around staplers, glue, and rolls of tape and ask the group to join the strips into a chain. Give them a few minutes to admire the chain and discuss what they can do with it. The group will probably suggest even more ideas, such as decorating the room or playing a game. Help them compare the usefulness of a single strip of paper with the chain's usefulness. Guide the discussion to have participants recognize that the whole group working together can be much more effective than any one individual working alone.

Parachute Pals—The same activities you do with the parachute and children are also great team-builders for adults. Using a purchased parachute and a ball, have a group of trainees try to keep the ball on the parachute without letting it go through the hole. Then change the goal and try to make the ball go through the hole as quickly as possible. Relate the activity to the need to work together to reach a goal. This activity also can illustrate that sometimes goals must change.

Jellybean Guessing—Hold up a clear jar of jellybeans or other small candies that you have counted. Have the number recorded in a hidden place. Ask each person to guess how many candies are in the jar. Announce the highest and the lowest guesses that you hear and write them on a flipchart or white board. Emphasize the broad range of numbers. Have participants now work in pairs to give one answer per pair. Solicit the highest and lowest guesses and again emphasize the range. Write the highest and lowest guesses on the chart. The range of numbers will usually be smaller than the first time. Work in groups of four to get one answer, then in groups of eight. Each time the range of numbers will become smaller. Keep enlarging the size of the groups until the range of guesses is very small or the whole group chooses one answer. Announce the correct number. The group answer will be much closer to the accurate amount than the individual, partner, or small group extremes. Lead the group to recognize and articulate that a group answer is usually more accurate than individual answers.

Discuss the various ways the participants approached the problem. Some will count a layer, then estimate; others will compare the quantity to something else. Discuss how pairs and groups arrived at one answer. Some will compromise by agreeing on an answer half way between the two extremes. Sometimes members of a group will accept the answers of the more outspoken individuals or the first one to speak. Sometimes one person will actively work to persuade the others. Compare this experience to how children need group activities to develop social skills, language, and problem-solving abilities.

Everybody Wins: The Value of Cooperation—This training exercise shows how people look at the same task in different ways. Draw an imaginary line on the floor, and ask one person to stand on each side. Ask them to try to persuade the other to cross the line. After they try several ways, help them to discover that an easy way is to simply say, "If you'll cross the line, I will, too." Then they both win. Use this activity to demonstrate the value of communication and cooperation.

Bountiful Ideas!—Hold up a paper towel tube. Ask participants to write as many uses as they can think of for the paper towel tube. After about a minute, ask participants to call out how many they listed. Usually it will be three to five. Then have them work in small groups to list their ideas. After about five minutes, ask the groups to call out how many uses they have listed. Call attention to how many more ideas they found when working as a group. Point out examples of how one person's idea generated another's idea and how ideas stimulated even more ideas when participants worked in groups.

The Value of Planning Together—Ask participants to make as many triangles on a piece of paper as they can in thirty seconds. They must work alone and not talk to each other. Use a stopwatch or count slowly to thirty. When the time is up, ask them to count the number of triangles they made and write down their numbers. Let them compare their work with each other. Then give them time to plan how they can make more triangles in the limited time. Ask them to make triangles again, and this time encourage them to work with others.

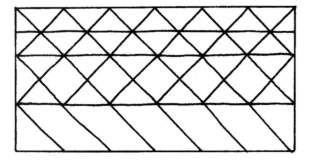

If no one discovers a quick way to make many triangles, demonstrate how to do it (see illustration). Relate the game to how there never seems to be enough time to plan, yet a little time spent planning and working with others can greatly improve performance. Everybody learns from others when they take the time to listen. People typically think of triangles as being separate from one another, but they sometimes need to look at situations from another point of view.

Tied up!—Give one person in a small group a ball of twine. That person holds the end of the twine and passes the ball to another person, who passes it to another, and so on. Continue until everyone in the group is holding the twine. Caution them to keep the twine taut but not to break it. Encourage participants to complicate the task by wrapping the twine around some people in the group. Return the ball to the first person after everyone is joined together by the twine. Next, ask the participants to follow your directions. For example, ask one person to take a step to the right, another to move to the middle, or another to sit down or turn backward. Then ask the participants to try to move to another location without breaking the twine. Have them see how cooperation is necessary for them to move as a group without breaking the string.

After several minutes, ask what they learned. Did some people show initiative while others deferred? Did leadership develop? What kinds of communication worked or did not work? Did the string break? If so, why? If not, how did the group prevent it from breaking? Help them relate the activity to the fact that every action a team member makes has an effect on the others. Just as they had to consider all other team members while they tried to reach the goal of moving, they must consider everyone's needs as they try to meet their team's goals.

Sharing Resources—Divide participants into teams of four to six persons each. Give each individual five to six pieces of construction toys or blocks. Ask them to build the most creative object they can. Do not tell them whether they should just use their own or whether to share with each other. They will quickly realize that they can be far more creative if they pool their resources.

Taking Risks—Before the session, put chocolate pudding and marshmallows in a clean, sanitized small plant pot. Cover with crushed chocolate cookies to look like dirt. Place a clean flower in the pot. During a training session, ask trainees if they will take a chance and "eat dirt." Offer a prize for the first person to volunteer. For fun, pull a gummy worm candy from the dirt and make a big show of how unpleasant it is. Eat it yourself in a very dramatic way. Relate the experience to thoughtful risk-taking. By this time, the volunteer will have figured out that the "dirt" is edible. Point out that the volunteer was willing to investigate the possibility even before knowing for sure that it was not really dirt. Relate the demonstration to the importance of trusting each other to work together. Point out how we are willing to take risks in a supportive environment. At break, serve chocolate cookies and gummy worms.

Judging by First Impressions—
When you have two winners for a game, offer each a choice of prizes. Have one wrapped attractively or in a pretty gift bag, the other in a plain, ordinary cardboard box or brown paper bag. Generally, the first winner will select the prettier wrapping. When the winner opens it, she will find a small trinket. Then the second winner will select the other package that contains a nice prize. Relate the experience to how one cannot judge based on first impressions. Point out how people should not jump to conclusions about each other's motives or capabilities, but get to know each other to work as a team. Relate the activity to how adults and children are all different inside. Stress the importance of taking the time to see what is inside and not judge based on what is seen.

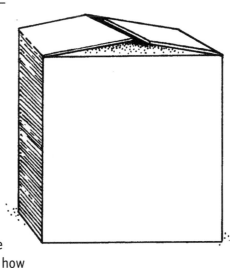

Finding Solutions to Problems

Puzzle Exchange—Mix up several children's frame puzzles. Place a frame and an assortment of pieces at each table. The pieces on each table should be an assortment from all of the puzzles, not just from the one with the frame on the table. Tell participants the goal is to complete the puzzle on their table during the training session. For group members to get a puzzle piece, they must share a tip or idea about the workshop topic. Instruct them that during the breaks, they are to give pieces to people who share a tip or idea with them. They are to give ideas to get pieces they need to finish the puzzle on their table. Use the experience to relate that learning is an exchange of information. Emphasize that no one has all of the answers (pieces), but that everyone has some. Through sharing, you can solve the puzzles and problems you encounter.

Folding Towels—Give volunteers an assortment of hand towels and bath towels. Ask them to fold them as they usually do at home. Compare the different ways each person folded the towel to the fact that there are often several ways to solve a problem. Ask the volunteers why they use the system they do. They usually say that their towels fit on the shelf better or that was the way their mother did it. Point out that there is usually more than one way to reach a goal and that the way selected will depend on individual needs.

Shedding Light on the Issue—Turn out the lights. Use a flashlight to show a small portion of a large picture or poster. Shine the light through a small hole cut in cardboard and held a few inches from the flashlight. Have trainees try to describe the picture from the small section that they can see. Then move the cardboard and shine the flashlight on the whole picture. Compare the two situations and how the flashlight alone illuminates much more of the picture. Compare the small beam of light to being too narrowly focused in an approach to solving a problem, and the larger light to a broader view. You can also go a step further and use a larger beam such as a portable lantern or shop light.

Bridging the Gorge—To demonstrate that creativity and imagination can overcome difficult obstacles, pose this problem to trainees:

> The Niagara gorge walls are 800 feet apart. The river channel is 400 feet wide with water flowing at 24 miles an hour. If no boat can go across and no helicopters are available to go across, how would an engineer get a cable across to build a bridge?

Encourage as many imaginative solutions as time permits. Then tell them how a kite was flown across, the kite string was used to bring across a slightly larger cord. Describe how larger items were pulled across the gorge until a cable was taken across and the bridge built. The beginning of the bridge was as simple as flying a kite. Use this solution to illustrate that we may solve even seemingly impossible problems with ingenuity and creativity.

Nine Dots—Show participants the arrangement of dots on a flipchart, poster, or overhead transparency. Have them copy the arrangement on a piece of paper. Ask them to connect all nine dots by making just four connected lines and without picking up their pencil after they start. Most participants will try to connect without going through the outer dots. After they try for a few minutes, show how they must go "out of the box" to find the solution. Relate this experience to how preconceived notions restrict problem-solving capabilities. One tends to approach a new problem based on prior experiences, in this case the dot-to-dot games played as a child.

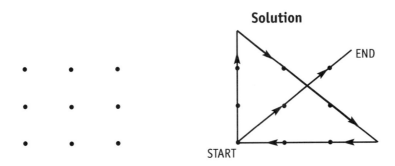

Solution

Five Thousand—To demonstrate the problems in jumping to conclusions, put the following addition problem on an overhead transparency, flipchart, or poster, but have all the figures covered. Tell the participants that you want them to add, in their heads, the figures that you uncover. Ask them to call out the answer. Uncover the figures starting at the top, showing only one line at a time, while the audience calls out the totals. When you uncover the final number, most will call out 5,000. Repeat the process to see if they catch on to their error. Then uncover all of the numbers at once so they can see them all together. Then they will see that the answer is 4,100 and not 5,000. Relate this activity to how we need to get all the information before we reach a decision. It also points out how we often jump to conclusions because of what we think should be the solution. The activity demonstrates the importance of taking time to be sure we are not too quick to make a decision.

$$
\begin{array}{r}
1{,}000 \\
+40 \\
1{,}000 \\
+30 \\
1{,}000 \\
+20 \\
1{,}000 \\
+10 \\
\hline
\end{array}
$$

SIX—To demonstrate how we make assumptions and look for incorrect or complicated solutions unnecessarily, write IX on an overhead transparency or flip chart. Ask trainees to add one line to make the number six. Most will assume that IX is the Roman numeral nine and will try to figure out how to make a Roman numeral six (VI). After they try for a few minutes, show them the simple solution of adding an S, or have a participant who has figured it out demonstrate it. Relate the activity to how we often look for solutions to problems based on false assumptions or not asking questions to get enough information.

Lemons to Lemonade—When addressing a particularly difficult problem, such as organizational change, personality issues, or conflict, here is a demonstration to take the edge off the issue. Prepare beforehand a few slices of lemon, a pitcher of water, and some sugar. Have a volunteer taste the lemon and describe it. Usually, she will give negative reactions, saying it is bitter, tart, difficult to eat, or unpleasant. Compare the lemon to the current situation being addressed. Then squeeze the other lemon slices into the pitcher of water. Add sugar and stir. Ask another volunteer to taste the lemonade and describe it. Relate the lemonade to the desired solution. Use this as a springboard to finding a solution to a perplexing problem. Have them think of the water as possibilities to consider. Ask them to think of the sugar as positive communication, that when blended with the lemon, can make a more pleasant solution—lemons to lemonade = problems to solution.

Communication Activities

Peanut Butter and Jelly—Show supplies to make a peanut butter and jelly sandwich. Ask for a volunteer to help you make a sandwich and have him turn his back to the audience. Tell him he cannot turn around to see what you are doing, and that you will make the sandwich following his instructions. He will usually begin by saying something like, "take out two pieces of bread." Deliberately misinterpret the directions by ripping out two slices of bread with a great flourish. Then let the volunteer continue to give directions while you continue to misinterpret them. Relate the misinterpretations to the need for clear directions and making an effort to understand what another is saying. The activity also demonstrates how people follow directions, but sometimes with a very different interpretation. This activity is especially good in directors' training.

Communication Blocks—Show how directions given only verbally cannot be easily understood. Have participants sit back to back with the same amount and color of small construction blocks. One of the partners constructs something and proceeds to tell the other person how to make one just like it. The person will have difficulty when they are unable to see what is being done. Relate the activity to the need to use vision to help understanding, and the need to show children and staff what we want them to do rather than just telling them.

A slightly different version demonstrates the limitations when directions are given only once without feedback. Start by dividing into pairs. Each person gets a set of small blocks that include exact duplicates. The partners turn their backs to each other. One person builds with the blocks and talks about what she is doing. The other partner tries to copy the pattern. Do not allow the directions to be given more than once, and do not allow any discussion or questions. Compare the constructions, which will probably be very different.

Repeat the activity, but this time allow discussions and questions. The results will be much better and far more similar. Lead trainees to recognize the problems in communication when there is no means of clarifying information. Relate this experience to the importance of giving feedback and to the need for reflective listening in working with children as well as adults.

Absence of Communication—Form groups of three to five people. Give each group some straws, playdough, or clay and toothpicks, and ask them to build a tower as tall as they can. Tell them that they may not talk while planning or constructing the tower. Tell them the group that builds the tallest tower will get a prize. Allow about fifteen minutes for the project. When time is up, ask them to reflect on the problems they encountered and how they overcame them. Ask how they were able to communicate and how effective those ways were. Relate the experience to children's problems in communicating when their language skills are limited and just developing. For those who work with toddlers, relate the experience to the strong desire for things coupled with very limited ability to verbally express those desires. The activity also can be used to understand the difficulties of children and adults with special needs or for whom English is a second language.

Ways to Communicate—Ask participants to line up according to their birthday month and day, starting with January. The catch is that they may not talk. After meeting some frustration, someone will recognize other ways to communicate such as hand signals or writing. After they complete the task, have them call out the birth dates and make any necessary adjustments. Lead into a discussion about the various means of communication that we use in daily life.

Use Clear Words, not Jargon—Print about twenty of the phrases on the following page on cards. Shuffle the cards and give them to a small group or to partners. Ask them to quickly make a speech out of the phrases by linking them together, adding as few words as possible. They should add mostly words such as "and," "yet," "but," "however". Have them read their speeches aloud, and lead the group to recognize that the phrases are jargon and open to wide interpretation as to meaning. Help the group to see that although the words and phrases sound good, they actually say very little.

Phrases

seeing commonalties	what we've seen
become societal problem	become more active stakeholders
in later time frame	tremendous enlightenment
can't afford price tag	the real key here
give a different perspective	strive for consensus
create innovative approach	opportunity to give free trial
integrate new approaches into system	attract economic growth
enjoy autonomy for awhile	vested interest to become more active
work on consensus	bring about positive change
get greatest return over time	take resources and focus them
does not compete with existing reform efforts	have a mechanism to get involved
	replicate a model
part of that effort	empower community
beginning to see synergy	buy into
coalition renaissance	unifying alliance
become world-class system	impact direction
link up through technology	collaborative effort
make certain commitments	embrace goals
regulatory relief would be incentive	commit to education
depends on local participation for success	support national goals
whirlwind tour	form partnership
open up for dialogue	cycle of improvement
get arms around design	reform education

Did You Read the Directions?—To demonstrate the importance of reading and following directions, give trainees a sheet of simple math problems involving addition, subtraction, multiplication, and division written out horizontally (such as 1 + 2 =). Write the following instructions at the top of the sheet:

For this exercise, the + sign means you should multiply, the − sign means you should divide. You do not need to work the multiplication problems. Work division problems as usual.

When they see the full page of arithmetic problems with their familiar math signs, many participants will assume that they know what to do and will fail to read the directions. Relate the experience to how one must introduce new ways of working with clear directions and discussion. This is a good activity to help directors understand why members of their staff do not always do what they are expected to do.

Clear Communication—Tell the following humorous stories to illustrate the importance of clear communication:

A grocer ordered an extra 200 turkeys to meet her customers' needs for Thanksgiving. The week before the big day, however, sales were very slow.

Afraid that she wouldn't be able to sell all the turkeys she had ordered, she called the supplier and told him to cut the turkey order in half.

When the order arrived, she found 200 turkeys, all cut in half.

A new employee was standing at the paper shredder holding a large report and looking very confused. "How does this thing work," he asked the secretary.

"It's simple," the secretary answered, taking the report from the new employee and feeding it into the shredder.

"How do I tell it to make three copies?" he asked.

Are You Listening?—To demonstrate how we stop listening when directions become too difficult, give the following instructions to trainees. Speak rapidly as you give the directions. Refuse to repeat the instructions if asked to do so. Afterward, have them discuss how they felt when they began to lose track. Relate the activity to how children feel if they do not have enough time to absorb information and to work at their own pace.

- Draw a square.
- Make a circle inside the square and a triangle to the right of the circle.
- Then make four small squares in each corner of the large square, putting a circle inside each of those squares.
- On the bottom of the triangle that is on the right of the circle, draw three lines, one shorter than the others.

Listening Skills—This activity demonstrates how people quit listening when they become bored or do not understand directions or the purpose of a task. Ask participants to work this simple math problems in their heads. Emphasize that the activity requires very simple math. Then read the problems fast so that participants cannot keep up with you.

$$
\begin{aligned}
&\text{Add } 2 + 4 \\
&\text{subtract } 3 \\
&\text{add } 4 \\
&\text{multiple by } 2 \\
&\text{subtract } 2 \\
&\text{divide by } 3 \\
&\text{add } 1 \\
&\text{subtract } 5
\end{aligned}
$$

The answer should be zero. However, most will become lost and quit if you read the problem fast enough. Repeat the procedure, and this time go slower or let them write down the answers as you read the problem one step at a time. Relate the experience to how, although this was a simple problem, the first time it was not presented in a way that made it possible for most to solve it. Tie the demonstration in with the importance of giving clear instructions in a way that others can understand them.

Musical Chairs—This activity helps persons to see that good communication can create a non-threatening environment for change. You will need a CD or tape player and some lively music.

Arrange chairs in a circle with the chair backs toward the center. Have one less chair than the number of participants. Play music while the participants move around the circle of chairs. Stop the music periodically for everyone to try to get a chair. The person left without a chair becomes an observer. Remove one chair each time the music stops. Continue until only one person remains. Ask participants to share their feelings. Opening up the conversation about change helps make people aware of feelings and stresses.

To relate to the importance of good communication during changing times, play the game again by making it obvious when the music is going to stop. Turn deliberately toward the CD or cassette player and reach for the controls in a highly visible manner. For comparison, then play the game while keeping a hand on the controls at all times, making no eye contact, and even deceiving participants by pausing occasionally. Discuss the different reactions that people experience when they know what to expect and when they are unsure. Discuss the problems caused by poor communication and ways to create open communication, especially during times of change.

Communication Self-test—Pass out the following questionnaire as a self-evaluation to help participants understand good procedures for communication. Discuss ways that listening and responding aid communication. Ask them to think of other responses that are examples of the principles given. Then ask them to watch for good responses as they work in groups throughout the session.

> Do you verify your understanding of what the speaker said by paraphrasing or restating?
>> "You are concerned about how to get your co-workers to understand why you want to have a meeting for the staff and parents."
>
> Do you demonstrate that you are listening by nodding, commenting, or offering other signs of understanding?
>> "You really wish you had more equipment, then."
>
> Do you attempt to expand your understanding of what is said by asking clarifying questions?
>> "So you don't think it will work unless you have some ways to involve the other staff?"
>
> Do you begin your response with agreement, then follow with any objections?
>> "I agree that it is hard to get staff to see the value of planning, but there are ways that it will work."
>
> If you disagree, do you state under what conditions you can agree?
>> "I can support the need to watch expenses, but reducing the budget for supplies is not the best way to do it."
>
> If you disagree, do you show respect for the individual's attempts?
>> "That's a clever idea, but it has some drawbacks that you may not have thought about."

THE VALUE OF OBSERVING

A Penny Saved—Ask participants to describe or draw a penny without looking at one. Remind them that they see pennies frequently and have for many years handled thousands of pennies. After they try for a few minutes with limited success, ask them to take a penny from their pocket or purse and look closely at it. Have some pennies available to pass around. Then have them draw or describe the penny. They will be much more successful this time. Relate the experience to the importance of observing children with a purpose in mind. Help them see that one can see often, but not necessarily observe. Emphasize that seeing is not the same as observing.

Phone Home—Ask participants to draw a touch-tone telephone and put the number, letters, and symbols in the right place. Typically, they will have some difficulty doing it. As they try, encourage them with such comments as, "Come on, now. You look at telephones many times a day!" or "I know you all have been using telephones for years!"
As they become frustrated, show them a telephone. Relate the experience to the difference between seeing and observing.

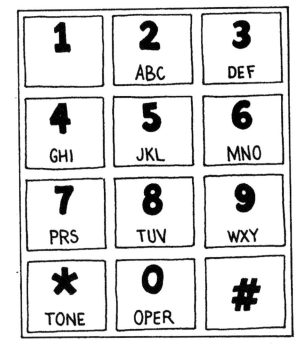

This activity also works when participants are negative and make comments about already knowing training content.

Note to the instructor: The 1 button has no letters, Q and Z are omitted, and the bottom row is * 0 #.

Cookie Characteristics—Pass out cookies for a snack. Use homemade chocolate chip or oatmeal cookies so there are noticeable differences among the cookies. Discuss how much the cookies seem alike when you look at the whole tray. Then have participants focus on differences in the individual cookies and describe the differences they see. They will see variations in the number of chips, in the sizes, or in the textures of the cookies. Relate the experience to the importance of careful observation and how, although things may seem exactly alike, many subtle differences can exist.

Have participants pick a cookie, then return the cookies to a tray that has the participants' names on it. Each one is to place her cookie over her name. Have a volunteer move the cookies, and place them over names on another tray where participants cannot identify their cookie from the location on the tray. Then see if participants can identify "their" cookie based on their memory of subtle differences. Everyone who does gets a prize.

Seeing the Whole Picture—To demonstrate the importance of teamwork and of seeing the whole picture, give each participant a piece of a children's jigsaw puzzle. Ask them to describe the whole puzzle based on just their one piece. They usually will not be able to tell much about the puzzle from the one piece. If the group is small, use a puzzle with about the same number of pieces as participants or use several small puzzles. Ask them to work the puzzle(s) at the break. If the group is large or the puzzle has many pieces, simply show them the picture on the box without working it.

You can use discarded jigsaw puzzles (even those with missing pieces) for large groups since they will not be working the puzzle and you probably will not get all the pieces back. Relate this experience to how we may see only our part in the lives of children. Help trainees understand that by working together (including parents and other professionals), teachers can see the whole picture and better understand a child's needs. You also can relate the activity to the need for understanding the total program in which one works, not just what one does.

Bird in the Hand—Put the following phrases on a flipchart, poster, or overhead transparency. Write the words on two lines and spaced exactly as they are here. Keep them covered until you are ready to do the activity.

A bird in the **the hand**	**A cup of** **of coffee**	**A stitch in** **in time**

To demonstrate the value of careful observation, ask participants to read the phrases rapidly. Most will read what they expect to see, not what is actually there. Relate the experience to the need for careful observation and not making assumptions based on what one expects to see.

CURRICULUM AND WORKING WITH CHILDREN

Teaching Is Not a Cookbook—This activity helps participants recognize that creativity is important in working with children. You can use it to make the point that working with young children requires knowledge, skills, judgment, and creativity. Pass out cards with various foods written on them, one item to each card. Give three cards to each person. Ask individuals to make up a recipe and describe it. They may add ingredients, but must use the ingredients on all three cards they received. The results will be humorous,

orange slices	green beans	pear halves
ketchup	tomatoes	mustard
whole-wheat bread	cabbage	corn meal
wieners	macaroni	eggs
grated cheddar cheese	spaghetti	skim milk
bean sprouts	lettuce	strawberries
marshmallows	tuna	potato
mashed potatoes	whipped cream	corn tortillas
shredded coconut	black beans	ground beef
onion	yams	sour cream
cherries	bagels	chicken legs
soy sauce	sesame seeds	pita bread
broccoli spears	green beans	soy sauce
chocolate syrup	corn	

especially from those who get combinations like cranberries, ketchup, and broccoli. Compare the difference in following a recipe and creating a new recipe. Emphasize that teaching is not a cookbook process. It requires problem solving, application of knowledge, and imagination. It involves making decisions based on prior experiences and the ability to predict outcomes. No one "recipe" always works with children, since children are all unique just as the combinations of food were unique. The participants created their recipes based on their experiences, skills, and knowledge of cooking, and on their ability to predict outcomes. We react to children in the same way when we make use of what we know and how we predict that children will respond to our actions. Even a prescribed curriculum (i.e., a cookbook) is not a substitute for skill and knowledge about how children learn.

Math Match—Make signs on index cards for the math concepts that children learn. Use Popsicle sticks or tongue depressors for handles. Make strips of paper with situations that are examples of children learning or using the math concepts. For example, one-to-one relationships: putting out napkins for snack. Participants with the strips find the right partner with the sign that relates to their situation. Then the two can describe the math concept and give other examples of activities that help children learn their concept. They can then be partners for another activity.

Seriation	Playing with nesting blocks
time	Recognizing the sequence of events in the schedule
temperature	Using a thermometer, putting on jackets to go outdoors, feeling the water
measuring	Cooking activities, comparing heights
counting	Counting the number that can be in the block area; counting to see how many children are present
one-to-one correspondence	Matching the cups to the saucers in the housekeeping area, putting a napkin at each place, getting a shovel for each pail
ordinal numbers	Deciding who will be first, who can use an item second or third
numerals	Seeing numerals on a calendar,
shapes	Using blocks, working puzzles
spatial relationships	Working puzzles
patterning	Making a pattern with beads or pegboards

classifying blocks, or beads	Grouping by color or size such as with pegboard,
comparing	Using blocks and other items of various sizes, shapes, and weights
ordering	Lining up unit blocks from shortest to longest
fractions	Cutting items in half, or dividing to share with a friend
vocabulary	Talking about math concepts as a part of the daily routine
numerical operations	Adding and subtracting by noticing how many there are all together or how many remain after some are removed

Unknown Rules—Roll a die. The instructor calls out a number, but it is often different from what is on the die. Ask participants not to tell the others if they figure out the trick. The secret is to not count the center dot. Consequently, a four is a four, but a five is also called a four. Relate the activity to the frustration of not knowing what is being done and not understanding the rules or expectations. Staff and children alike want to know what is expected of them.

Children's Coordination—To help trainees understand the coordination limitations of young children, let them cut something with their left hands if they are right-handed or with their right hands if they are left-handed. Ask them to cut a picture out of a magazine or give them construction paper to cut. Discuss with them the difficulty they experience and relate it to children's difficulty in attempting to master a task before they have the coordination to do it.

For another version, pass out crayons or markers and coloring book or worksheet pages with a very detailed drawing. Ask the right-handed people to color the pictures with their left hand; the left-handed people to use their right hand. As they experience difficulty and frustration, relate their experience to the struggles and frustration of young children when we expect them to do something that is too difficult for their coordination or capabilities. While participants are working, criticize them and tell them to hurry. Help participants recognize how that way of reacting to children does no good because of the lack of coordination.

Workbook Wisdom—To demonstrate that most workbook experiences can be presented as hands-on activities, have trainees look through several readiness workbooks. Ask them to select a page and figure out another way to present the same concept with real materials. For example, a page requiring children to match shoes by drawing a line between the ones that are alike could be replaced by real shoes that children pair up in the housekeeping area. Trainees also can be helped to see that the real shoes can be used in many other ways such as learning to buckle or tie shoestrings and to classify in several ways. Compare the rich experience using real materials to the artificial, limited experience of the workbook.

Classification and Categorizing—To help participants understand classification, have them select several items from their purses, wallets, or tote bags. Ask for a volunteer to classify the items. Then have someone else re-classify the items using different categories. For example, one person may classify by use and put all the money together. Another may classify by shape and put the coins with other round objects. Still another might classify by color and put all the black items together. Help participants recognize that there are often several ways to classify items and not just one way. Relate this activity to giving children real materials and letting them select ways to classify.

Short Attention Span—Tell trainees you are going to read something that you know will interest them. Emphasize how important the information will be to them. Then read a boring passage such as an insurance form, an IRS document, a section of the Federal Register, or other boring document. Have someone time the reading. Read slowly in a monotone, expressionless voice. It will usually take only a few minutes for their minds to wander. As you see listeners begin to get restless, lead them to understand that the information was not interesting to them, consequently their attention span was short. Emphasize how long two or three minutes can be when an activity is not interesting to you. Relate the experience to the short attention span of children and how activities and expectations must be appropriate and related to their interests. You also can make a point of how an expressionless voice makes it difficult to pay attention.

Toddler Tour—Have trainees get down on their hands and knees and look at a classroom from the view of a child. For infants, they should be as low as possible, even on their stomach or back. For toddlers and preschoolers, they should sit on the floor. Have participants describe the room using each of their senses. Then have them navigate around the room as a child would. They will notice things that they may not have been aware of before by viewing the room from this level. Look for safety or health hazards. Check to see how the room arrangement affects what children see since they are shorter than adults. Ask about how children can be independent in the present arrangement. Look to see what items are in the child's view, and what are above their eye level. As a group, compile a list of the differences in how a child might view the room and how an adult would view the same room.

The Child's Viewpoint—For an example of how we sometimes fail to see actions from a child's viewpoint, have each participant select a partner. One will be the child and the other will be the parent. Have the "child" sit on the floor and the "parent" stand nearby. Have the parent hold the child's hand for several minutes while the parent chats with another person. Continue until it becomes a little uncomfortable for the child partner. Participants see how adult actions may not be pleasant for the child and how long time can seem to a child. Discuss how we often hold children's hands or put them in an uncomfortable position because we do not take time to see how it might feel for the child.

For one more example, change roles, and this time the child sits on the floor and talks to the parent who is standing. Help participants recognize that they should get down to children's eye level to talk to them. Lead them to see that it is difficult for children to be looking up for much of the time, and that the adult seems very big from the child's viewpoint.

How Children Feel about Activities—Divide the group in half. Have one group make a step-by-step craft with someone giving specific and complicated directions, etc. Make sure that everyone at the craft table makes the craft "correctly." Add inappropriate teacher comments (for example, sound very controlling) as they work. Solicit comments about how they feel about the way they are treated. On the other side of the room have a table set up with an open-ended art activity with no directions to follow. There, trainees just sit down and use the materials. After ten to fifteen minutes, have the groups switch sides. After everyone is through, ask how they felt about both projects. Help them see how much more fun the open-ended activity was and compare the comments by the teacher.

How Children Respond to Adults—Walk over to a participant and whisper a question such as, "What is your name?" The participant will usually whisper the answer. Relate this experience to how children will take their cues from us. If we are loud, they will be loud; if we talk in a low voice, they will likely do the same. Help participants understand the importance of walking over to a child and getting the child's attention rather than calling across the room.

Role Models—This activity demonstrates the importance of adults as role models. It shows how we should demonstrate appropriate behavior rather than just telling. Give these instructions to participants, demonstrating them as you say them slowly:

1. Put your right arm out in front of you.
2. Make a circle with your forefinger and thumb.
3. Now, put the circle on your chin.

As you give the last instruction, place your own forefinger and thumb circle on your cheek, not on your chin. Most participants will do what they see you do rather that what you say. This activity demonstrates the value of practicing what we preach and of involving a combination of several senses.

Feeding the Hungry—To help participants recognize children's need for attention, ask them to think about being very hungry. Have them visualize going into a nice restaurant for a special treat—a birthday dinner, a holiday meal, or a celebration. They order a steak, which arrives on nice china, served with flair by attentive wait staff. Have them imagine that they look at the steak that they have eagerly anticipated only to discover that it is very small; in fact, it is only about two inches in diameter. Have them think about being very hungry. When they address their disappointment to the waiter, he assures them that quality is what counts most and that this steak is the best money can buy.

Use this scenario to open discussion about quantity versus quality. Since you are really hungry, quantity counts just as much or more that quality. How does this relate to working with children? In various studies, doing things together usually ranks at the top of "What makes a happy family." Quality time is important, but the quantity of time spent together is, too. It is essential to spend time with each child.

Language Development—To help participants recognize the importance of children having experience before language is meaningful, have participants each get a snack. Each person uses one word to describe the snack based on what she sees. Each participant gives a new word and does not repeat words already given. Next, let each person feel her snack and use a word to describe the way it feels. Then have each participant eat her snack and use a word to describe the taste. Discuss how experiences, combined with language, are meaningful. Relate this experience to the need for children to have experiences before language has meaning for them.

Graham Crackers—This activity will help trainees recognize how the way they present activities affects children's behavior. It will help them recognize the importance of offering choices. Give individual packages of graham crackers or other individual snack foods to some participants. Place one package between two persons for some of the others. Put an assortment on a nearby table for still others to choose at will. Compare this experience with children's activities: When the teacher makes a decision, the child's only choice is to do it or not to do it. Discuss how when children are toddlers, they will "fight" over an item, but if they are older, they will share. Others may be given a choice of when and what they do. Compare the autonomy of children and ways to develop it by giving children choices and presenting activities according to the ages of the children.

Child Development Activity—Have several clothing shapes cut out of construction paper with various developmental milestones on them. Place them in a small laundry basket, then have a piece of clothesline stretched across the room or have two people hold the ends. Sort the laundry and hang it on the developmental clothesline. Participants may come up and get a piece of "laundry" out of the basket, and hang it up in appropriate order. Discuss the task or milestone and why it belongs where it does. The activity gets people up and moving. You can adapt it for different developmental areas or spans, and make it as broad or as narrow as you like.

Using Child Development Knowledge to Choose Materials and Activities—Compare puzzles of various difficulty. Relate the choice of materials and activities to child development knowledge.

The Value of Real Experiences—An effective way to demonstrate the difference between real experiences and artificial, paper experiences is to demonstrate that children learn best when actively involved with concrete materials.

1. Pass around apples of different colors and varieties. Have participants explore their apples for about five minutes and talk to each other about their experiences. Give them paper plates and knives to use if they wish.
2. Have participants generate a list of descriptive words about their apple.

Record their words on an overhead transparency or on a flip chart.

3. Now pass out artificial red apples.
4. Have participants look at the list they generated and draw a line through each word that describes the artificial apple.
5. Now pass out a black and white coloring book or hand-drawn picture of an apple.
6. Cross out any words on the list that describe the coloring-book apple.
7. Now hold up the word "apple" on a flashcard. Have the participants say the word. Then have the group spell the word out loud several times in unison.

Lead participants to understand how much more learning occurs with the real experience. All the words left show how much more effective the experience with the real apples was. Help them identify the various levels of abstraction proceeding from the real, concrete object to the written word.

Pogo Stick—To demonstrate the value of first-hand experiences, have a volunteer hop on a pogo stick. Then ask other participants to describe in words how to do that as if they were instructing someone who had no idea how to use a pogo stick. Ask them how they would teach someone to hop on a pogo stick without demonstrating it or showing them how. Help them see how difficult it is to understand something that you only have been told about and with which you have no experience. Relate it to learning-by-doing. You must use a pogo stick to be able to use a pogo stick.

Reflections—Have a trainee hold a mirror perpendicular to a desk or table. Then have them attempt to copy a design by looking in the mirror. They may have to ask another trainee to hold the mirror so they can hold the paper in place. This is a good exercise to demonstrate that tasks that may seem easy to us are not to children who have much less experience upon which to draw.

Sensory Learning—To demonstrate how people may be better at learning through one sensory area over another, do this demonstration: Blindfold two to three volunteers and have them smell several items you have prepared in advance. Ask each volunteer to whisper to an assistant what she thinks the item is. The assistant writes down their answers. Then have the volunteers remove their blindfolds and compare their answers. The answers will usually be different. Relate the experience to how some people may be able to recognize items by smell better than others. Some good items to include are: rubbing alcohol, milk, dish detergent, vanilla flavoring, apple slices, dried roses, cantaloupe or other melons, orange, cinnamon, onion, leather, or coffee grounds.

Transition Visualization—Give each participant a copy of the form, "What Do We Want Children to Do During Transition?" found on page 276 in the Appendix. Have the participants close their eyes and visualize what they want to happen in their classroom during a transition time. Guide them to focus on what it looks like when it is happening, what it sounds like, and how it feels to them. Then have them open their eyes and answer the questions on the form. Guide them through deciding what they need to do to make their visualization happen.

Delegating Difficulties—Sometimes demonstrating what not to do is effective in helping trainees to see what they might be doing wrong. To demonstrate the wrong way to delegate, ask two volunteers to make a peanut butter and jelly sandwich. Provide only three slices of bread, one knife, peanut butter, grape jelly, and apple jelly. After you give the directions, leave the room in a hurry, and wait outside the door (where you can't be seen) for a few minutes. The volunteers will try to figure out what you want them to do and how to do it. Stay out long enough for them to make a sandwich. When you return, be very critical of how they have done the task. Tell them you wanted the apple jelly, not grape, and ask why they used the same knife in the peanut butter and the jelly. Criticize the way they cut or did not cut the sandwiches. Tell them you wanted each person to make one if they worked together, or that you wanted them to make a sandwich together if they each made one. Relate the experiences to the problems created when directions are not clear and precise, supplies are inadequate, and support and guidance are not available while the task is under way. This activity also points out a common problem with directors who give directions in a rush and do not have time to offer support.

The Value of Being Organized—Ask several participants to find a specific card in a deck of playing cards organized by suit and by number from smallest to largest. Let them know the order, then time them with a stopwatch to see how long it takes them to find the card. Shuffle the deck and ask the participants to find a specific card in the deck when there is no order. Relate the difficulty in finding the card to the difficulty one has in finding teaching materials or records when they are not organized in a consistent manner.

Doing Things Right the First Time—Read the following letter of apology from a company as a humorous example of the problems that mistakes can cause.

> *Dear Sir:*
>
> *It has come to our attention that our instruction booklet for the Acme Jet Ski omitted one final page. Consequently, we are enclosing a copy of the last page, which addresses "How to stop your Acme Jet Ski." We apologize for any inconvenience this may have caused. We will ship overnight free of charge to any requests from hospitals.*
>
> *Sincerely,*
> *Miss Takes Hurt*

Plop, Plop, Fizz, Fizz—Ask trainees to watch as you put an aspirin in a glass of colored water. Then put an effervescent antacid tablet in and ask them to describe the difference. Use this activity to demonstrate pizzazz and to lead into a discussion of the importance of enthusiasm.

Keep Your Eye on the Goal—Ask several volunteers to try to balance a peacock feather on their palm. Typically, they will not be able to do it. Then demonstrate it yourself. The secret is to watch the feather at the end, not your hand. Use the experience to lead into a discussion about staying focused on the desired goal and not becoming side-tracked by other tasks.

The Power of Suggestion—To demonstrate the power of suggestion, have trainees clasp their hands and hold their forefingers extended about one to two inches (three to five centimeters) apart. Lead them through a visualization of pretending there is a rubber band pulling their fingers together. Say, "Your fingers are being pulled closer and closer together. You can feel them moving, moving, closer and closer in a monotone, hypnotic voice. They will be surprised to see that their fingers actually seem to be pulled together.

Dealing with Stress—Have participants list their stresses on flipchart paper. Then ask for ways to address those stresses. After suggestions are given for all of them, remove the sheets, pass them around, and let each person tear part off until there is nothing left. Refer to this as eliminating stress.

Attitude is Everything—Write in large letters on a poster or chart:

A T T I T U D E = 100

Ask participants to write a number under each letter that tells where it is in the alphabet. A is one, T is twenty, etc. Then add the numbers across to get 100. Make the point that attitude means a lot in working with children and co-workers. We need 100% positive attitudes!

A	T	T	I	T	U	D	E = 100
1 +	20 +	20 +	9 +	20 +	21 +	4 +	5 = 100

LEARNING GAMES

Learning games are a fun way to stimulate discussion or review material. Games are an excellent means of reinforcing learning and reviewing content without becoming monotonous. Games offer a novel way to summarize material, to stimulate interaction, and to motivate participants. Because it is difficult not to participate, using games will alleviate many problems with reluctant participants. Games offer a safe way to try out responses to situations.

Variations of television game shows such as Jeopardy, along with adaptations of traditional games such as Bingo and board games, can be used for training. The difference will be in the content of the questions asked or slight changes in the procedures. Although games can take much time to prepare and may require a large block of time to play, they are highly effective. When trainees have fun, they enjoy learning and enjoyment is a key element in mastery. At times, competition may be added by offering prizes for the winners.

Games have some factors in common with role-play. Both are activities that bring in an element of reality and include rehearsal for skills that trainees will need on the job. Consequently, both types of experiences are good ways to allow trainees opportunities for using information and applying skills that they have learned.

An important component of the game process is communication during and after the game. For games to be effective, they must generally include interactions between players with a debriefing by the instructor. Without the opportunity to assess the actions that they take and the results of those actions, the game may not support growth in problem-solving skills.

WHEN ARE GAMES APPROPRIATE?

Having fun and using information are both important components of the adult learning process. Games are one of the ways to provide both. Additionally, games allow the trainees to actively recall information and concepts as a reinforcement of learning.

Games may be used to:

- Introduce a topic or a concept.
- Apply knowledge.
- Reinforce concepts and aid retention of information.
- Energize, motivate, and increase interaction.
- Facilitate team-building.
- Add humor and fun.
- Support the transfer of learning to the job.
- Provide an opportunity to assess mastery.
- Review and summarize information.
- Provide a culmination activity.

Games should not be used just for the sake of having them. The right games will add to the training plan and not simply serve as a way to fill time. Here are some guidelines for using games to help you decide when a game is appropriate.

- Assess your audience. Some groups may see games as silly and not react well to them.
- Evaluate the size of the group. If the group is too large, there may be too much waiting time for the game to be effective.
- Be sure the game relates to the training objectives.
- Be creative and use your imagination in designing games.
- Keep the rules simple and provide them in writing for reference by the players.
- Be very familiar with the game. Know the rules well and play it yourself ahead of time.
- Use mostly open-ended questions to reduce incorrect answers and prevent embarrassment.
- Have enough game materials to involve everyone.
- Play the games in small groups to minimize waiting when the games involve taking turns.
- Provide a way to communicate about the content and actions.
- Circulate among the players, adding information and supporting their interactions.
- Have fun and enjoy yourself.

- Remind participants when time is almost over to help them end the game.
- Make provisions for those who complete a game early.
- Debrief afterward to ensure that players relate the game to the learning objectives.

Several of the games described require questions. Number the questions and you can use them again with different games. For example, the same questions will work for Bingo, Carnival Ducks, or Go Fishing. Thus, you might use the questions several times during a course, but each time with a different game offering variations for reviews. You also may use a game several times in a course but with different questions each time. In fact, it is often easier to repeat a game with a new set of questions because the trainees will already know how to play.

BINGO GAMES

Bingo is good for becoming familiar with terminology or answering questions to review information.

To make a Bingo game:

1. Make a list of thirty open-ended questions related to the training topic. Number them.
2. Write numbers on cardboard tokens. Have one token for each question.
3. Make Bingo cards for participants, putting numbers randomly on the cards.
4. Use the same number range as the tokens and questions.
5. Select from numbers 1-6 in the first column, 7-12 in the second, 13-18 in the third, 19-24 in the fourth, and 25-30 in the last column. If you have more than thirty questions, adjust the number range accordingly.
6. Write FREE in the center.
7. Have enough buttons or beans for participants to mark their cards.

Another way to make many cards quickly is to give participants blank Bingo cards and let them chose the numbers they want to put in their grids. Tell them the range of numbers from which they may choose. Ask them to write the numbers randomly in the squares, with 1-6 in the first column, 7-12 in the second, continuing as described above. Tell them to not duplicate any numbers. Have them write FREE in the center.

To play Question Bingo

1. Pick a Bingo token with a number.
2. Read the question corresponding to that number.
3. Ask for a participant who has that number on her card to volunteer to answer the question. All participants who have that number on their card cover it with a button or bean.
4. The first person to cover five squares in a row wins a prize. As with regular Bingo, the row may be horizontal, vertical, or diagonal.
5. Continue playing until all tokens are drawn, all prizes are won, or the group begins to lose interest.

For a shorter version, use nine-square grids and have a winner for three in a row. For the shorter version, select from the numbers 1-5, 6-10, 11-15, and 16-20. Make twenty questions for the shorter version.

You will need more numbers from which to select for the cards when you have a large group of trainees. Consequently, you will need more questions. For large groups, make fifty questions. Select numbers for the columns on the cards from 1-10, 11-20, 21-30, 31-40, and 41-50.

For more extensive reviews or if you want the play to continue longer, play "X," "frame," or "cover the card" versions of Bingo.

BINGO
Here are examples of questions for an overall review of early childhood competencies. You may easily adapt these questions to review any training program or to relate to a specific workshop topic.

Supplies Needed for Question Bingo:

1. Bingo cards and tokens made per instructions on page 95, under "To make a Bingo game."
2. Beans or buttons to cover the cards
3. List of question related to the topic of the workshop
4. Small prizes

Professional Development Review Bingo Questions

1. Tell how professional development benefits you.
2. Give a tip for classroom management.
3. What does it mean to be a professional?
4. When should you wash your hands?
5. Share a time-management tip.
6. Give a tip for good discipline.
7. How do you personally handle stress?
8. Name a community resource that you use.

9. Describe how children learn.
10. Give an idea for communicating with parents.
11. Name a professional organization.
12. Give a tip for making parents feel welcome.
13. How can you be an advocate for children?
14. How can your classroom be multicultural?
15. True or False: Children should be required to clean their plate.
16. Give a tip for getting children to eat nutritious foods.
17. Share a tip for getting children to clean up.
18. Why is it important to talk to babies?
19. Tell how to set up an interest center.
20. Name your favorite book to use with children and tell why it is your favorite.
21. How do you encourage language development?
22. Why is it important to observe children?
23. Why do you need to know about child development?
24. What are some advantages of outdoor play, even in the winter?
25. Why is hand washing so important?
26. What are some benefits of water play?
27. Tell some things children learn from blocks.
28. Why is corporal punishment not desirable?
29. Give some signs of possible child abuse.
30. Why is it important to have art activities daily?

Terminology Bingo—This adaptation of Bingo is a matching game that works especially well as a review of new vocabulary. Pass out blank Bingo cards without numbers but with FREE in the center square. Write common early childhood terms on a dry-erase board, chalkboard or flipchart. Have trainees write the terms randomly on their Bingo cards. Play Bingo as usual, except instead of numbers, call out the definition and let the players mark the terms they have on their Bingo card. Give the winners a small prize.

Health and Safety Terminology Bingo

Terms to Write on Bingo Cards	Definitions to Read
1. Accident	An occurrence that is not expected or intended.
2. Accident prone	Describes one who is a frequent victim of unexpected accidents.
3. Caries	Cavities in the teeth or decay of teeth.
4. Choking hazards	Items that are at high risk of causing children to choke such as grapes, hard candy, or wieners.
5. Communicable disease	A disease that can spread from one person to another.
6. Coordination	How well one is able to work various parts of the body together; seeing an object and being able to pick it up with one's hand.
7. Daily health check	Observing a child upon arrival for signs of illness.

8. Deciduous teeth	A child's first set of teeth.
9. Egocentrism	The way children view the world during the pre-operational stage when they only see things from their own perspective.
10. Enrollment forms	Forms used to secure needed information on children.
11. Environment	The total surroundings in which we live, including all people and all things.
12. Exercise	Physical activity.
13. Fire drill	An orderly procedure for getting children out of a building quickly.
14. First aid	The immediate care given to an injured person or to one who is suddenly ill.
15. Gross motor activities	Those activities (such as climbing, running, and jumping) that require large muscles to be used.
16. Hazard	A situation that creates the chance of accident or risk.
17. Health	A state of physical and mental well-being, not merely the absence of disease.
18. Health records	Records signed by a health professional that assess the physical health of the child.
19. Immunization record	Record signed by physician or local health authority showing what immunizations the child has received.
20. Incubation period	The time between exposure to a disease and when its symptoms appear.
21. Inspection	The act of checking to see if a specific criteria is met.
22. Liability	A person's responsibility for an accident as a result of negligent acts.
23. Negligence	Failure to exercise the care that the circumstances require.
24. Nutrition	The quality and amount of food eaten.
25. Poison	Any substance gas, liquid, or solid that tends to impair the health or cause death when introduced into the body or onto the skin surface.
26. Prevention	Acts and procedures that reduce the incident or risk of illness or accidents.
27. Safety	A means of keeping a person free from harm, danger, or risks.
28. Safety checks	Specific times to evaluate conditions relative to safety.
29. Safety goals	Desired outcome one strives to reach in maintaining the physical well-being of children.
30. Sanitation	The overall cleanliness and freedom from bacteria of the specific facility or area.

Idea Review Bingo—Another version of Bingo may be used for training that involves ideas that are lists of words or short phrases. Have trainees list the words randomly on the cards, then mark them as they are called. For example, in a session on dramatic play, list props that can go in the dramatic play area on a chalkboard or flipchart. Then ask each participant to list the twenty-four props they are most likely to use, writing one prop in each square. Randomly select one prop at a time from the list on the chalkboard or flipchart and circle it. Players who have that word listed get to cross it off their Bingo cards. Continue until there is a winner according to typical Bingo procedures. Have a small prize for the winner.

This version will take longer if you have much more than twenty-five words from which to choose or a small group of trainees. Shorten the time if you wish by reducing the grid to nine squares. Lengthen the time by continuing until there are several winners. This version of Bingo is a popular way to review anything that involves word lists such as characteristics of good early childhood personnel, directors' skills, equipment for a classroom, or outdoor play equipment.

The benefit of Idea Review Bingo is that it provides an opportunity for participants to select the ideas they want to implement or to review information. Writing the ideas or information helps retention. The Bingo card listing the information can then be a handout that participants can take home with them for future reference.

Carnival Ducks

Carnival Ducks is the childhood carnival activity where one picks a floating duck, reads the number on the bottom of the duck, and wins a prize corresponding to the number. In this version, adapted for training, the game has questions for trainees to answer. Carnival Ducks works well as a review or reinforcement technique toward the end of a session. This version does not include a prize with every duck, but has enough prizes to maintain interest. Participants take turns selecting a duck, then respond to a request that matches the number of the duck they picked. Carnival Ducks can be a small group or large group activity.

- Make a list of requests for information and number them.
- Write a number on the bottom of rubber or plastic ducks or other floating items. Use a permanent, waterproof marker and put the number on a part that will not be seen while the item floats. Use about eleven ducks with numbers.
- Mark another duck "WINNER."
- Have a prize related to the workshop topic for those who pick winning ducks.

The requests should be general enough so that most persons could give a response since they will be answering publicly. Make several sets of requests in order to have more choices of requests than you have ducks. For example, if you have three sets of requests, the first time duck number four is drawn, read request four from set one. The second time number four is picked, read request four from set two. The third time number four is drawn, read request four from set three. Have printed lists of requests that you can check off as each one is used when using fewer ducks than you have requests.

Supplies Needed for Carnival Ducks

1. Small plastic ducks or other floating items
2. A small, clear pan of water
3. List of requests for information related to the topic
4. Small prizes

Health Review Requests for Information for Carnival Ducks

Set One
1. Share a tip for getting children to wash their hands.
2. Give a tip for teaching children good eating habits.
3. Name a story, song, or game that involves nutrition—one about fruits, vegetables, or other good food.
4. Give some signs that let you know a child might be sick.
5. Suggest a way to encourage children to brush their teeth.
6. Tell when caregivers should wash their hands.
7. Tell some ways to get children to settle down and relax at rest time.
8. True or False: Going outdoors in winter will give children a cold.
9. What should you do if a child has a fever?

10. True or False: Sandboxes should be covered to keep them from getting wet.
11. Name two items that are choking hazards for young children.

Set Two
1. Share some activities to promote children's physical activity and exercise.
2. Why is outdoor play important to healthy development?
3. True or False: All children of the same age will need the same amount of rest.
4. True or False: A child with a rash should always be sent home.
5. True or False: Caregivers only need to wash their hands when handling food.
6. Demonstrate how staff should wash their hands.
7. True or False: Children should always be encouraged to clean their plates.
8. Describe one of the communicable diseases common to children.
9. True or False: Children do not need dental care until they have permanent teeth.
10. True or False: Most accidents children have cannot be prevented.
11. Describe how one can tell if a child has head lice.

Set Three
1. Give some reasons why smoking around children is harmful.
2. Describe how to make a solution to sanitize toys.
3. Tell how you would comfort a child who is upset because of an injury.
4. What should you do with a sick child if you cannot reach the parent right away?
5. Give some signs of child abuse.
6. What is the normal temperature of young children?
7. Why is milk so important in young children's diets?
8. Tell some ways you support good emotional health.
9. What should you do if you suspect a child is being abused?
10. How do you communicate the importance of a regular bedtime to parents?
11. Describe how to take the temperature of an infant.

Carnival Ducks may be played with questions, too. Make questions instead of requests for information and play as above. The questions should be open-ended so that most persons could give a correct answer since they will be answering publicly. For true or false questions, ask the participants to explain their answers. Ask such questions as, "Why is that false?" or "Under what circumstances could it be false?"

Go Fishing

Make a list of questions or requests that relate to the training subject and number them. Cut fish shapes from poster board. Attach a paperclip near the mouth of each fish. Make as many fish as you have questions or have several sets of questions and change the questions for a repeat play using the same fish. Number the fish. Purchase or make a fishing pole with a magnet on the end.

Participants in turn "catch" a cut-out fish using the pole. Then they respond to the question or request that corresponds to the number on the fish that they caught. For variety, trainees may ask for a volunteer in the group to answer the question or to give an example of why the question is important. For true and false questions, ask trainees to explain or elaborate on their answers.

Supplies Needed for Go Fishing:

1. Poster board fish, numbered, and with a paperclip attached to mouth
2. Fishing pole with a small magnet on the end
3. List of questions or requests related to the topic

Outdoor Environment Questions and Requests for Information for Go Fishing

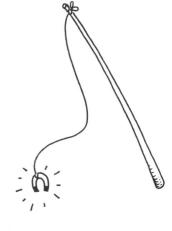

1. Give two reasons why children should go outside even in winter.
2. True or False: Most playground accidents cannot be prevented.
3. Discuss some ways you can prevent misuse of equipment.
4. True or False: Sandboxes should be covered to keep them from getting wet.
5. Share two activities to do with balls.
6. True or False: Children should not go outdoors if the temperature is below 50 degrees or above 80 degrees.
7. Discuss the types of equipment needed on a playground.
8. True or False: Infants should not be taken outdoors.
9. Describe what teachers should do on the playground.
10. True or False: Toddlers should not go outdoors because they will put grass and things in their mouth.
11. What are some hazards to avoid on playgrounds?
12. Name some ways that children misuse equipment.
13. Share some ideas for free or inexpensive outdoor equipment.
14. Give a tip for keeping playgrounds safe.
15. True or False: Since wading pools are shallow, it is not necessary to watch them as closely as swimming pools.
16. What do you think we mean about playground needing a balance of shade and sun?
17. True or False: It is OK to have art activities outside.
18. True or False: Going outdoors in winter will give children a cold.
19. True or False: A playground should be checked frequently for hazards.
20. Since playgrounds are larger than indoors, it does not matter where you put equipment.

21. If you have $100 for outdoor equipment, what will you buy?
22. How can you be sure you have enough for children to do on the playground?
23. What are some signs you need to rotate equipment or add more activities?
24. Give some reasons outdoor play time is important.
25. True or False: Since outdoor time is for play, teachers need not talk to or interact with children.

Jeopardy

Jeopardy is a good game for reviewing definitions and relationships. In Jeopardy, participants choose a category, then they are given an answer. They must ask a question to which the answer they picked relates. Make a poster with the categories and the points on it. Select a Host to give the answers and three or more participants to be players. You will need a bell or small xylophone for each of the three players.

To play Jeopardy:

1. One player selects a category and point level.
2. The Host gives the answer that goes with the selected category and point level.
3. Each of the players tries to be first to state the question.
4. Players signal their readiness to answer by ringing a bell or tapping a xylophone.
5. The first one to answer correctly gets the points and picks the next category and point level.
6. When all categories and point levels have been picked, the player with the most points wins.

Here are some Jeopardy categories, point values, and questions about observing and recording children's behavior:

Observing and Recording Children's Behavior
Jeopardy Answers and Questions

Point Value	Infant / Toddler Development
100	How infants and toddlers learn.
	Through their senses
200	The ages of an infant
	Birth through one year
300	By talking and singing to infants, caregivers enhance this.
	Language skills, language development
400	Two-year-olds are known for increasing this.
	Independence, autonomy
500	Lack of this for a child under three can lead to later learning problems.
	Stimulation, quality experiences, nurturing, nutrition, and health care

Point Value	Preschool Development
100	Stimulating experiences help this.
	Cognitive development, intellectual development
200	Comes from interacting with others.
	Social development
300	Soft, slow music has this effect on active four-year-olds.
	Calms them down, helps them rest
400	Playing outdoors helps this.
	Physical development, gross motor skills, large muscles
500	When we reward appropriate behavior and redirect or substitute activities, we are providing this.
	Positive guidance

Point Value	Recording Methods
100	A written narrative that gives only facts.
	Anecdotal record
200	A record of how many times an event occurs.
	Tally sheet, interest sheet
300	A record that measures particular skills exhibited by children.
	Checklist or developmental screening
400	A place to keep examples of children's work.
	Portfolio
500	You can use these to show children's progress and development.
	Records

Point Value	Testing Children
100	Tests that are inappropriate for young children.
	Standardized tests, paper and pencil tests
200	Testing may be appropriately used to screen for these.
	Developmental delays or health problems
300	Some standardized tests are not free of this.
	Bias or cultural bias
400	Tests that identify a child's skills and measure developmental level.
	Developmental screening tests
500	Examples of standardized tests.
	Developmental screening test, achievement, readiness, diagnostic, and intelligence tests

Point Value	Using Records
100	A good time to share observations with parents.
	Parent / teacher conferences
200	Samples of children's work are in this.
	Portfolio
300	This will not happen if we do not use records.
	Recognize potential health or developmental problems; children reach their potential
400	Teachers should use observations to plan this.

	Curriculum, classroom environment, or activities
500	The concept that information collected is kept private and used ethically.
	Confidentiality

CARD GAMES

Card games are good to use for reviews or for sharing ideas and information. Make cards from index cards or poster board since players will handle them a lot. Cards also can be made by printing or writing directly on the card. Or follow the directions below to make labels on a computer to use to make cards.

Card games will work best with two to four players. The number of cards needed will depend on the number of players in a group. Because you will need several sets of cards for a class, make each set a different color to keep them sorted when put away. For some games, numbering the cards is helpful in matching pairs. Encourage discussion when play is under way. Small prizes add humor and friendly competition.

Print the rules for each set of players for reference. Once players understand how to play a game, the game may be played using other topics or questions.

Making Cards with a Computer—The instructions that follow are an easy way to make cards on the computer using Microsoft Word. If you have another word processing program, check the instructions for making labels and adapt the procedure as needed.

Using Microsoft Word and Windows:

1. List the information you want to put on cards in a computer file.
2. In Tools, select Envelopes and Labels.
3. Select Single Label.
4. Select the label size you want to make. A good size is Address Labels 1" x 2.63."
5. Select New Document. A page of label gridlines will open.
6. Paste the list of information you want to put on labels at the bottom of this document.
7. In Window, select Split so you can see the label gridlines and the list of information at the bottom.
8. Cut and paste until your information is on the labels.
9. Adjust font size to fit the labels if needed.
10. Print the labels and affix them to index cards or poster board cut to size. You can also print directly on purchased blank business cards designed for the computer.

Simple Card Games for Review—To review and reinforce learning, card games provide opportunities to discuss information and apply knowledge. Card games for review may be as simple as drawing a card with a question or situation on it. Players then discuss the answer or appropriate response with others in a group of two to four players. To make a simple card game, follow these directions:

1. Write one question or describe a situation that calls for a response on each card.
2. Turn the cards upside down in the center of the players.
3. Guess a number or roll a die to select the first player.
4. The players draw a card from the stack.
5. The player answers the question or reacts to the situation described.
6. The play continues clockwise until all cards are drawn.

Here are some questions for a safety review card game. In this version, players receive scenarios to describe what they would do under the given circumstances. This game also can be played with the Draw One rules that follow.

Safety Review Questions for Card Games

1. Donita hit Natalie with a wooden block. There is a large bump on her forehead and she says her head hurts. What do you do?
2. One of your preschoolers fell and knocked out a tooth. What do you do?
3. During lunch, Allison chokes on a carrot stick. What do you do? How could you have prevented the incident?
4. At the end of the day, Latoya is crying and says Clayton pushed her and her arm is hurting. What do you do?
5. Rio was running on the playground and tripped over a tree root. What do you do?
6. Haley is crying and says her eye hurts. Another child has tossed a handful of sand in the air. What do you do?
7. Early in the morning, you notice a bruise on Cedrick's arm. What do you do?
8. Jean Claude fell off the swing. He says his arm hurts really bad. What do you do?
9. LaDerick suddenly has a nose bleed in the middle of circle time. What do you do?
10. Mario was stung by a bee on the playground. What do you do?
11. Mia fell and cut her lip. What do you do?
12. Michelle steps on a nail during outdoor water play. What do you do?
13. Anthony fell from the climbing frame and has a skinned knee. How do you take care of the injury?
14. You are doing a cooking activity with your children. Sophia puts her hand on the electric toaster and burns it. What do you do?
15. You see a small item lodged in Jo's ear. What do you do?
16. You take your toddlers on a walk around the block. A stray dog bites Cassandra. What do you do?
17. Jeannette wants to go barefoot on the playground. Will you let her?
18. Juan tries to climb on his cubby to reach his toys on the top shelf. How do you prevent injury?
19. Your aide moved a table for circle time. The table blocks the exit. What do you say to her?
20. Babs tries to open the gate. How can you prevent her from leaving the yard?

Pairs—Make questions in categories and write or print them on cards. Include the category on the card. For example, make six questions each in some of the following categories: Health and Safety, Learning Environment, Families, Professionalism, Classroom Management, and Child Development. The number of players will determine the amount of cards you will need. The more players you expect to have in a group, the more categories you will need. A pair in this game consists of two cards from the same category. Here is how to play:

1. Deal the cards, giving five to each player.
2. Stack the remaining cards in the center of the group of players.
3. Guess a number or roll a die to see who will play first.
4. If the first player has two cards from the same category, the player may ask the two questions of another player, then place the pair on the table in front of her.
5. If the player asked the questions cannot answer both, another player is asked to respond.
6. The first person who answers both questions gets to draw a card from the stack.
7. Play continues clockwise.
8. A player who does not have a pair from the same category must pass. Thus there is an incentive for players to answer questions and draw a card to make a pair when their turn comes.

The player who places all cards in pairs first is the winner. For another version, make duplicates of each question and make pairs when a player has the same two questions.

Draw One—Make a set of cards with questions on them. Make duplicates of each question (twenty questions will mean forty cards). Having an answer key sometimes is helpful for players to refer to if the players do not agree on an answer.

To play Draw One:

1. Deal the cards, giving five to each player.
2. Place the remaining cards in a stack in the center of the players.
3. Guess a number or roll a die to see who will play first.
4. Each player in turn reads one of the questions on the cards in his hand. He answers the question, discusses it with the other players, or gives examples.
5. That player lays the card down in front of him, discarding it.
6. He draws another card from the stack.
7. A player who has a duplicate card, or draws one during the game, lays his card on top of the matching discarded one.
8. The play continues until a player has discarded all of his cards and is the winner.

Author/Book Match—Use the rules for Draw One for this game. Make card pairs where one card has a picture of a classic children's book (cut from a catalog) and the other card has the name of the author. A pair consists of a picture of a book and the author of that book. If the names of the authors are not visible on the pictures of the books, have a list where players may verify their answers.

BOARD GAMES

Simple board games can be made on poster board. You also can adapt playing boards from purchased games such as Candyland. Make sure the board does not have too many steps or require so many moves that the game lasts too long. Make a prototype and time the game before you make your final version. Generally, about thirty minutes is as long as groups will stay interested in a board game. Try to have enough game boards and parts that you will have four to six players for each game. If players have to wait too long between turns, they may lose interest. If there are too few players, there will usually not be adequate interaction. Board games are wonderful for reviewing information. They are an excellent way to involve participants and get them to share ideas and experiences. For board games to be most effective, follow these guidelines:

- Keep the rules simple.
- Give players written instructions for reference as they play.
- Keep the groups between four to six players.
- Encourage discussion of cards and situations.
- Offering prizes for the winners interjects a spirited bit of competition.
- Have something to do for those who finish early while the others complete the game.

Making Board Games—To make a board game on poster board, draw a path and divide it into segments. Include some landing spaces that require going back several spaces and some that require drawing a card. You can make a path of "stepping stones" with one-inch (three-centimeter) dots using blue for the path and red to indicate where a card must be drawn. When players draw a card, it can have a question they answer or they may ask the group to answer. The same playing boards can be used for different training topics if you make several sets of cards to use.

You may wish to laminate the playing boards to make them last longer. However, if you are transporting them often, the lamination may not be desirable. Lamination makes them difficult to carry because they slide and are hard to hold.

Making Cards for Board Games—To make labels for cards on the computer, follow the directions with card games. Cards for board games may be on construction paper since they will not be handled as much as in card games.

To make a set of cards, cut construction paper into pieces that are three by one and a half inches (eight by four centimeters). You can cut three across and eight down on a piece of nine by twelve inch (twenty-three by thirty centimeter) construction paper to get twenty-four from each sheet. Cut extras since there are thirty labels to a set for this game. It is also a good idea to have extras in the event that one is misplaced so you can quickly make a replacement. Make each card set a different color to keep the sets together when they are stored. Put a label on each construction paper card. Laminate if desired. You also can simply write the information on the cards.
Here are the instructions to give to players and situations to make cards for a board game on professionalism. The game will typically take about thirty minutes for a group of six to play.

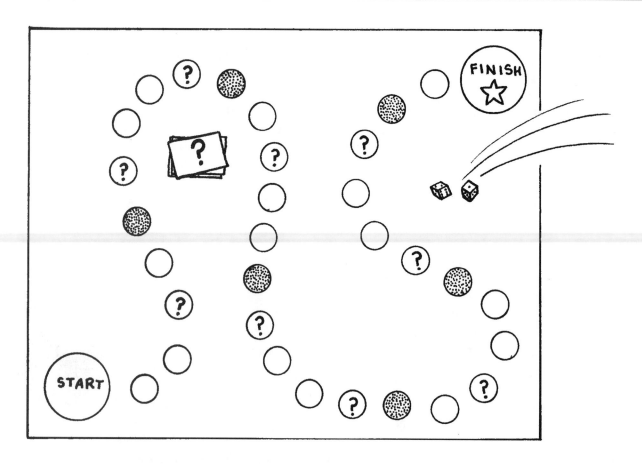

**Professional Board Game
Instructions for Players**

Each player chooses a playing piece and puts it on the space marked START. Put the set of cards in the designated place on the board. Roll the die to see who goes first, then proceed to play in a clockwise direction.

Each player in turn rolls the die and moves forward the number of spaces as the dots on the die. If you land on a red dot, draw a card from the stack, read it aloud, and move accordingly. The card may have something positive that will allow you to move forward or it may have something negative that will require you to go back. After drawing a card and moving, put the card at the bottom of the stack.

Two or more players may land on the same space. When a player gets to the end, she may continue to participate in the discussion. Players are encouraged to discuss the situations on the cards that they or others draw. The first one in each group to reach the end will receive a prize.

Professionalism Board Game
Cards to Draw

1. Your aide does not dress professionally most of the time. You make a point to compliment her when she does dress appropriately. Go forward 2 spaces.
2. You wonder if a child may have a nutritional deficiency. You discuss it with the nurse. Go forward 3 spaces.
3. You have a chance to attend a conference on brain research. You register and plan to attend. Go forward 3 spaces.
4. A parent worries because her child mispronounces many words. You help her arrange for a screening. Go forward 2 spaces.
5. Your co-worker had to leave early to pick up her son. You clocked out for her so she wouldn't lose pay. Go back 3 spaces.
6. You have a decision to make and you consult the Code of Ethics. Go forward 3 spaces.
7. One of your co-workers is having marital difficulties. Another co-worker asks you what's wrong. You tell her all you know. Go back 2 spaces.
8. You're mad because a parent hasn't sent a change of clothes for a child. You decide to tell her what you think. Go back 2 spaces.
9. All your friends are getting tattoos. You decide not to because you think it isn't professional. Go forward 2 spaces.
10. You know you'll have to be off next Friday. You give the director plenty of notice so she can get a good substitute. Go forward 3 spaces.
11. You arrive early for a parent meeting to be sure your room is set up to greet parents. Go forward 2 spaces.

12. Your aide is working hard to get her CDA. She asks to copy your competency statements because she works nights at another job. You let her. Go back 3 spaces.

13. Your aide is working hard to get her CDA. She asks to copy your competency statements because she works nights at another job. You politely tell her she will learn more by doing it herself. Go forward 3 spaces.

14. You see a child left on the playground when a class goes inside. You ignore the situation because you feel you are only responsible for your class. Go back 3 spaces.

15. You are required to leave the room orderly and ready for the next day. A child is late leaving, so you do not straighten the room. Go back 2 spaces.

16. You know the cook prepares too much food just so she will have leftovers to take home. You ignore the situation because she sometimes gives you some. Go back 3 spaces.

17. Your director asks if you will help a new aide. You refuse, because no one helped you when you were new. Go back 2 spaces.

18. You leave the children with a parent volunteer while you take a child to the restroom. Go back 3 spaces.

19. A co-worker comes in your room to visit when she is on break. You keep your attention on the children and tell her you will see her after work. Go forward 2 spaces.

20. Your director has asked staff to wear dresses or neat pant suits to a parent meeting. You wear your old slacks anyway. Go back 2 spaces.

With a change of cards, you can use the same game board for another topic. Here is a version for working with families. The instructor can select the situations related to the current content of the training from the many listed. Another way to vary a game is to make two sets of cards, playing with one set one time and another set at a later time.

Family Relationships Board Game
Cards to Draw

1. You remembered to call Mrs. Rodrigues by her name. Go forward 1 space.

2. You spent at least five minutes with each parent this week talking about their child. Go forward 2 spaces.

3. Ms. Jacobson told you she wanted some information about discipline. You ignored her request. Go back 1 space.

4. You decided that Bessie should not be allowed to take the medicine her mother sent and did not give it to her. You did not consult anyone. Go back 3 spaces.

5. You planned the parent meeting all by yourself. You did not involve any of the parents because you knew what they needed. Go back 2 spaces.

6. You missed an opportunity to invite a parent to help in your classroom. Go back 1 space.

7. You speak to each parent, call them by name, and greet their child by name each day. Go forward 2 spaces.

8. A parent suggested that the families hold a picnic for the end of the school year. You helped her contact the other parents and plan the event. Go forward 2 spaces.

9. You got angry with a parent who was late picking up her child. You said some things you should not have. Go back 3 spaces.

10. You told another teacher that you thought LaQuita's mom didn't really want the new baby she was expecting. LaQuita overheard you. Go back to the beginning.

11. Your classroom has photos of traditional families only. Four of your children are from single-family households, three are being raised by their grandmothers, one lives with her stepdad, and two more are in foster care. Go back 2 spaces.

12. You know that Maria's mother works two jobs. You spend extra time with Maria because you know she doesn't have much time with her mother at home. Go forward 1 space.

13. You heard a parent say something unpleasant about another mother. You did nothing even though you considered the statement untrue. Go back 3 spaces.

14. You wrote a section for your center newsletter to let the parents know what you have been doing with their children. Go forward 2 spaces.

15. A parent is upset because you didn't follow instructions for medicine. You reply, "It won't hurt them to get more. That's what I always did with my children." Go back 2 spaces.

16. At the end of a trying day, you tell Jason's mom that he has been really bad and you don't know what you will do with him if his behavior doesn't improve. "I've just had it with him!" you tell her. Go back to the beginning.

17. Your new assistant is not doing as well with the children as you think she should. You tell a parent concerned about her child being prepared for school that the new aide is not teaching her child anything. Go back 3 spaces.

18. You call a parent and demand that she immediately return the shirt that her child wore home two weeks ago when his got wet. Go back 2 spaces.

19. A parent asks you to tell her who hit her child. You tell her and even give the phone number so she can call the other parent. Go back 3 spaces.

20. You are mad at a teacher down the hall. You tell one of the parents who is your neighbor about the incident. Go back 2 spaces.

21. You call a parent when you hear she has been sick to let her know you are thinking about her. You ask if there is anything you can do for her son, Derrick. Go forward 1 space.

22. You let the children make thank you cards for a parent who brought refreshments for a party recently. Go forward 2 spaces.

23. You make sure every parent gets a copy of the information about an upcoming field trip. Go forward 2 spaces.

24. You wear your blue jeans and a T-shirt to a parents' meeting. Go back 1 space.

25. You tell a parent that you might not be able to keep her child in your class unless he quits wetting his pants. Go back 3 spaces.

26. You hold a parent conference and talk only about the problems with the child. Go back 2 spaces.

27. You watched for Miss Williams to tell her about the way her daughter helped another child that day. Go forward 2 spaces.

28. You wrote a personal thank you note to a parent who had helped on a field trip. Go forward 2 spaces.

29. You called a parent who forgot to send a permission slip for a field trip to work out a plan for her to get it to you. Go forward 2 spaces.
30. You make a point of telling each parent something good their child did each day. Go forward 3 spaces.
31. You ask a parent if there is anything you can do to help her daughter, LaShonda, adjust to the new baby sister. Go forward 2 spaces.
32. You make sure that you personally invite each parent to the parents' luncheon at the center. Go forward 2 spaces.
33. You select a good brochure about how children learn each week to send home to parents. Go forward 2 spaces.
34. You select books about a child who lives with his father to read to Josuah when you learn he is now living with his father. Go forward 2 spaces.
35. A parent feels that children should learn to hit back if someone hits them first. You tell her, "You're wrong. We can't do that here." Go back 1 space.
36. A parent wants her child to keep clean during the day. You explain to her the value of art and playing outside. You also provide a smock and ask the parent to let you know when she has to go somewhere after work so you can help her child clean up before she arrives. Go forward 2 spaces.
37. A parent doesn't like for her child to play in the housekeeping area because it seems sissy. You explain how children learn through play and give her a brochure about the value of play. Go forward 2 spaces.
38. You tell a parent that her child is the worst behavior problem you have ever seen. Go back 3 spaces.
39. Your Lucky Card! Roll the Die and get another turn!
40. Your Unlucky Card! Skip your next turn!

The possibilities for using board games are vast. Here is yet another set of cards for a board game:

Health And Safety Land Board Game
Cards to Draw

1. You forget to send the injury report home with Haley's mom. Go back 1 space.
2. Bad news! Your children are throwing blocks in the block area. Go back 1 space.
3. A large wooden truck stored on the top shelf of your block cabinet is pulled over on a child's head. Go back 2 spaces.
4. Children are playing on the tumbling mat unsupervised. Jeremy does a forward roll and knocks Thomas to the floor. Go back 1 space.
5. Uh-oh! LaToya ate a berry from the Poinsettia plant in the science area. Go back 3 spaces.
6. You demonstrate how to carefully and gently pet the new guinea pig. Go ahead 2 spaces.
7. You put the medicine back in the cabinet, but you forgot to lock it. Go back 1 space.
8. Stacy uses the child-size dust pan and mop that you put by the sand table to sweep up spilled sand. Go forward 1 space.

9. Taylor is being very careful with the stapler as you observe him from nearby. Go forward 1 space.

10. Too bad! Maria cuts her finger on a rusty broken sifter in the sand table. Go back 3 spaces.

11. You ask Allen to unplug the blender for you as you finish a cooking project. Go back 2 spaces.

12. You report to your director exposed pipes in the gym that could get hot enough to burn a child. Go forward 2 spaces.

13. Nicholas has a runny nose. You give him some medicine that helped another child who also had a runny nose. Go back to the beginning.

14. You demonstrate proper handwashing to the children. Go forward 3 spaces.

15. You came to work even though you were running a fever. Go back 4 spaces.

16. You return the clearly labeled disinfectant to the locked storage cabinet out of children's reach. Go forward 3 spaces.

17. You sand several blocks in the block area that have rough edges. Go forward 1 space.

18. You remove a toy with rough edges. go forward 1 space.

19. Go boom! Jessica slips on a slice of canned peaches left on the floor after lunch. Go back 2 spaces.

20. Samuel trips on the long dress in the housekeeping area and cuts his chin. Go back 2 spaces.

21. You notice an electrical outlet with no cover. You replace it. Go forward 2 spaces.

22. You make sure every child has a seatbelt buckled before you start the van. Go forward 3 spaces.

23. Two-year-old Matthew puts a small bean up his nose. Go back 3 spaces.

24. Jenny has wrapped the cord from the blinds around her neck. Go back 4 spaces.

25. You have bolted your cubbys to the wall to keep them from being knocked over where they might injure a child. Go forward 2 spaces.

26. You forgot the supply of tissue you need for circle time so you quickly run to the supply room, leaving your classroom unattended. Start over.

27. Briana's mother is concerned because she is not yet potty trained even though she is 18 months old. You explain to her that children will learn when they are ready. Go forward 1 space.

28. You explained to Cynthia's mother about how to look for head lice. Go forward 1 space.

29. You recognized that Juan might have a hearing problem. You get to go forward 4 and draw again!

Another Version of Board Games—Make cards with labels on construction paper using the questions below. You may use the same playing board as for the other games or design a new one. In this version, the players answer questions about the topic as they move around the board. Any topic can be used in the same way. Just make cards from a set of questions rather than situations. For groups of four to six players, twenty-five to forty questions give a good variety.

Establishing Relationships with Families
Directions to Players

Select a playing piece. Roll the die to see who will play first. Then the play proceeds in a clockwise direction. Each player rolls the die and moves that number of spaces. Draw a card when you land on one of the red circles. Answer the question on the card that you draw, then return the card to the bottom of the stack. All players are invited to discuss the questions or give examples of similar situations. The first person to reach the end is the winner. When finished, please continue to contribute to the discussion. Play continues until everyone finishes. For true or false questions, please explain your answers.

Establishing Relationships with Families Board Game Questions

1. True or False: Children's families will consist of a mother, father, and sister or brother.
2. Why should parents be involved in the program?
3. True or False: The child care center is responsible for teaching the child and developing social skills. The parent is responsible for all physical care.
4. A good resource for health information for parents is:
5. True or False: The caregiver can expect that all children in her program will come from families similar to her own and will have the same values.
6. Why is confidentiality important in the child care setting?
7. Tell about a time you helped a parent with a separation problem.
8. Why is it important to send home samples of the children's work?
9. Tell about a time you helped a parent understand the value of play.
10. Tell how you would explain to parents the learning opportunities in everyday household tasks and routines.
11. Name a resource for parents of children with disabilities.
12. Tell about a time you helped a parent understand the child's point of view.
13. How can a caregiver show that she respects a child's cultural background?
14. Tell about a time you shared a special event or experience in the center with the parents.
15. Give some ideas about how to discuss a child's problem behavior with a parent in a constructive, supportive manner.
16. Tell how a caregiver can help a child make the transition to school.
17. How can the caregiver help a child with alternative care arrangements when a child is sick or if a parent has to work when the center is closed?
18. Have you ever had a parent who felt you were competing for the child's affection? Tell about it.
19. How can a caregiver help a child or family under stress?
20. Give a suggestion for parents to help their children relax after group time at the center.
21. Give a suggestion that will help parents enjoy their children.
22. Tell about a time you helped a parent recognize their feelings or attitudes about handicaps.
23. A resource for diagnosing and treating children with handicaps is:

24. A good resource for information about children's handicaps and right to services is:
25. Tell about a time you helped a parent communicate with or get help from a government or community agency.
26. How can you help a child feel he belongs in his family?
27. Name some activities and materials that parents can share with their children at home.
28. How can the caregiver encourage parents to talk to their children about important family events and the children's special interests at home?
29. Tell about a suggestion you got from a parent that helped you improve the program for their child.
30. Tell about a time you shared a child's achievement of a new skill with a parent.

Professionalism Board Game

Here is another version of a board game. The goal of this game is to help players become more familiar with the requirements of the Child Development Associate (CDA). It could be adapted for any other early childhood credential as well. In this version, clever names are given to some of the places where players draw cards and other spaces.

1. Make a set of cards for the situations that follow the instructions for players.

2. Make a playing board on a piece of poster board. Draw squares or put dots to represent the path and moving spaces. Make a set of labels to identify some of the locations on the board where players will draw Professional Development Cards. Put the instructions on the path of the playing board in the order listed. Give the spaces the names to which the Professional Development Cards refer. Also give spaces the names referred to in the Places to Draw Cards. Put the Professional Paradise "Congratulations" statement at the end of the path. Add some additional places to draw cards. A total of about ten to twelve places to draw cards is desirable. If you put fewer than that, the game may not be challenging; if more, it may take too long to play to hold players' interest. Mark all the spaces to draw cards with a red dot.

3. To play the Professional Game, you will need a playing board, a set of Professional Development cards to draw, and a die for each group of four to six people.

4. You will need playing pieces, one for each player. Playing pieces may be purchased or you can use different buttons or coins. Have enough variety that the players will easily recognize their pieces. You will need one die per game.

5. Print these instructions for each group of players:

**The Professional Game
Instructions for Players**

The purpose of this game is to help you become familiar with the steps that lead to the CDA credential. The goal is to reach the end, which is to get your CDA credential. Each player chooses a playing piece and puts it on the space marked START. Put the set of cards in the designated place on the board. Roll the die to see who goes first, then proceed to play in a clockwise direction.

Each player in turn rolls the die and moves forward the number of spaces as the dots on the die. If you land on a red dot, draw a card from the stack, read it aloud, and move accordingly. After drawing a card and moving, the player puts the card at the bottom of the stack.

Two or more players may land on the same space. When a player reaches the end of the path, she may continue to participate in the discussion. Players are encouraged to discuss the situations on the cards that they or others draw.

Professional Development Cards
Make cards to be drawn when players land on the red dots. The player who draws a card follows the instructions on the card. These scenarios are based on CDA procedures, but could be easily adapted to fit the requirements of other credentialing systems.

1. Your adviser has observed your classroom, completed your Formal Observation Book, and left it with you in a sealed envelope. Finish the Observation Obstacle Course.
2. Over 75 percent of your parents have returned the Parent Questionnaires in the sealed envelopes. You made it past Questionnaire Quicksand.
3. You've sent in your application by the due date. You're traveling down Deadline Drive. Watch out for the Deadline Detour.
4. You receive a call from your CDA Representative who tells you that when she receives your materials, she will contact you to schedule your assessment. Now you coast down Schedule Street.
5. You complete your Oral Interview, Early Childhood Skills Review (written exam). You turned in your Parent Questionnaires, Formal Observation Book, Resource File, copies of your Autobiography and Competency Statements. You've made it to Assessment Avenue!
6. Congratulations! You have just been notified that you are awarded the Child Development Associate Credential. Welcome to Professional Paradise.

Places to Draw Cards

Make stopping places along the path on the playing board that require drawing a card. Place a red dot on the spaces. Here are some ideas to label the stopping places:

1. Get on the Training Trolley. You've completed sixty training hours.
2. You've selected your adviser. Travel through Adviser Alley.

3. You have at least ten training hours in each content area for the CDA. Go around Competency Curve.
4. You've written your autobiography. Turn on Author Avenue.
5. You've completed 120 training hours. Go to Training Thoroughfare.
6. You've completed the seventeen items for your Resource File. Come to the end of Resource Road.
7. You've written half of your competency statements. You're in the Competency Circle.
8. You've written all of your competency statements. Turn the Competency Corner.
9. You've sent home your Parent Questionnaires and provided envelopes for their return. Careful. Don't fall into Questionnaire Quicksand.

Tic Tac Toe Games

Partners can play Tic Tac Toe by asking or answering a question before they place their X or 0 on the board. Once trainees understand the process, they can use the game for almost any topic depending on the questions used.

Make or purchase a Tic Tac Toe board for each pair of players. Make a set of cards with Xs and Os the same size as the spaces on the Tic-Tac-Toe boards. Make a list of questions or requests for information pertaining to the subject, and give a copy to each pair of players. Provide written instructions to players if they have not played the game with questions before.

Here is how to play Tic Tac Toe as a review:

1. Give one partner the cards with Xs on them.
2. Give the other partner the cards with Os.
3. The person with an X asks a question or makes a request from the list, then places an X card on a Tic Tac Toe grid. She marks the question or request off the list so that it will not be used again.
4. The participant with the 0 responds, then places an 0 card on the grid. The asker must accept the response for the play to count. If the asker does not accept the answer, she chooses another answer or request until she is satisfied with the other player's response.
5. Play continues with the players attempting to place cards to get three alike in a row.
6. Give a small prize to the winner of each game. If you want the play to last longer, play more games and let the winner be the one who wins the most games.
7. For the next game, the person who is 0 becomes the X and the X becomes 0.

This game can be introduced to a whole group and then played by partners. Discussion of responses should be encouraged.

Supplies: Tic Tac Toe grids
               0 cards

X cards

A list of questions or requests for information related to the workshop topic

Tic Tac Toe

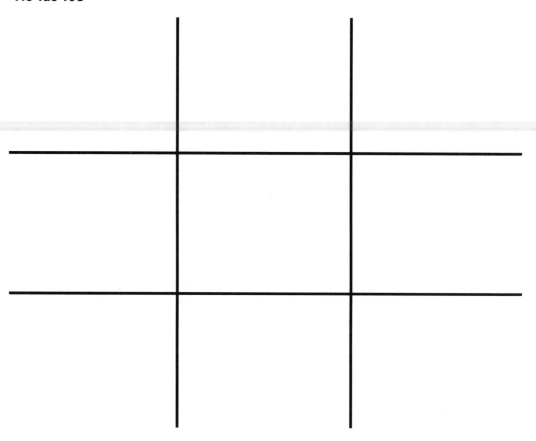

Tic Tac Toe

1. Tell about a way you help children move from one activity to the other.
2. Describe some materials you have made for your children to use.
3. Tell about a way you help substitutes fit into the center's routine.
4. Name a social service, health, or education resource in your community.
5. What would you tell a parent who has experienced family violence?
6. Tell about a time your observation was helpful in understanding a child.
7. Why is it important for every staff member to understand their responsibilities?
8. Tell about a time you coordinated plans with parents, specialists, or other program personnel.
9. Tell about a problem you helped resolve by discussing it with the appropriate personnel.
10. Describe a time you helped other staff members.
11. It is not necessary to choose substitutes carefully since they will only be there a few days. (True or False)
12. Tell about a time you shared information about a child's growth, health, behavior, or progress that helped a parent.

13. How can a caregiver adapt plans to include a child with special needs such as a developmental delay?
14. Since each caregiver has her own class, there is no need to plan together.
15. Tell about a time you worked with parents or specialists to help a child with handicaps.

OTHER GAMES

Alphabet Game—To play this game, select a topic, concept, issue, task, or job and use the alphabet to structure information about the topic. Use as many letters of the alphabet as possible to start words that relate to the subject. In many cases the game will be humorous. For some letters, players may need to use their imaginations quite a bit.

Divide trainees into teams and announce a time limit. Usually ten to fifteen minutes is long enough. When the time is up, the winning team is the group that has the most letters with one or more words that start with the letters. If each team lists a word for every letter, the winner is the team with the most words overall. Here is an example of possible answers to the alphabet game with a goal of identifying the various roles of directors and the skills required of them:

Director Roles and Responsibilities Alphabet Game

Accounting, Administration	Nutritionist, Nurse
Bureaucratic Expertise, Bill Collector, Bookkeeper	Opportunist, Optimist
	Purchasing, Psychologist, Promoter, Planner
Contract Negotiation, Counselor	Quality Control Specialist, Questioner
Delegator, Dietitian	Resource Developing, Regulator
Evaluation, Encourages	Supervisor, Sanitarian, Safety Engineer
Finding Resources, Financial	Trainer, Treasures, Teacher
Grantmanship	Unifier
Habit Former, Helper, Hatchet Person	Visionary
Insurance Expert, Imagination	Wizard, Writer, Waitperson
Juggler, Justice, Janitor	X-tra Hard Worker!
Keeping Records, Kind	Yo-yo—Able to handle the ups and downs
Listener, Liaison	Zoologist
Motivator, Mother, Monitor	

Charades—Charades can be played with small groups of three to five participants. Give each group a set of index cards with the situations they are to act out without speaking. Each person in the group takes a turn, draws a card, and acts out the situation. The others try to guess what situation the person is demonstrating. Here is an example:

Playground Charades
Write the following playground hazards on index cards, one on each card. Each person draws a card. One at a time, players act out the hazard until someone in the group guesses what it is. After all hazards are identified, the group lists ways to alleviate the hazards.

1. Broken glass is on the playground.
2. The fence is broken.
3. Too many children are on the playground at one time.
4. Staff members are talking to each other and not paying attention to the children.
5. Children are not taught how to use equipment safely.
6. Not enough equipment is on the playground.
7. Children are allowed to walk in front of swings.
8. Teacher leaves the playground to get something.

Match-up—This game is good for anything that can be matched such as words and definitions. Simply write on index cards what you want to match. Pass out a set of the index cards to small groups or partners. Ask the trainees to match them. Here is an example:

Book Match—Pass out index cards lettered with the authors and names of popular children's books. Ask the trainees to work in small groups to match them. Provide catalogs of children's books or the actual books for checking their work.

Book Title	Book Author
A Chair for My Mother	Vera Williams
A Tree Is Nice	Janice May Udry
Alexander and the Terrible, Horrible, No Good, Very Bad Day	Judith Viorst
Ask Mr. Bear	Marjory Flack
Bedtime for Frances	Russell Hoban
Brown Bear, Brown Bear	Bill Martin, Jr
Good Dod, Carl	Alexandra Day
Chick-a-Chicka Boom Boom	Bill Martin, Jr
Crow Boy	Taro Yashima
Curious George	H.A. Rey
Frederick	Leo Leoni
Good Night Moon	Margaret Wise Brown
Madeline	Ludwig Bemelmans
Make Way for Ducklings	Robert McClosky
Mike Mulligan and His Steam Shovel	Virginia Lee Burton
My Father's Dragon	Ruth Stiles Gannett
Nobody Asked Me if I Wanted a Baby Sister	Martha Alexander
Once a Mouse	Marcia Brown
Peter Rabbit	Beatrix Potter
Petunia	Roger Duvoisin
Sam, Bangs, and Moonshine	Evaline Ness
The Little House	Margaret Wise Brown
The Very Hungry Caterpillar	Eric Carle
Umbrella	Taro Yashima
Where the Wild Things Are	Maurice Sendak
Whistle for Willie	Ezra Jack Keats
William's Doll	Charlotte Zolotow
Winnie the Pooh	A. A. Milne

Acronyms—Give teams a word related to the topic of the training session. For example, if the topic is physical development, you might give them the word "PHYSICAL." Then, as a team, trainees come up with as many facts as they can think of related to physical development that start with the letters in "PHYSICAL." Set a time limit of ten to fifteen minutes for the activity. The team with the most answers that are appropriate and not greatly contrived wins a prize. Here are some possibilities that a team might suggest:

P atterns of development are predictable
H appens at various rates
Y awning is a reflex, not a controlled movement
S itting up is usually accomplished at ___ months
I s continuous
C reeping occurs at about___months
A rm movements are controlled before fine motor
L eg muscle development allows the child to pull to a standing position at about ___ months

Pizza Game—This is a matching game that introduces novelty into a common matching activity. The game can be used for such activities as matching words to definitions or identifying relationships. Here is how to make a pizza game.

1. Draw a pizza on poster board, cut it out, and cut into pieces.
2. Make a pizza pan from poster board. Cut it out. Draw the same number of slices on the "pan" as you have pizza slices, but do not cut them out.
3. Write words on the pizza slices. Write the definitions of the words in the slices drawn on the pan.
4. Players match the words to the definitions by placing the pizza slices with the words on the matching definitions on the pan.

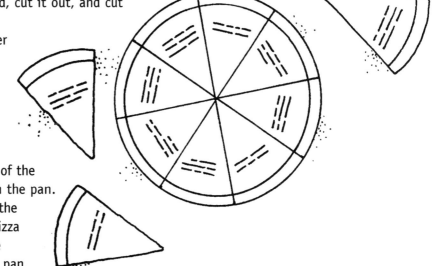

Other possibilities are to write a theorist's name on each pizza slice and write something about the theories on the slices on the pan. Other uses are matching the ages of children with developmental tasks, math terms with examples of their use, or matching science concepts with the experiences that lead to understanding the concepts.
For fun, add props such as pizza boxes, aprons, checkered tablecloths, and pizza cutters. This game can be a small group activity or played with partners.

Amelia Bedelia—Read the story of *Amelia Bedelia* by Peggy Parish. Ask small groups to illustrate the story using an assortment of scrap materials—construction paper, straws, fabric and lace, small boxes, etc. Each group will do it very differently. One group might work on a single project to recreate it together; another group may choose to have individuals do their own version. Still another group may assign parts and have each person complete one part. Give very little direction to stimulate the groups' problem solving and creativity.

As the groups work, watch for examples of cooperation, language development, problem solving, literacy, and other important skills to use as examples of the value of working in small groups. Offer materials and supplies as trainees request them or as you see the need. Deliberately do not include enough scissors or glue. Failing to offer enough will create a need for the groups to share. Look for examples of someone using the book as a resource. Some trainees will usually check the sequence of the activities with the book as they plan their display. Offer paper stapled into a book for anyone who wants to make an individual book to retell the story.

When the groups have become thoroughly involved, suddenly announce "STOP, it's now time to ..." in a loud voice. When the participants begin to grumble that they are not finished, relate the experience to how children feel when they are interrupted. This experience points out what happens to children when we do not give them enough time or their time is arbitrarily limited. It points out how they dislike being interrupted when they are very involved in an activity. Then allow the groups to continue their work. A few minutes before the time is really up, announce how much time is remaining. Call attention to this announcement to demonstrate the correct way to move into transitions.

Let each group describe to the others what they did so everyone sees the various ways people interpreted the story. Help them to see the value of group work by having them list what they experienced as they worked. If they do not identify any of the following, describe instances you observed of cooperation, problem solving, leadership, language development, literacy, small motor skills, and other benefits of the activity. Help them to see that the skills they used are more important than the product they produced. Relate their experience to what children experience when they have open-ended activities in an art area, housekeeping area, or block area. Lead them to recognize the value of such open-ended group activities and how books can stimulate creative activities.

OTHER LEARNING EXPERIENCES

BRAINSTORMING

Brainstorming is the rapid generation of many ideas without evaluation. Brainstorming is a good tool for stimulating creativity. While it is often difficult for participants to resist judging ideas as they are presented, brainstorming can be an effective way to generate many ideas and solicit a large amount of information quickly. For successful brainstorming, observe the following guidelines:

1. Explain the process of brainstorming and review these guidelines:
   - Quantity rather than quality is the goal. Think of as many ideas as you can; the ideas may be as bizarre as you wish.
   - Piggyback on others' ideas. Look for variations on the ideas suggested by other participants.
   - Evaluation is not allowed at this time. All ideas are accepted without comment and no discussion of the feasibility of ideas should occur at this stage.
   - Stop when time is called.
2. Select a recorder to write down all the ideas or suggestions.
3. Clarify what is to be brainstormed by being as specific as possible.
4. After the brainstorming session, go back and evaluate the ideas by asking:
   - Which ideas are not feasible?
   - Which ones are possible?
   - How can ideas be combined to create a plan?
   - What barriers are anticipated? Can they be overcome? How?
   - Which idea(s) should the group pursue at this time?
   - What resources are needed to make the plan(s) work?

Warm-up—Sometimes a group may need an example of brainstorming to warm up to the concept. Demonstrate the technique with an easy example. Ask them to brainstorm what they can do with a simple object such as a paper cup, unsharpened pencil, or even an apple or orange. Starting with a simple idea helps a group understand the concept of brainstorming. Many humorous suggestions as well as useful ones generally are offered, helping the group to enjoy and understand the technique.

Another Warm-up—Have participants brainstorm all the ways they can get from one side of the room to the other. They will list the obvious such as walking, running, or skipping. Ask them to be as imaginative as possible, and you will get everything from being carried by a rickshaw to riding an elephant. Then ask them to evaluate the suggestions to determine which ones are feasible, given the resources available to them.

And Yet Another Warm-up—Brainstorm the ways one might eat bread. Lead the participants from the obvious—toasted, as croutons, as a sandwich—to unusual ways such as with chop sticks, as a dessert, rolled up into a ball.

Role-play

Role-play allows learners to act out a scenario and to practice behavior before they need it on the job. Role-playing is more effective than just discussing what they might say. Role-play allows learners to actually rehearse what they will do in specific circumstances. Role-play gives participants a chance to think about and rehearse what they will say in response to a given situation. It can be a fun and active experience during training.

The roles may be prescribed or spontaneous. In prescribed role-play, participants receive specific role descriptions and may even receive scripts or starter scripts. In spontaneous role-play, the participants play themselves and demonstrate how they would respond to a situation.

Role-play can be very effective in helping participants develop responses to real-life experiences that they likely will encounter on the job. Some examples of good uses of role-play are:

- Responding to a parent's concern about academic learning.
- Explaining the value of play to a parent or co-worker.
- Talking to a staff member about tardiness.
- Describing the value of art experiences to a parent or co-worker who is concerned about messes.
- Addressing the reluctance of an assistant to follow through on activities and procedures.
- Speaking to a legislator or policy maker about the needs of children.
- Talking to a parent of a child who appears to need special services.
- Discussing concerns about a co-worker with a supervisor.
- Contacting a parent whose child has been bitten by another child.
- Addressing a parent whose payment is late.
- Contacting a parent whose child is sick or injured.
- Explaining a late pick-up policy to a parent.
- Handling a situation involving late fees.
- Talking to the news media about children's needs and issues.

How does one set up and conduct an effective role-play situation? Follow these easy steps for guidance:

1. Use role-play to help learners rehearse behaviors they are likely to need on the job.

2. Choose a scenario that includes a problem or situation that relates to one of the training objectives.

3. Describe the problem or situation, giving enough information to help players assume roles.

4. Describe the circumstances that set the stage for the role-play, including the location, personalities, and motives.

5. Keep the situation simple to reduce "hamming" or irrelevant behavior.

6. Give the information in writing for participants to study ahead of time and for reference as the role-play unfolds.

7. Decide who will play each role. Ask for volunteers when possible.

8. Involve the observers by giving them specific things to watch for or to evaluate.

9. Prepare the actors by giving them time to read, think about, and plan their roles.

10. Conduct the role-play.

11. Discuss and debrief what happened during the role-play experience.
    - Give the learners in the role-play an opportunity to comment on their roles first. Allowing them to evaluate themselves first seems to make any constructive criticism more acceptable.
    - Discuss with the observers what they saw, how they felt, and any suggestions for other ways to react.
    - Provide feedback and suggest additional ways to respond.

12. Repeat the role-play with different participants or to have the original role-players change their responses.

Here are examples of script starters for a prescribed role-play scenario. Also included are questions for the players and observers to think about as the role-play is under way and after it is completed.

For easy-to-use scripts, make separate sheets for each role with the name printed in color or in bold print. In the example below, Mr. Jackson's name could be in blue on his sheet. On Mrs. Montez's sheet, her name could be in red. Color helps the role-players easily see and focus on their parts.

Role-play Scenarios
Parent Participation in Center Activities

PARENT, MR. JACKSON: "I really wish I could come to the Parents' Night, Mrs. Montez, but you know I am working two jobs now, and trying to raise the two boys on my own is really hard. On top of everything, my car's brakes need an overhaul, and I can do it myself, but I just do not know when I can get it done, what with the two jobs and all."

TEACHER, MRS. MONTEZ: "I understand, but the boys really would like you to come. Is there anything I can do to help?"

MR. JACKSON: "Well, if there was another parent that we could carpool with, that would really help. It's just almost impossible for me to get my car fixed by that date when I have so little time to work on it."

The role-play continues with Mrs. Montez offering to help arrange a carpool, and Mr. Jackson expressing appreciation.
Questions for group discussion:

1. What are some other ways Mrs. Montez could have helped Mr. Jackson?
2. What obligation do teachers or directors have to assist parents?
3. How far should a teacher or director go to help parents participate in center activities?
4. Why should center staff help parents in their roles?

Differences in Staff and Parent Expectations
Supporting Children's Independence

TEACHER, MISS ADLEY: "Mrs. Smith, could we talk for a few minutes? I'm concerned that Maria always wants someone to help her, even with things she can easily do for herself. She's almost five now, but she refuses to even try to tie her own shoes. It's a real problem for me, since there are eleven other children in her group."

PARENT, MRS. SMITH: "I know you want the children to do things for themselves, but at home we always help Maria with her clothes. I think it is important for children to know that adults care enough to help them."

The role-play continues with Miss Adley, the teacher, attempting to support the parent, while helping Mrs. Smith understand the importance of self-help skills.

Questions for group discussion:

1. What are some other ways Miss Adley might have approached Mrs. Smith?
2. What problems does it create for children when parents and staff have different expectations?
3. How can the needs of parents and teachers be met?
4. What problems can lack of communication between center staff and parents cause?

Viewpoint—Viewpoint is a structure for role-play wherein each participant attempts to persuade the group that her viewpoint is best. The viewpoint structure works in a variety of situations to examine conflicting opinions. Viewpoint requires five players. Others in the group serve as observers. To play Viewpoint, each participant receives a sealed envelope with instructions that include a scene description, the role to play, and a sign identifying the role. Here are some examples of instructions for Viewpoint:

**Viewpoint Instructions
A Child Refuses to Eat**

Do not discuss your viewpoint with others before the activity. Discuss only the role you selected and any props you might wish to use.

Let the observers understand your viewpoint through the things they see and hear you do.

Decide how you can persuade the observers and members of the group that your viewpoint is the best approach. The observers will decide which person has the best solution.

You may use chairs for props and you will have three minutes to act out your role. Please put the sign around your neck so the observers will know the part that you play.

Scene:

The family is eating a meal at the table. The three-year-old absolutely refuses to eat, a situation that happens often. Everyone—Mother, Father, Aunt, and Uncle— all have a different solution to the problem.

Mother

Tell her she can have dessert if she eats all the food on her plate.

Father

If you put the food in her mouth, she will have to eat.

Aunt

Ignore it. If you do not feed her in between meals or allow snacks, she will eat at the next meal.

Uncle

Make her stay in the high chair until she eats.

> **Child**
>
> You act out the scene.

After the role-play ends, the observers discuss the various viewpoints presented. Then they decide which solution is the most appropriate and why it is the best course of action.

Viewpoint is a structure that is effective in many early childhood situations. Some unique features are the time limit for the role-play and the evaluation of the points of view, not the players. However, the observers may wish to offer suggestions to the player whose viewpoint is considered the most appropriate so that viewpoint is effectively conveyed. Here is another Viewpoint episode:

Viewpoint Instructions

A Child Cries When Not Given His Way

Do not discuss the content of your viewpoint with others before the activity. Discuss only the role you selected and any props you might wish to use.

Let the observers understand your viewpoint through the things they see and hear you do.

Decide how you can persuade the observers and members of the group that your viewpoint is the best approach. The observers will decide which person has the best solution.

You may use chairs for props and you will have three minutes to act out your role. Please put the sign around your neck so the observers will know the part that you play.

Scene:
An aide in a childcare center refuses to give a four-year-old a piece of candy that he saw in some supplies brought for a party later in the week. The boy begins to cry, something he often does when he does not get what he wants. The staff members discuss what to do about the problem and offer some solutions.

Assistant Director

Children who cry often may be insecure and should be given sympathy.

Mother

He is spoiled and must learn he cannot get what he wants by crying.

Aide

He is insecure, and that is why he should get what he wants.

Teacher

We should pay attention to him when he is behaving well and ignore him when he cries.

Child

You act out the scene.

Cautions about Role-play
Several disadvantages to role-play are:

- Some people may resist or be reluctant to participate. Do not force them to take part.
- Others may not take the activity seriously and will play the "bad child" or the "class clown."
- Some will greatly exaggerate their actions.

However, the more realistic the scenarios, the more likely participants will take the role-play seriously. To maximize and encourage participation, conduct the role-play in small groups to include more people at one time. Participants are more likely to take the experience seriously in small groups; participants who are uncomfortable with role-play will be less intimidated in a small group setting.

Here are some additional variations in conducting role-play activities:

Sports—Use a sports metaphor to vary role-play. Divide participants into teams. One person is designated to be a coach, the role-players become team members, and the others are fans. The fans' task is to encourage the team members. The coach offers suggestions and guidance. If a specific sport is very popular in your area, add sport terminology to the role-play such as: "You really hit a home run with that idea!" or "Let's huddle and come up with a game plan."

Fishbowl—Conduct a role-play or other task in the center of the group. The group not involved in the role-play will be observers and will offer encouragement and suggestions to those in the fishbowl. This activity is for groups where participants are very comfortable with role-play and with each other because it means all eyes are on them.

LEARNING STATIONS

Learning stations are guided, "hands-on" active experiences that provide trainees opportunities to experiment with materials. Learning stations offer adult learners opportunities to choose activities and to focus on their areas of interest. The stations allow learners to work at their own pace and to work without concern for mistakes. The stations allow for discovery and thus help participants see the value of the activities. Learning stations help participants understand the value of interest centers for children. Because learning station activities are hands-on, they increase the chance that learners will actually do the activities at the job site. The learning station approach gives trainers a chance to practice what they preach about how learning occurs.

The major disadvantage of learning stations is that they can be very time-consuming to prepare and set up. They usually require a lot of materials and equipment that must be gathered, organized, arranged for trainees, and removed when the session ends. However, some topics are best taught through learning stations. Topics and activities that work especially well with learning stations are:

- Art activities
- Sensory experiences such as water play
- Science activities
- Cooking and food preparation activities
- Block play experiences
- Making learning materials for children

To set up good learning stations, consider the following:

- Make each station self-contained and self-explanatory. Have everything that is needed for the activity at the station.
- Prepare clear, simple, written directions for each station since participants will be working with little direct guidance from an instructor.
- Have enough stations that everyone can be involved and still have a choice of places to move to when finished with a particular activity.
- Provide a means for trainees to evaluate or respond to the activities so you are certain that they understand the concepts.
- Plan a way to address barriers to implementation.

Consider how many people can work at each station. Then plan to have enough stations to have space for twenty-five to fifty percent more than you expect to attend. The goal is to ensure that everyone has a choice of other activities when they are finished with one and ready to move to another. Leaving room for choice is important since everyone may not be interested in doing every activity. Having enough stations also means that there will be little waiting or crowding.

Science Learning Station–Changes in State of Matter
Put out cornstarch, water, and a large bowl. Place a sign near the bowl that suggests what the learners should do. The sign should stimulate learners to think about what happens.

Making and Exploring Goop

1. Put some cornstarch in the bowl.
2. Add water until the mixture is slightly runny.
3. Put your hand in the mixture.
4. How does it feel?
5. Lift your hand and let the mixture run down through your fingers.
6. What do you notice happens to the mixture?
7. Why do you think it happens?

Give each trainee a sheet of paper to write about her experiences at each station. The sheets might include this information for the learning station on states of matter.
What words can you use to describe how the mixture felt? What words would children use?

1. Can you remember anything else that felt similar to the mixture?
2. What happens as the mixture rests for a while?
3. What happens when you squeeze the mixture?
4. What could children learn from this experience?
5. How will the children clean up after this activity?
6. What problems do you anticipate with this activity? How will you address the problems?

As an example of positive and negative ways to interact with children, talk to the participants as they work, criticizing them, telling them to hurry, dominating the activity, and interfering with their work. For comparison, react appropriately to some trainees, showing interest in their work. Ask about their experience and engage in open conversation with them. Offer encouragement to experiment. The trainees will soon get the point about interacting positively with children.

Learning Station for Transition Time
This activity helps trainees understand the importance of structuring the environment to allow for smooth transitions and to provide for children who need more time to complete a task. Use this activity to welcome participants to training, as a demonstration of how to handle transitions, or as an icebreaker. Set up the materials in advance so that early arrivals can begin to create as soon as they arrive. Allow about fifteen minutes at the beginning of the session to finish if they need to do so. Give them a five-minute warning that time is about up. Help them understand how to provide for early arrivals and how, when children finish one task, other activities should be available. Point out the indirect guidance you used and how participants were free to be creative. Be sure

trainees understand that instructions for children would include pictures and might instruct the children to look at a book or to select a picture if they are nonreaders. Encourage trainees to use this idea and create their own version for a parent meeting.

Put out these supplies:

- Construction paper, ribbon, lace
- Name tags
- Markers in assorted colors
- Pipe cleaners and scraps of fabric
- Playdough and accessories
- A selection of quotations in a decorated box (some are at the end of this section)

Display posters with these instructions:

1. Help yourself to a snack.
2. Make a name tag that is uniquely yours!
3. Enjoy participating in one or more of these activities:
   - Fancy Initials—make your initials with the materials provided.
   - Book Fair—select a book that appeals to you. Read it to see how it reminds you of your childhood.
   - A Pipe cleaner Sculpture—build yourself with pipe cleaners.
   - Playdough Pet—make a playdough figure of an unusual pet you would like to have.
   - Favorite Quotes—select a quotation from the box to share with others.
4. Be prepared to share what you did and how it relates to planning transition time when you introduce yourself.

Field Experiences

Remember how you looked forward to field trips during your elementary school days? Remember climbing aboard the big yellow school bus full of excitement and taking off to the airport, zoo, or museum? Field trips are valuable for adult learners, too. "Going to see" is an excellent way to learn how other programs work and what they do for children and families. Field trips can be a group activity or an assignment for participants to go on their own.

Field trips to other early childhood programs are an excellent way to learn about other settings and to get ideas for activities and see them in practice. Field trips are a great way to find out about services for children and their families. Here are some ideas to make field trips valuable and productive:

- Have a clear goal and purpose. Will trainees learn new teaching ideas or strategies? Is the goal to understand the eligibility for services? Are they to see what a quality program for infants and toddlers is like? Are they expected to learn about licensing requirements? The goals and purpose of the field trip determine how to plan for it.

- Provide an overview of what visitors can expect to see. Visitors will want to know what a day might be like at the site they are visiting. They need to be informed about what part of the daily schedule they will see.
- Give trainees some guidelines for the visit. Let trainees know whether they should talk to the children or if they should go by the office before going to the classroom. Directions to the site are a great help if they are going on their own.
- Provide some structure to the experience. Give trainees a check list of things to look for, an assignment to summarize their experience, or some questions to answer. Ask them to compare and contrast methods or to be alert to certain things at the site.
- Debrief as a group. Trainees will not have noticed the same things. Each person's experience will be different. There will be many things to see and learn on a field trip, and each trainee will focus on aspects that interest her. Debriefing as a group helps each person benefit from everyone's experience.

Disadvantages and Cautions

- Field trips can be expensive or difficult to arrange when transportation is involved.
- Participants may not see what they were expected to see, or they may misinterpret what they observe. If the instructor is not with the trainees, misunderstanding is more likely to arise.
- A tendency to be critical of other programs or to see them as "not as good as ours" may exist.

All field experiences do not have to involve a trip, however. A field experience can be right in one's own backyard. Here is an example of an on-site field experience for trainees to become familiar with the learning opportunities and variety of materials on playgrounds:

Playground Detective

Walk around your playground and look for the following:

1. Something smooth and something rough
2. Something to get in and something to get on
3. Something scary and something reassuring
4. Something that moves and something that stays still
5. Something little and something big
6. Something purchased and something teacher-made
7. Something man-made and something natural
8. Something living and something non-living

Find five examples of:

1. sounds
2. growing things
3. things to climb
4. things with interesting textures
5. things with unusual shapes

After the field experience, provide a way for participants to share and discuss what they found as playground detectives.

Stories, Quotations, Proverbs, and Analogies

Short stories, vignettes, and anecdotes can be motivational or used to emphasize a point. Stories in the form of fables and parables have been used to transmit values and culture throughout history. Good teachers through the ages have been skilled at telling tales to reinforce values. Stories engage listeners by relating their experience to the issues at hand. Stories should not preach or tell participants what to do, but should encourage them to think and to draw their own conclusions.

To use stories effectively, consider the following:

- Be thoroughly familiar with any story selected.
- Practice telling the story to tell it smoothly and with expression.
- To jog your memory, write the key story components on an index card in the order that they occur.
- Do not read stories unless the stories are short and you read with vocal variety.
- If reading a story, look up frequently at the audience to maintain good eye contact.
- Use different voices for the various characters to hold trainees' attention.

For good story sources, see page 277 in the Appendix.

Sometimes children's books can be used to demonstrate truths or concepts that you want to present to adults. *William's Doll* by Charlotte Zolotow can be effective in helping adults to see the value of play with dolls for boys as well as girls. *Nobody Asked Me if I Wanted a Baby Sister* by Martha Alexander is a good introduction to sibling rivalry or how to help children adjust to a new baby in the family. *Ira Sleeps Over* by Bernard Waber can help adults understand the conflict between children's desire for independence and their need for dependence. *Nana Upstairs and Nana Downstairs* by Tomie dePaola can be used in a session on children's relationships with their extended families or ways to help children adjust to the illness or death of a grandparent. For more information on children's books and the topics that they can illustrate, see page 277 in the Appendix.

Your own experiences can be rich sources for stories and anecdotes. Write down those great examples of children learning and all of your experiences that are examples of the concepts you want to develop.

Quotations
Short quotations, sayings, and poems can emphasize a point in an effective—and sometimes inspirational—way. Presenting information in a catchy or unique manner is attention-grabbing as well as more memorable. Put the quotations on a poster or overhead transparency or periodically read one throughout a training session. Have "a quote of the day" or "quote of the week" for a class.

Proverbs
Have trainees relate old sayings to their work situation. Ask them to describe how one applies to them or to tell about an experience they have had to which the proverb refers.

Some possibilities are:

Time is money.

(A participant might relate this to how a director or caregiver must be able to manage their time and prioritize their responsibilities.)

Waste not, want not.

(Caregivers likely will compare this to the need to use inexpensive or recycled materials for activities.)

A stitch in time saves nine.

(Could relate to the need for preventive maintenance.)

The proof of the pudding is in the eating.

(The success of training is in the change in behavior on the job.)

A bird in the hand is worth two in the bush.

(Work with what you have rather than waiting for something you do not have.)

Penny wise, pound foolish.	(Purchase good equipment that will last.)
Never put off until tomorrow what you can do today.	(Children grow up fast; we must make every day memorable.)
Behind every cloud is a silver lining.	(There is always something good that can come from seeming disaster.)
A penny saved is a penny earned.	(Spend money on early childhood to save money on social problems.)
It is better to light one candle than to curse the darkness.	(Look for a solution, even if the action is small, rather than complain about the problem.)
Many hands make light work.	(If everyone helps, any job will be easier.)
A journey of a thousand miles must begin with a single step.	(We must start somewhere. Even when the task seems overwhelming, we can make it manageable if we take small steps.)
Give a man a fish and you feed him for a day. Teach a man to fish and you feed him for a lifetime.	(Education prepares us for life.)

Analogies

Analogies, like quotations, proverbs, and stories, can emphasize a point. Analogies can be discussion starters for partner or small group activities. The instructor can read a selection of analogies, then ask trainees to think about them and choose which one best fits them. Here are examples of analogies:

For sessions on cooperation and interpersonal skills:

Time to Plant

Let us plant:
One row of lettuce—let us practice caring and concern for each other
Two rows of turnips—let us turn up our willingness to help each other
Three rows of squash—let us squash gossip, criticism, impatience, and arrogance
Four rows of beets—let us beat everyone in kindness and respect
Five rows of mint—let us keep our mind clear and in mint condition
Six rows of thyme—let us use our time well, and spend it wisely
Seven rows of sage—let us heed sage advice from which we can learn

Eight rows of sunflowers—let us shed sunshine and light wherever we go
Nine rows of carrots—let us remember the carrot, not the stick
Ten rows of peppers—let us pepper our speech with kindness

For sessions on planning or classroom management:

As a planner, I am most like:

- a canoe
- a race horse
- a circus train
- a jet plane
- a horse-drawn carriage
- a hot-air balloon
- a dump truck
- a space shuttle
- an ocean liner

My motto is:

- Do it now!
- Time is money.
- Take time to smell the roses.
- Time flies when you're having fun.
- What you see is what you get.
- Life is like a box of chocolates.
- Let the good times roll.

For sessions on staff relationships or coping with stress:

A day at work is like:

- a soccer riot
- a Mardi Gras party
- a football game
- a parade
- an amusement park
- a rock concert

This song describes how I feel:

- I Am Woman
- Everything's Coming Up Roses
- Sunshine on My Shoulder
- Wind Beneath my Wings
- We've Got Trouble
- We Shall Overcome

- Memories
- Getting to Know You
- What's Love Got to Do with It?
- Take This Job and Shove It

For sessions on administration or supervision:

When I must address a staff problem, I feel like (or I wish I could be like):

- an ostrich
- a lamb
- a wolf in sheep's clothing
- a snapping turtle
- a pit bull
- one of the three little pigs
- Tyrannosaurus Rex

My problem-solving skills are like:

- a sledge hammer
- a pair of tweezers
- a chain saw
- a bulldozer
- a plumber's friend
- a surgeon's scalpel
- a pair of scissors
- a paintbrush
- an egg beater

CHAPTER 4

Making and Using Effective Workshop Materials

Audiovisual Aids—VCRs and Other Monsters

Using audiovisual aids helps learning take place by incorporating both visual and auditory modalities. Audiovisual aids should supplement personal contact and interaction, not be used as a replacement for such contact. Audiovisual aids focus attention on what is being discussed and increases interest in material. They can improve retention by engaging more than one of the senses.

One of the most frequently used aids for training is the videotape. Videos and VCRs are readily available, and videotapes are becoming increasingly common in the training field. However, videos are not the cure-all that some may think, and there are limitations to what they can do.

Videos

Videos selected for training should take advantage of the unique property of video recordings, which is showing movement. A video that only shows people talking has limited usefulness and will rarely hold trainees' attention. The advantage of videotapes over other aids is that they can illustrate behavior and interactions. Unless videos do so, they may not be the best means of presenting information.

As the technology becomes less expensive, videos can be found for almost any training need. Effectively used, they are a good medium for many training situations. However, they also can be an excuse for participants to doze in the back row of a darkened room. Here are some guidelines for selecting and using videos effectively:

Prepare for Viewing
Preview the video before using it. Even if you have seen it many times, a quick review will refresh your memory. You may see new opportunities for follow-up activities or new points to emphasize.

Ensure that the content is appropriate. A good video conveys a message. If the message is not apparent and requires too much explanation, then consider another way to present the information. Never use a video as a substitute for adequate planning. Videos should be used only when they specifically demonstrate a situation that cannot otherwise be seen.

Consider the quality of the video. Videos have a distinct advantage over still pictures because they show action. They can show, for example, children involved in real situations and adults interacting with children. If a video does not show action, then a better medium likely can be found. Videotapes are competing with the trainees' favorite movies and television programs. If the video is not well made, find another activity. If the tape itself has been damaged, do not use it.

Consider the length and keep it short. Even the best video will not hold participants' attention if it is too long. If you must use a thirty-minute video, find a good place to end and break it into two parts. Show only a portion at a time with discussion or an activity between the parts. About fifteen minutes is as long as one can usually hold an audience's attention when they are passively sitting and watching. It is not necessary to show a whole video. If only part of a long video is relevant, just fast forward beforehand and be ready to show the relevant part.

Plan a means of interaction during or immediately after showing the video. Use a viewer's guide sheet that calls for the participants to record certain information they learn from the video. You might have viewers write an anecdotal record about something they saw. Tell trainees before they view the video what they will be asked to do following the viewing.

Consider the time of day when you use a video. If you use one late in the day after a heavy lunch or full day of training, a darkened room is a sure recipe for inattention. Scheduling videos before lunch is the best approach. A video often stimulates impromptu discussion during the lunch break. You also can give an assignment based on the information in the video to complete during lunch.

Showing the Video

Give a reason for viewing and an overview of the video's content. Spend a few minutes explaining what the video will depict. Describe briefly what viewers will see and some specific things to watch for. Tell viewers some of the things they will learn from the video to help them see its importance. Let viewers know that there will be a discussion or activity following the video.

Keep the light level bright enough for taking notes. It is often helpful to dim the lights, but sitting in a darkened room, especially after lunch, makes concentration difficult.

Ensure that everyone can see. If the screen is too small for the whole group, consider dividing into small groups and use two monitors and two tapes. Or have one group do another activity while a second group watches, and then have the groups change places.

Make the video available for trainees to use on their own at a later time. A major advantage of video is that one can watch tapes many times if information is complex. Participants who watch the video in their own homes may feel more freedom to view it several times.

VIEWERS' GUIDES

To make a video most useful, viewers need something to do other than watch. One way to involve viewers is to use a viewer's guide for any video used in training. If no guide is provided with a video you wish to use, devise one yourself. Watch the video and make notes of specific points or techniques shown. Sometimes videos will even have graphics or list major points to make it easy for you to develop a guide. Make questions based on the information presented. An example of a viewer's guide is on page 278 of the Appendix.

MAKING AND USING YOUR OWN VIDEOTAPES

With the proliferation and ease-of-use of video cameras, it is possible to make your own videos for training. By capturing the actions of children on tape, you can create an excellent source of material for learning observation skills, assessing and evaluating practices, and learning interaction techniques.

If you use a camcorder often in a classroom, the children will become accustomed to it, and they will react normally. Taping a child's intense concentration as she works to complete a puzzle, a child's struggle to perform some self-help skills, or a child's exploration of the properties of water are a few of the numerous opportunities to create your own training materials.

To use videos you make in a workshop setting, give trainees a guide or overview of what you want them to watch for. Perhaps you want them to look for the learning that can come from open-ended materials. Maybe they should watch to see how a child learns from exploring materials. Perhaps you want them to observe one child's responses to a teacher or to another child.

You also can have them simply watch the video and note what they see. Be sure to allow time to discuss the observations after viewing the video. These discussions will emphasize the importance of observation skills.

ACTIVITIES USING VIDEOS

Video Observation—Have half of the class (Group A) watch a ten-minute video of an active toddler. Tell them to try to remember as much as possible about what the child does. Have the other half (Group B) review a developmental checklist for toddlers. Ask them to prepare to use the checklist to watch the same video. Group B watches the video using the checklist, while Group A tries to record as much as they can of what they see as they watch the video. Following the viewing, have both groups write down everything they remember. Have each person in Group A find a partner from Group B. Ask each pair to discuss its experience. Trainees with the checklist will typically report more information. Help the group identify the benefits and limitations of a checklist over memory or note taking. Help them recognize the circumstances under which one technique will work better than the other. This video observation activity demonstrates the convenience and benefits of using a checklist to observe children's behavior. It is a good introduction to observation and recording children's behavior.

Overhead Transparencies

Overhead transparencies are one of the most versatile mediums to use for training. Overhead projectors are relatively inexpensive and often available in meeting rooms and classrooms. Overhead projectors offer a distinct advantage in that they can be used while facing the audience and maintaining eye contact. If transparencies are properly made, they can be seen by a large group. Overhead projectors are simple to operate—just set up, turn on, focus, adjust the image, and you are all set.

Creating Effective Transparencies

Since transparencies are viewed from a distance, they must be easy to read from anywhere in the room. To make them easy to read, use a minimum of words and lines of text. If you have a lot of information, separate it into several transparencies. Here are guidelines for making effective overhead transparencies:

- **Keep the message simple** Stick to one idea or concept per transparency to help participants absorb the information. If there is too much information to read or if it is difficult to read, they will lose interest. Follow the T-shirt guide—put only as much information on an overhead transparency as you would likely see on a T-shirt.
- **Use the six-by-six rule** Limit the printed information to six lines on a transparency and six words per line to make transparencies readable from every seat in your room.
- **Use large type.** Make the letters at least one-quarter inch (one centimeter) high; 16-24 point size.
- **Use a grid** to make the lettering neat when you write information by hand.
- **Consider the transparency an outline** of your ideas, not as your entire presentation.
- **Include bullets or numbers** to make points easy to follow.
- **Add color, art work, and graphics with restraint.** Too many pictures may take away from the message. Graphics can clarify, but keep them simple. Too many colors can be distracting. Generally, two to three colors will suffice. Highlight key points or use the same color for parallel items. Just because one has a great color printer, it is not necessary to show everything it can do. If a color printer is not available and you want variety, use different colors of transparencies or make the background dark with white text.
- **Mount transparencies in frames** and write notes on the frames to use as memory joggers.

Software programs such as Microsoft Power Point or graphics programs can be used to make a series of transparencies quickly and professionally. You can print a transparency right off your computer. Be sure you use the correct transparency film material. Transparency film for printers is designed to "take" the ink from your printer.

To make a transparency with a copy machine, print the information on regular copy paper. Insert the film into the paper holder of the copier. Use the paper copy as the original, and just copy as you normally do. If your copier is adjustable, experiment with making the transparency lighter or darker for the best results. If your copier will enlarge, you may wish to enlarge some materials used for transparencies. Be sure to use the recommended film for your copier.

Using Overhead Transparencies

- Turn the projector on, show the transparency, then turn the projector off unless you are showing several transparencies in a row. The bright light from the projector can be a distraction.
- Make an arrow shape from a business card to help the group focus on a specific part such as an important statistic or key word. Turn up about one-half inch (one centimeter) of the shaft to make picking up the arrow easier. Use the arrow to point to important points or sections of transparencies. Or simply use a pencil to point to an item you wish to emphasize.
- When you have several items in a list on a transparency, use a cover sheet to expose one item at a time. Thus, you will not have participants looking ahead and not focusing on the item under discussion. Use a piece of poster board or other sheet of paper heavy enough to block light and not be blown off the projector.
- If you want part of the transparency covered to remove for emphasis, tape a paper flap to the frame. Make it large enough to cover the part you want hidden. Turn the flap aside to expose the whole transparency.
- Present your transparencies in an order that is logical and apparent to the audience.
- Provide copies of the information on the transparencies to reduce note taking by trainees during the presentation.
- Put a small piece of masking tape on the projector to properly line up each transparency. The tape will prevent having to move transparencies around to line them up by trial and error.
- Use a piece of cardboard or poster board to shield the overhead projector light when you are not using it.
- Colored page protectors or report covers can be used as overhead transparencies, just do not try to run them through your copy machine. Try cutting out arrows or sunburst designs from them to emphasize a part of an overhead.
- Always have a spare bulb. Bulbs burn out at the most inconvenient time.
- Consider purchasing folding projectors. Although they cost more initially, they are a good investment in convenience since they can be carried like a small suitcase.
- For projected images, whether overheads or slides, make sure the images are at least forty-two inches (one meter) from the floor. Often the best arrangement will be to put the screen in the corner of the room and angle it toward the center of the room.

Slides

Slides are beneficial visual aids in large groups where projecting an image on a large screen may be preferred to using a VCR with a small screen. Slides can show specific settings or illustrate activities. Slides are especially useful when discussing room arrangement or playground ideas where it is impossible to bring items with you.

MAKING YOUR OWN SLIDES

Any 35-mm camera will make slides. Simply purchase film that is designated slide film. Usually slide film has "chrome" in the name. Generally, slide film comes in 100, 200, and 400 speed. The speed to use depends on the lighting situation—the lower the number, the more light is needed for best results. Take the pictures as you would prints.

Most print processors also will process slide film. It may take longer, so allow extra time. If you plan to use the slides frequently, have duplicates made because projection may eventually fade slides or damage them. Another solution is to take several shots for each slide you want to use. Taking extras is less costly than making duplicates, and will give you a "working set" with extras for safekeeping.

If you need a slide with writing on it such as a title slide, photograph alphabet blocks or magnetic letters spelling the title. Or, simply make a poster and photograph the poster. Slides are also useful to show examples of children's artwork. To photograph flat items such as posters and artwork, be sure you line the camera parallel to the surface of the paper.

SETTING UP FOR SLIDE PRESENTATIONS

Joe Jabot is headed out to give a slide presentation about a new program his organization is instituting. On the way into the meeting room, he drops the slide tray. To his dismay, slides scatter around his feet like fall leaves. Quickly scooping them up, he now must spend twenty minutes reorganizing his slides—time he should have used greeting his audience. During the session, several slides are upside down, some backward, and some are out of order, messing up the continuity of his carefully planned presentation. What did poor Joe do to deserve this? He failed to tighten the ring on the carousel tray.

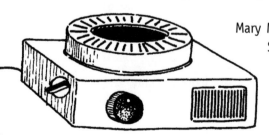

Mary Martinez has been preparing her presentation for months. She carefully selected her slides and arrived in plenty of time to set up and be ready. However, halfway into the session, the screen goes dark. After waiting several minutes while she tries to fix the problem, the audience gets restless and some people even leave. Mary finds the bulb is out, and now must wing it without her important visuals. Mary forgot a cardinal rule of using a slide projector—always bring a spare bulb.

Latonia Lancaster has been giving slide presentations for years. She has learned the hard way to carry a spare bulb, check the carousel, and be sure the slides are in order. Still, her presentations just are not what she thinks they should be. They have an amateurish quality that detracts from the message. Her slides are sometimes too dark or too light, leaving her to explain what people would be seeing if the slides were better. And then there is the awful bright glare when she finishes that causes her audience to flinch. Latonia could improve the technical aspects of her presentation.

How do we prevent the disasters described above? Follow these guidelines:

- Arrange slides in a logical order. If you are showing examples of room arrangement, show a slide of the whole classroom, then closer views of each interest center. This order helps viewers see relationships. If you are showing activities, group them by categories such as teacher-made math manipulatives or props for dramatic play.
- Use only well-exposed slides. Poor quality images add nothing to a presentation.
- Do not switch between horizontal and vertical views frequently. A constant change from horizontal format to vertical and back again is distracting.

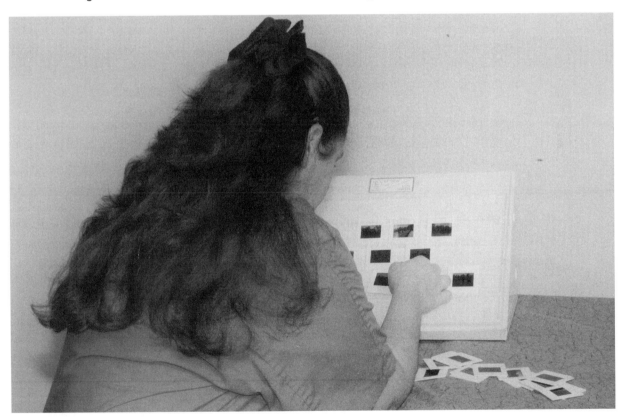

A slide sorter will be helpful in arranging your slides in the proper order. Slide sorters are lighted racks that allow you to see the slides by placing them on the rack. You can easily move the slides around until you have them in the order that you want.

Use carousel trays that hold eighty slides for presentations. Although some hold one hundred and forty, the openings are smaller. You risk slides hanging up in the projector during a presentation. Tighten the center ring on the carousel tray. Spilling and scattering slides just before a presentation gets you off to a very poor start!

To put slides in the tray correctly, hold the slide in front of you where you view it the way you want the audience to see it. Put a mark in the bottom left corner. When you insert the slide in the tray, turn the slide to where the mark is on the upper right side away from the screen. This procedure will eliminate backward or upside down slides.

Use coding dots or colored markers and number your slides to keep them organized. Because the slide frames are plastic, be sure you use a marker that writes on plastic.

Always bring an extension cord with a grounded adapter when you plan to use projectors. Inevitably, the electrical outlet is not in the most convenient place for your projector. A three-outlet accessory for your extension cord is handy if you use a tape recording or compact disc player with your slides. The extra outlets are handy if you are using several types of audiovisual equipment and want to get everything set up prior to opening. If the cord blocks a pathway, keep it unplugged until you need it or tape it down with duct tape.

Always preview your slides at the training site. Ensure that both vertical and horizontal slides are clearly visible from all parts of the room. Be sure the projector is the right height so that the slides are visible from all over the room. Also ensure that no one sits in the seats directly in front of the projector where they will block the light.

Have someone prepared to change a bulb and turn the projector on so that you will not need to leave the podium. Check the room lighting to see how to dim it. Have someone prepared to lower the lights at the appropriate time.

Showing Slides

Leave the slides up long enough for the audience to study the image. If the slide includes much detail, the audience may need time to identify exactly what they are seeing. Since you will be very familiar with the slides and know the content, there may be a tendency to change too rapidly. It is distracting to have a member of the audience say, "I missed that. Will you show it again?"

If you must control the projector from a location other than the podium, walk to that location before the lights are turned out. If the room will be very dark, moving around becomes a safety issue. Avoid standing at the projector if it is not at the very back of the room since that may put your back to many in the audience.

Change the slides yourself with a remote control or work with an assistant who knows when to change them. Frequently saying, "Next slide, please," to a helper can be distracting. You also may decide on a signal for when you want the slides changed.

Laser or battery-operated light pointers are useful tools with slides. Similar to flashlights, they project an arrow or small dot on the screen. Use them to point out a specific item without walking up to the screen. For example, if you are showing a slide of a classroom and want to call attention a small item that might not be noticed, point to it with a light pointer.

A bright screen at the end of a slide presentation is startling since it is such a strong contrast in the darkened room. Prevent this startling effect by using blanking slides to block the light. Make blanking slides by cutting two-inch (five-centimeter) squares (the size of slides) from poster board. Put them in the slide tray at the beginning and end of the set of slides. Make the blanking slides from colored poster board to use them as separators when you have several sets of slides in the same slide tray. Having a blanking slide at the beginning means you can turn the projector on before you need it without the distracting bright light on the screen.

Use your slides as notes. The visual image can remind you of points you want to make. If your slides are in a logical order and you associate certain points with the images, they serve as cue cards.

Always take along an extra bulb. Projector bulbs have a long life, but you can be sure that one will give out just before a session where you absolutely need the slides to convey the message. Make sure you know how to replace a bulb quickly or have someone available who does. Asking for someone in the audience to volunteer to replace the bulb will label you an amateur.

Useful Accessories for Audiovisual Equipment

- Duct tape to hold down your extension cord if it has to run across an area where someone may walk.
- A grounded adapter—a small item that will save the day in an older building that does not have the right kind of outlets.
- A twenty-five-foot (eight-meter) extension cord with a holder and extra outlet accessory.
- A small flashlight in case the projector needs adjusting after the lights are turned out. A flashlight is far less distracting than asking someone to turn on the lights to fix a problem.
- Something to prop the projector on in case you have to raise it higher.
- Laser or other light pointers.
- A remote control so you are not tied to the projector.
- A slide sorter to help in arranging slides in the correct order for a presentation.

Flipcharts

Flipcharts are useful for making a permanent record of information. For visual learners, a flipchart helps them focus on the discussion. There are two major uses for flipcharts— to provide information to participants and to record information from participants. Flipcharts may be prepared in advance to present information, an especially important factor where audiovisual equipment is not available. They also may be used to record information and ideas from the participants in such activities as brainstorming or group discussions.

Flipcharts to Inform

Prepared flipcharts are an effective way to convey information. Use these guidelines to make informative flipcharts:

- Keep sentences short.
- Use bullets or numbers to help clarify content.
- Use illustrations or graphics as appropriate.
- Make letters large enough to be easily read, considering the distance from which they will be viewed. Usually letters will need to be about one and a half inches (four centimeters) high. Leave about two inches (five centimeters) between the lines.
- Do not try to put too much on a flipchart. Too much information means it likely will not be read or understood.
- Think of a flipchart as a billboard. The message must be conveyed quickly and succinctly.
- If you make a mistake, cover it with a stick-on label. Or cover a mistake with a piece of paper cut from an old chart and attached with rubber cement.
- Vary colors to help understanding. Highlight key points with color markers or graphics. Use one color for major headings, another color for explanations or examples.
- Use markers that do not bleed through, making the information on other pages difficult to read.
- Write on every other page and leave a blank page between each page you use if the next page shows through.
- Make use of the surprise element. Keep the information covered until it is needed. Uncovering a page attracts attention to the information. Keeping information covered prevents participants from reading ahead and being distracted from other matters.
- If you wish to have participants compare or contrast information, use two charts.

Flipcharts to Record Ideas and Suggestions

Another use for flipcharts—and probably a more common one—is to record the suggestions or ideas of participants. When using flipcharts for this purpose, the same guidelines above apply. Additionally, here are others:

- Write memory joggers lightly in pencil on the blank pages to serve as reminders of key points to include.
- Work from the side of the chart if you are the one writing on it. Turning your back on the group reduces the contact you have with them.

- Use as few words as possible; you are recording key ideas, not exact quotations.
- If you will refer to the suggestions later, place the pages around the room for reference.
- For a permanent record of the information, copy to a small sheet of paper or take the sheets with you and enter the information into a computer file.

Using Flipcharts

For prepared flipcharts, use colored stick-on flags to quickly find the page you want. Another way to find pages fast is to write the topic of the flipchart vertically in small print on the side. You can flip pages back and forth as much as needed without delay.

Another way to find a specific page is to cut off the bottom corner of each sheet in an ascending manner. This process helps one to see the bottom of several sheets at once. Write the topic of the sheet on the diagonal edge of the cut corner to quickly find the one you want.

Use adhesive pages or hang pages on the wall with drafting dots. Drafting dots are small adhesive circles that may be removed without damage.

To avoid wrestling with an easel, try taping prepared flipcharts to the walls if allowed to do so. Tape the bottoms up over the top to create an element of surprise as the material is uncovered for discussion. Reveal each page as you make the presentation.

Props

Props include any item or object used in training, usually excluding audiovisual items, handouts, and other paper products. Props may be used for demonstrations of specific steps or to illustrate a point in a presentation.

Why Use Props?

Props allow the participants, especially visual learners, to focus on the instructor. They give trainees something to help them remember. Props add interest, aid retention, and add humor to training. They can stimulate discussion, interaction, and creativity. When possible, let the participants tell how the props relate to the issue. Props can be as varied as imagination allows.

Prop Ideas

Key chains—Give to participants when they identify the "keys to good ..."
An eraser—Because we all make mistakes.
Rulers or measuring tapes—Give out when participants "measure up" in some way.
Blocks—Stack as you build a "tower of learning."
A compass—Relate to "finding your direction," "feeling lost at times," "not knowing which way to go," or "pointing you in the right direction." A picture of road signs (or cardboard representations) or a road map also can be used. Use to relate to how instruc-

tion books or manuals serve as guides or give to participants to "help them find their way to good..."

Bubble gum, tape, or fancy paper clips—To hold things together when they seem to be falling apart.

A toy dinosaur—To remind us that change is inevitable, and without adaptability, we will become extinct.

Funnel—Relate to how we take in a lot of information, but we do not retain it all—especially if we do not use it in our work.

Toy train and track with switch—Use to "sidetrack" a train. Relate to how "we will not reach our goal if we become sidetracked." Lead a discussion of some of the ways we can get "sidetracked" and on how to "get back on track" by focusing on goals.

Magnifying glass or binoculars—Relate to "seeing the details," "focusing on parts of an issue or subject," "don't get lost in small issues," "don't fail to see the 'big picture'," "don't make a big issue out of a small matter."

Yo-yos—Life is full of ups and downs, but just as a yo-yo is designed for ups and downs, we can be equally resilient.

Cup of water and various containers—Relate to how we must adapt to work together or to fulfill expectations, yet we are still the same people. The water must adapt to the different containers, but it is still the same amount of water.

Tool kit with assorted tools—Relate to the tools you need to do a job or to fix things. Emphasize the need to have the resources to do necessary tasks. One tool (or activity) is not enough. One solution will not fit every problem.

Umbrella—To protect you during stormy times.

Telephone book—Relate to how there are many ways to do things, but they may not be useful unless they follow a system. The telephone book is in alphabetical order, a system we all know. Stress the importance of organizing and having a consistent procedure for how you do things. Relate to the importance of procedures, practices, and policies. Use a small musical instrument such as a xylophone to demonstrate that all music is made from a few notes that follow a system.

A penny—For good luck!

Flashlight or candle—Relate to "shining light on a subject," "having help if you feel you're in the dark," "to help you focus on a topic," or to "light the way."

A small trophy—To remind us of our goals; to celebrate our successes.

Paper clips—Relate to how even a small, simple item can be extremely useful and important. Everyone's ideas are good and should not be considered too small or simple. Some of the most useful inventions such as the paper clip seem very simple today!

Spoons, forks, knives, and chopsticks—Relate to how everyone selects the right tool that they know how to use for the task they want to do. Relate to selecting the right activity, method, or strategy for children. Several ways might work, but one will likely work best for each person.

Toy telephone—To keep in touch with reality, to improve communication.

Mask—To help you try out new roles without risk.

Candy hearts—To remind us of what we believe and why we work with children.

A candy bar—For remembering the sweetness of success.

Box of gelatin—Sometimes when you "get in hot water," the best comes out.

Mirror—For taking a close look at your strengths.

Any sports equipment and glasses or toy binoculars—Learning is not a spectator sport; participation is important for adults as well as for children.

Braino—Use it to unclog brains. Wrap an empty cylinder can with a label that says "Braino."

Roadmap—You can't get lost if you don't know where you are going; sometimes there is more than one way to get somewhere. There is no roadmap to success.

Rubber ball—Relate to bouncing idea to each other.

Microphone—To broadcast news about children, to broadcast information to parents.

Flour sifter—To find the information that is important, one must sift through a lot of information.

Small globe or inflatable globe ball—One person can make a world of difference in the lives of children.

Fruit and Veggie Props

Pass around an assortment of fruit and vegetables. Have participants think of a way each fruit and vegetable relates to the training topic. Give one or two ideas to get them started. Use the name of the food or some characteristic of it. Here are some possibilities:

Banana—I am "appealing" to you to...

Beet—You just can't "beet" these ideas and suggestions!

Orange—"Orange" you glad that...

Pepper—This is a great "pepper-upper!"

Pear—We will now get a partner and "pear" up to...

Lettuce—"Lettuce" work together.

Apple—This is the "apple" of my eye.

Carrot—Use the "carrot" rather than the stick.

Peach—This is a "peachy" idea.

Turnip—Let's see what new ideas we can "turnip!"

Plum—Are you "plum" tired of . . . ?

Occupation Symbol Props

Hold up items to symbolize various occupations. Ask participants to tell how their job or responsibilities are like the professions represented. Some possibilities are:

Item	Occupations Represented	How It Relates to Working with Children
Band-Aid, thermometer, or other first-aid items	Nurse, emergency medical technician	Providing first aid, treating illness
Checkbook, calculator	Banker, accountant	Keeping financial records, paying bills, collecting tuition
Cooking utensils, apron	Cook, dietitian, nutritionist	Planning and preparing meals and snacks
Tool belt, tool box, assorted tools	Electrician, carpenter	Keeping things in good repair
Hard hat, hammer	Construction worker	Building quality programs, constructing lives
Briefcase	Lawyer, manager	Knowing the laws, supervising others
Graduation cap, diploma	Teacher, graduating student	Knowing about children, teaching others
Stop Sign	Crossing guard, police officer	Keeping children safe
Toothbrush	Dentist, dental hygienist	Helping children stay healthy
Fire hat	Firefighter	Conducting fire drills, protecting children
Gardening tools	Gardener	Nurturing children, helping them grow
Megaphone, pompoms	Cheerleader	Encouraging children, parents, and other staff
Dance shoes	Dancer	Helping children learn gross motor skills and coordination
Musical instrument	Musician	Using music throughout the day
Artist beret or supplies	Artist	Providing art activities, supporting creativity
Cleaning supplies	Janitor, custodian	Keeping facilities clean
Sports gear	Athlete	Staying in good physical shape, working as a team

Traffic Sign Props

Hold up traffic signs and ask participants to identify how the signs relate to their work. For example:

Sign	How It Relates to Our Work with Children
Bridge out	Sometimes one must find another way to reach a goal rather than the usual one.
Bump	There are ups and downs, and hazards to avoid.
Construction Ahead	We are building children's futures.
Curve Ahead	Often we must change directions to meet the needs of families and children.
Deaf Child Area	We address the needs of children with special needs.
Deer Crossing	We protect "dears" from harm by watching out for them.
Do Not Enter	Our values should not be imposed on those of other cultures; we respect privacy.
Fire Lane	We make sure that exits are not blocked.
Hospital	We keep children healthy.
Keep Out	Respect families' confidentiality.
Lane Ends	We need warnings or notice of change.
Loading Zone	We communicate with parents, supervise pick-up and drop-off times.
No Parking	There is no time to stop advocating on behalf of children.
No Passing	We cannot rush children's development.

One Way	Sometimes there may be one best way to accomplish a goal.
Passing Lane	There are sometimes barriers we must go around to reach our goals.
Pedestrian Crossing	Children develop at different rates.
Railroad Crossing	We must constantly be alert to potential hazards and risks.
Scenic Overlook	Help children appreciate beauty and nature.
School Zone	We educate children.
Slippery When Wet	We watch for hazards.
Slow	Do not rush into decisions about children.
Soft Shoulders	We must not forget the importance of nurturing.
Speed Zone	There are windows of opportunity that should not be missed.
Stop	We help children learn to stop misbehavior.
Yield	Help children learn to share and respect other's rights.

Dry-erase Boards

Dry-erase boards, often called white boards, are increasingly available in meeting rooms. One also can find various sizes of boards that are easy to transport. These boards are especially useful when small groups are making lists of ideas. Having boards readily available helps the trainer to react to unexpected needs of a group. For example, the boards can make it possible for small groups to have a writing surface for their ideas. Here are some tips for using white boards:

- Use several colors of markers to aid understanding.
- Have someone copy the information from the board if you must reuse the board and want a record of the discussion.
- Keep statements short since space is limited.
- Clean boards periodically with cleaner designed for that purpose.
- Keep permanent markers away from boards to avoid accidentally using them.
- Small easels can hold the board at the right height.

White boards also can be used in much the same way that traditional chalkboards are used. Chalkboards, however, are often difficult to see, especially if glare is present or if the words are written lightly. If you use a chalkboard, experiment with the amount of pressure it takes to make the letters easy to read.

Posters

Posters are inexpensive visual aids that can convey information to trainees and focus their attention on a concept or idea. Participants also can make posters as a learning activity. Making a poster describing the value of block play to post in the block area can be an effective learning technique. Making a poster serves to reinforce learning and to help implement new ideas on the job site. Many of the same guidelines for making flipcharts apply to making posters. Here are some reasons to incorporate posters into your training plans:

Why Make Posters?
- Posters made as part of the training can be a means for participants to summarize content or identify key points.
- Posters can serve as job aids and reminders to assist transfer of learning.
- Poster-making offers opportunities for participants to express creativity.
- Posters can communicate important information to parents, co-workers, and others.
- Making posters involves hands-on learning.
- Poster-making can be an individual, partner, or small group activity.

Making Effective Posters
- Keep sentences short or use phrases.
- Use bullets or numbers to help clarify content.
- Use manuscript printing to make neat, readable letters.
- Include illustrations as appropriate—they may be cut-outs, freehand drawings, or an enlargement of a drawing.
- Use color judiciously. Too many colors may reduce the effectiveness of the poster by making it appear cluttered.
- Consider the distance from which people will view the poster. Make letters and illustrations large enough to read from the typical viewing distance.
- Do not try to include too much on a poster. Too much information means it is not likely to be read.
- Think of a poster as a billboard. The message must be conveyed quickly and succinctly.

For posters that you make to use in training, the same principles apply. Posters are useful in training rooms where the layout is not conducive to overhead transparencies.

To make a graphic or to enlarge a drawing for a poster, make a transparency first. Project the transparency on poster board, using an overhead projector. Draw around the projected image. Then add color or details as you like. This same technique works in making flipcharts as well.

Poster-making Activity Ideas
Vision of Better Childhood—Have statistics about children printed on labels or index cards to distribute. Good sources for the statistics are the *Kids Count Data Book* and the *Children's Defense Fund Annual Report*. Have participants select some of the labels or index cards and attach them to poster board. Then have them complete the poster by illustrating their vision of how they will change the statistics they selected. For exam-

ple, if the statistics a trainee selected concerned health care, the trainee might use a drawing of a healthy child with a caption "Your baby depends on you! Get up-to-date on immunizations." The Vision of Better Childhood activity can be an individual, partner, or small group activity.

Sandwich Boards—Make sandwich boards from poster board or flipchart pages to promote a cause or to introduce yourself. The sandwich boards can be a stimulus for discussion during breaks. They will add a touch of humor to the training as well as provide a way for trainees to share information. To make sandwich boards, use tape to connect two pieces of poster board with the tape draped over your shoulders. There will be a poster in the front and one in the back. Trainees will be walking billboards.

A Perfect World—Ask participants to make a poster of what they consider an ideal classroom or playground. They may use cut-out pictures from catalogs or draw their own. Ask them to write a sentence about what makes this classroom or playground world perfect. To stimulate ideas, ask them to think about their own childhood and what they liked to do outside.

A Good Place to Be a Child—Have trainees cut out pictures or draw things that they remember fondly from their childhood to make posters. The posters can focus on outdoor or indoor items and activities. Ask them to make captions telling their fondest memory. This activity is a good way for trainees to understand the influence of the environment and early sensory experiences on children.

Handouts

Handouts are one of the most common training aids. Good handouts serve as resources for many years; poor handouts are not read and find their way promptly into the trashcan. Carefully consider the format and layout of text and graphics when making a handout. Well-planned, attractive handouts will invite trainees to read and understand the information. Taking the time to make good handouts pays off in their increased effectiveness.

Formatting for Comprehension

The layout of text and graphics affects not only the appearance of a handout, but influences the reader's ability to understand and use it. Consequently, where and how you place information on the page is as important as getting the information down in writing. Here are some techniques and suggestions to create well-designed handouts:

White Space—Do not try to cram too much into one handout. A full page of single-spaced text with narrow margins will be read only by the most interested trainees. Leaving adequate blank, white space helps prevent a cluttered look. White space is almost as important as the text in making a handout attractive to the reader. This blank space gives the learner a place to write information and to jot down notes and reminders. The placement of white space helps the learner judge the relative importance of information. Generally, about one-fourth to one-third of a page is a good guide for how much blank space to leave.

Bullets and Numbering—Listing important points with bullets (putting dots or other markers beside items) will often make information easier to understand. Bullets are good memory aids for learners when there are three or more related items or ideas. Lists should include only key words or ideas without excess verbiage. Numbered lists are good to use to identify steps in a procedure, rules to follow, or facts to remember. Numbering is helpful if you will be referring to specific items on a list during training.

Font Styles—Varying the text with different fonts can make handouts more appealing. However, avoid the temptation to use too many different fonts since that may be distracting by making a handout look cluttered. Too many font styles will make it difficult to tell what is most important. As a rule, about two or three font styles per handout are enough.

If you make many handouts on a computer, a good way to select a font quickly is to create a sample line of type of each font you have on your computer. Type "The quick brown fox jumped over the lazy dog" or "Now is the time for every good man to come to the aid of his country." Or you can simply type the alphabet. Copy the line as many times as you have fonts. Then put a font name in alphabetical order beside each line of type. Continue until you have all the font styles that are on your computer. Select each line and change the font for the whole line to the one named at the end of the line of type. When printed, you have a reference sheet to use in selecting fonts for handouts. This reference will allow you to see how the font looks so you can decide if you want to use it for a handout. Some fonts may be too difficult to read to be useful; some may be too decorative for easy reading; and some fonts may get tedious if used too often or for too much text.

Boldface, Underlining, and Italics—Boldface, underlining and italics can be used to introduce new terms and to call attention to specific words. Boldface is good to use for headings to help a reader find information. Underlining sometimes makes material a little more difficult to read, but can call attention to specific information. These formatting aids can be used to vary the text without using another font. However, if these techniques are used too much, they lose their impact. If you emphasize everything, you emphasize nothing!

Headings and Subheadings—Headings and subheadings help trainees see the relationship of information. A heading identifies a general topic and subheadings further break down the information related to the main heading. Leave white space before and after headings and subheadings to set them apart from the body of the text and show relationships. Headings and subheadings enable participants to quickly locate information. Hence participants are more likely to use the handouts as a reference once they are back on the job.

Columns—When handouts have a lot of text, dividing the pages into two columns will make them easier to read. Generally, readers find that reading columns is faster than reading a single page since they can rapidly skim much of it. Word-processing software makes it easy to convert text to columns. Columns also allow one to make several lists of words or short phrases on a page rather than one long list.

Justification—Justification refers to how the lines of text are arranged on the page. Left justification is when the left margin is even and the right uneven; right justification is when the right margin is even and the left uneven. Sometimes it is desirable to fully justify text where margins on both sides are even. With handouts created on a computer, it is easy to justify text as desired.

This is an example of left-justified type. As a rule, left justification is the most readable and the style to which we are most accustomed. Left justification is used much more often than the others.

This is an example of right justification. Right justification refers to lines of text arranged in line down the right-hand side of the page or the column. Right justification can be an interesting technique, but may be tiring if overused.

This is an example of fully justified type. Note that both sides are even. Fully justified type may be difficult to read and sometimes leaves odd-looking or uneven spaces in the text. Fully justified type is what we are familiar with in newspaper columns.

Graphics—It is easy to add pictures to handouts due to the proliferation of clip art and computer graphics. However, do not put in a graphic just because you can. Any graphic used should add to the handout. A picture of a child bathing a doll would be great in a handout about water play or outdoor activities. A drawing of a beach scene adds nothing to the article, regardless of how attractive the scene may be.

- When using several graphics, make them related sizes. A large picture of a child on a tricycle looks odd if it is placed beside a small picture of a child on a sliding board.
- Do not put graphics too close to the edge. Doing so may give the impression the picture is "falling off" the page.
- Putting a graphic in the center of the page may make the text seem awkward around the graphic.
- Use rubber cement rather than glue when attaching pictures to a piece of paper. Rubber cement will allow time to position the picture and will not cause wrinkling as glue will.

Guidelines for Effective Handouts

- Give each handout a distinctive title. When several handouts are used in a session, participants will need to be able to refer to the right one. Having handouts with very similar titles such as Relationships with Families, Family Relationships, and Developing Family Relationships at the same session will be confusing. Use different colors of paper if you must use very similar titles.
- Use headings, bold print, font styles, underlining or capitalization for emphasis and organization.
- Consider the format. Space information so it is easy to understand and read. Use lists, bullets, and left justification with text.
- Use short, active sentences with clear language.
- Include only relevant information.
- Leave enough white space that the page is appealing to read.
- Give references for additional information when appropriate.
- Include your name, address, and telephone number for future contacts.
- Number the pages if a handout has more than two pages.
- Date handouts or identify the training session date.
- Make sure handout copies are readable.
- Identify why the handout is important and how it will be used.

KISS—Keep It Short and Simple

Follow the KISS system for handouts as well as for visual aids. Beware of confusing participants by giving them too much information or giving information in a complicated way. Participants are better off if they get a hundred words of information that they will read and understand than if they get a thousand words that they set aside or find unclear. For fun, compare this bureaucratic document from a more common version of the same information:

Compare:

We respectfully beseech, petition, and entreat that proportionate and commensurate provision be made, this date hereinafter subscribed, for the satisfying of these petitioners' nutritional requirements and for the organizing of such methods of allocation and distribution as may be deemed necessary, befitting, and proper to assure the reception by and for said petitioners of such abundance of edible baked cereal products as shall, in the sole judgment and discretion of the aforesaid petitioners, constitute an adequate and sufficient inventory thereof.

To:
Give us this day our daily bread.

Types of Handouts and Their Uses

The table below describes some of the various types of handouts and when they might be used. The chart provides guidance in varying the types of handouts one uses. On pages 279-286 of the Appendix are examples of the first seven handout types. Examples of others are found in various locations throughout this text.

When your goal is to . . .	Use this type of handout
1. Have participants record their ideas or information that they learn.	An interactive worksheet
2. Help learners apply knowledge, participate in a debate or solve problems.	An action sheet, a decision sheet
3. Let learners evaluate themselves, what they do, or the training they have attended.	A self-evaluation sheet, a checklist
4. Guide independent reading and help learners understand what they read.	A reading guide
5. Provide guidance in the specific steps of a task or help learners understand a sequence of steps.	A checklist, an instruction sheet
6. Help learners think about their experiences and ideas to stimulate reflective thinking.	A recall sheet or comparison sheet
7. Help learners see other points of view or critical thinking skills.	A debate sheet or comparison sheet
8. Set the stage for role play.	A script starter, a description of
9. Help learners know what to expect.	An agenda of the activities
10. Evaluate what participants already know and need to learn.	A pretest, a questionnaire
11. Help learners focus on the content of a video or field experience.	A viewer's guide, an observation sheet
Help learners remember the main points of training.	A summary sheet, a checklist, an interactive worksheet
Provide materials to read or for reference.	Brochures, copies of articles, reading guides

Tools for Handouts

Here are some possibilities to consider for keeping up with handouts.

Padding—Handouts or forms that are used frequently can be made into tablets inexpensively by most quick-copy services.

Spiral binding—If you are going to be giving each participant many handouts, consider spiral binding. Binding equipment is relative inexpensive, and the participants get a book they can keep for reference. Quick-copy services and office supply stores also can do it for you.

Drilling—A quick-copy service can punch holes in your handouts to make it easy for trainees to put them in loose-leaf binders. Drilling is good when you will be giving handouts over a series of sessions such as a class. Or you can use a manual hole punch.
Laminating—Laminating can make job aids or materials that will be handled often last longer.

Using a variety of colors for handouts is helpful whenever many handouts are used at a single session. Various colors help participants locate the proper handout fast. Having distinct titles also helps trainees quickly find the handout to which you are referring during training.

If you did not have holes drilled or drill them yourself, pass around a three-hole punch in ongoing classes for trainees to punch holes in their handouts for notebooks. Punching holes right away helps trainees to organize their handouts. Trainees can keep up with their handouts if they put them in a loose-leaf binder immediately.

Tent Cards

We are most familiar with tent cards as used on the tables in restaurants to advertise specials. Tent cards are simply heavy paper folded to stand up, often like a tent. In training, tent cards can be used to provide guidelines for the training or they can be a job aid that trainees take with them. Tent cards can be a means to pose provocative questions to stimulate thinking or they can announce or promote upcoming training opportunities. They may include inspirational sayings or welcome messages. Tent cards are a means of providing information to a small group to read upon arrival or when they finish a task early. Tent cards can designate or identify a place to conduct an activity or even be used as place cards for participants. Tent cards can be as simple as a folded piece of heavy paper. Or, they can be fancy, die cut forms either made or purchased from paper supply companies.

Tent cards can be used to give instructions to small groups. When tent cards are used in this way, they clearly imply that activities are indeed group activities. The fact that there is only one set of instructions on a table is a subtle reminder that groups are expected to communicate and work together. Because tent cards stand up, they attract attention and are more visible than a piece of paper. Here are some possible uses for tent cards:

- Print the agenda on them so participants can use them for reference throughout the session.
- Post questions for discussion.
- Post things to think about such as motivation or inspirational messages.
- Color code the tent cards and give tickets or color-coded name tags to mix up participants as they arrive.

- Print the names of registered participants to separate participants who come together. Or use them to separate into groups based on job responsibilities.
- Include reminders of key points in the training.
- Print instructions for an activity for early arrivals to complete while waiting for the session to begin.
- Provide guidance for participants in appropriate behavior during training.

MAKING TENT CARDS

Use the template on page 287 in the Appendix to make a tent card. By putting the fold marks on the sheet, participants can fold the tent cards themselves. Use paper clips to hold them together. Another advantage of using tent cards is that they can be flattened and filed after use. If a tent card without a base begins to spread apart and will not stand up, fold back about one inch (three centimeters) of a corner. Folding the corner will restrict the spreading that causes the tent card to fall. You can tape a paper strip to the inside to keep the bottom from spreading.

PARTICIPANT GUIDANCE

Tent cards are a good place to provide written guidelines for participants such as the Participants' Bill of Rights in Chapter Five on page 185. Here are some examples of what might be included on guidance tent cards:

●●●

What you can do during this training:

- Ask any question that you wish.
- Share examples from your experience.
- Think about how you will use the information.
- Ask for clarification when something is not clear.
- Take a break whenever you wish.

Getting the most from this session:

1. Prepare yourself—List questions that you want answered and ideas you want to share.
2. Network—Talk to the people around you. Find out what you have in common.
3. Take notes—Write down ideas you want to remember. Review them soon after you get home.
4. Share with co-workers—Tell your colleagues back at work what you learned.
5. Keep in contact—Talk to other participants following the session. Contact the speaker if you have additional questions.

●●●

Six Cs of Learning Together:

Commitment—to the task at hand

Creating—using our talents to learn
Connecting—getting to know each other as resources
Communicating—sharing our ideas and information
Celebrating—valuing what we learn and how it will help children
Caring—about each other and our mission

• •

To get the most from this workshop, just **RAP!**

R eview—Take notes for reference.
A nalyze—What in this session will work for you?
P lan—Decide how you will implement what you have learned.

Inspirational and Motivational Messages

Rights of the Child
Tent cards are a good place for inspirational messages. For example:

• •

Children have. . . .

The right to affection, love, and understanding
The right to a family and stability in the home environment
The right to adequate nutrition and medical care
The right to protection from physical and emotional harm
The right to free and appropriate education to reach individual potential
The right to time and opportunity for play and recreation
The right to be among the first to receive aid in times of disaster
The right to learn to be a useful member of society and to develop individual abilities
The right to be brought up in peace and brotherhood
The right to enjoy these rights, regardless of race, color, sex, religion, national or social origin.

• •

Good Mistakes
The electric light bulb got its present shape because Thomas Edison accidentally dropped a screwdriver on an early light, knocking it out of its original shape. When he saw that the accident caused it to burn more brightly with increased power, he knew he was on to something. If you make mistakes today, it is simply part of the learning process. We are all here to learn and to make discoveries. Let your light shine!

Good Enough
Sometimes it is easy to think that almost right is good enough as we complete the numerous tasks that fill our days. But is almost right good enough? If as much as 99.9% correct is good enough, then:

22,000 checks will be deducted from the wrong bank accounts in the next 60 minutes

12 babies will be given to the wrong parents each day

107 incorrect medical procedures will be performed by the end of today

20,000 incorrect drug prescriptions will be written in the next 12 months

18,322 pieces of mail will be mishandled in the next hour

114,500 pairs of mismatched shoes will be shipped this year

103,260 income tax returns will be processed incorrectly this year

Two million documents will be lost by the IRS this year

Discussion Starters

Tent cards are a good way to get small groups at tables talking to each other. Put several questions on a tent card to stimulate discussion before the session starts. Tent card questions may even be an icebreaker. Here are some questions from which to choose to encourage participants to reflect on their past experiences and to become acquainted.

- What was the most disappointing experience you had as a child?
- What brought you the most recognition or satisfaction as a child?
- What do you remember learning in school first?
- What play activities do you remember?
- Who read stories to you when you were a child?
- What was your favorite book as a child?
- What do you remember about learning to read when you were a child?

Introduction Nameplates—Pass out heavy sheets of paper and markers. Ask trainees to interview someone they do not know. After they find out several things about that person, have them make a name card to identify the person, decorating the card according to the person's interests or hobbies. Provide construction paper, glue, greeting cards, magazines and catalogs, and even ribbon and lace scraps to make the cards.

Congratulations or Thank You—Find inexpensive items in party stores that say "Congratulations" or "Thank You." These items can be used to make interesting tent card awards to recognize accomplishments or to express appreciation. Place them in front of the person being recognized.

Questioning Techniques

Good questions require trainees to sort out their ideas. Answering questions gives trainees a chance to express themselves and reinforce their learning. Answering questions helps trainees plan how they will implement new skills and techniques and overcome barriers to implementation. Good questions help trainees learn how to respond to parents and others who may not understand why they do things as they do. In many ways, answering questions can be a rehearsal for advocating what is good for children.

Good questions do not just happen. Effective trainers spend time and energy to plan and design questions that meet a variety of needs in the learning setting. Good questions serve many important purposes in training. They can:

- Assess prior experience and knowledge

    "What do you know about setting up for unit blocks?"

    "How do you communicate with parents?"

- Arouse interest and hold attention

    "What do you think I am going to do with this?"

    "How many ways can you think of to use . . .?"

- Start discussions

    "What materials do you use in your art area?"

    "Why is it important to allow blocks of time for play?"

- Solicit suggestions and ideas

    "Who will tell us about . . .?"

    "What are some ways you can help children with transitions?"

- Evaluate learning and understanding

    "What are some things you will put in your housekeeping area now that you've attended this workshop?"

    "How will you explain to parents the importance of outdoor play?"

- Enhance learning through the expression of ideas

    "Who can tell me about . . .?"

    "Why do you think that . . .?"

- Validate the expertise that participants bring to the session

    "Who has had experience with . . .?"

    "Has anyone found a solution for . . .?"

CATEGORIES of QUESTIONS

There are four general categories of questions:

1. Factual questions check participants' background knowledge or mastery of material;
2. Application and interpretive questions help trainees recognize relationships, analyze facts, understand applications of information or procedures;
3. Problem questions are based on real or highly probable situations and designed to help trainees apply knowledge; and
4. Opinion questions ask for reactions to situations or information.

Factual questions are usually those that ask for specific information such as "When should you wash your hands?" or "What should you do if a child is stung by a bee?" Application and interpretative questions are those such as "Why do you think it is important to communicate with parents?" or "How do you know when to make a report to Child Protective Services?" Problem questions are generally descriptions of situations for which responders are asked to determine a course of action. Examples of problem questions are those such as "What would you do about a three-year-old who says only a few words?" or "How will you react if a parent is so angry with her child that she wants to spank him at your center?" Opinion questions include such as "What do you like about . . .?" or "How do you feel about . . .?"

Constructing Good Questions

Good questions do not just happen. A competent trainer determines the types of questions that will best stimulate thinking and learning. She will base her decisions on knowledge of the participants' needs. A competent trainer carefully plans the questions with the objectives in mind. She has in her repertoire several ways to ask for the same information to meet her goals. Follow these guidelines in creating questions to facilitate learning:

- Use words the participants will understand. Omit jargon and explain unfamiliar terminology.
- Consider the knowledge and experience of the trainees. Remember that recognition is easier than recall. A trainee may be able to tell you that a statement such as "It is good to read books to children" is true, but not be able to identify the many other ways to include literacy in the classroom.
- Avoid being too abstract or hypothetical. Trainees want real solutions to real problems. They want practical answers to the problems they face every day. If a question is too abstract, trainees will view it as irrelevant.
- Frequently use questions that require thought rather than just recall or recognition. Excessively simple questions will leave trainees feeling unchallenged.
- Use a variety of question types. Each type of question serves a different purpose, so variety is essential to meet the needs of the participants and the instructor.
- Keep the objectives of the session in mind as you prepare questions.

Types of Questions

Different types of questions serve different purposes in training. Variety helps the trainer ensure mastery of content. Select or construct questions based on the goals desired. What are some types of questions and what purposes do they serve? Here are some suggestions:

Divergent and Convergent Questions (Open and Closed Questions)—Convergent questions are those that call for a specific answer. They are questions such as "What is the name of the agency that is responsible for licensing?" Convergent questions call for recall or recognition of a single, correct answer. Divergent questions, by contrast, have a variety of possible answers. An example of a divergent question is, "How many ways can you identify to involve parents?" Divergent questions require participants to think of several possible answers. These questions frequently are referred to as open and closed questions. Each type serves a different purpose in training.

General and Specific Questions—General questions are those that ask for global concepts such as, "How do you handle discipline?" and "What are some ways to encourage dramatic play?" Specific questions are similar to "How can you redirect a child who is being aggressive?" or "What should you do if a toddler bites another child?"

Situation Questions—These questions are the "What would you do if . . .?" ones that call for participants to identify the actions they would take under certain circumstances. Real-life situation questions can be easily developed from the many instances that occur when working with children and staff. These questions seek very practical responses and help trainees make decisions about appropriate action before occurrences. Situation questions help trainees see the relevance in the training and play a key part in supporting change. When trainees are able to think through an appropriate response to a situation, they are prepared to cope with the situation correctly when it occurs. Situation questions form a core component of effective training.

Speculative Questions—These questions are the "What if . . .?" questions. They ask participants to use their imaginations or, as the term implies, to speculate. Speculative questions call for trainees to consider situations that they will probably not face, but in the process of answering them, trainees focus on priorities. Questions such as "What if you had all the money for equipment that you needed and more?" or "What if you could change your job in any way you wanted?" are some examples of speculative questions. The main difference between speculative and situation questions is that the situation scenarios are common and very likely to occur, whereas speculative questions are unlikely to occur.

Useful Questions and Responses for Trainers

To clarify:

"Will you tell us more about..?"

"Can you give me an example of...?"

To restate:

"Are you saying that...?"

"You're wondering if...?"

To refocus:

"A good point, but we haven't finished discussing..."

"That would take more time than we have here, but I wonder if you've thought about...?"

To disagree:

"Another way of looking at it is..."

"One problem I have when I think about that is..."

"I understand, but have you considered..."

To seek support for suggestions:

"Can you give us some reasons for...?"

"What circumstances lead you to believe that...?"

"What have you observed that made you feel...?"

To assess prior knowledge and experience:

"What do you know about...?"

"Tell us some ways to..."

"What have you tried and how has it worked?"

To evaluate learning:

"Which of these do you think is most important and why?"

"Based on what we've done today, what do you...?"

"What is the difference between _____ and _____?"

WAYS TO DIRECT QUESTIONS

Asking questions in the same way is tiring for participants. There are many ways to include opportunities to answer questions throughout a training session. Here are a few ways to ask:

- Directly, to specific individuals
- On flipcharts or posters for small groups to answer
- On an overhead transparency to the whole group
- Written on worksheets as discussion guides
- On tent cards for group discussion
- Rhetorically, without expecting an answer but to make a point
- By bouncing questions from the group back to the group for answers

Allowing Time for Response

Many instructors find the silence following a question somewhat unsettling. They tend to want to move on to the next activity, call on another participant to answer, or even answer the question themselves. Do not fear the period of silence following a question. Give the person who is called upon ample time to respond. Adults may want to consider their reply before speaking or decide how they wish to word their answer. If you give up and answer the questions yourself, the trainees will begin to depend on you for answers. The purpose of questioning is to stimulate thought, and not allowing enough time can block thought.

Try counting to ten before you ask another person to answer a question or go on to the next activity. Show with your body language that you are interested in what participants have to say.

Watch body language to identify persons who are thinking about responding. Look for tentative attempts to raise a hand or facial expressions that show evidence of a desire to reply. When you see that an individual shows some interest in answering a question or commenting, recognize and call on that person.

Remember that if you have done a good job conducting the training, the participants may be still thinking about what has just happened. They may need time to digest the new information before they will have a question to pose. The time you wait will seem much longer to you than it will to the participants.

In a large session, be prepared for the possibility that there might be an awkward silence after a call for questions.

WAYS FOR PARTICIPANTS TO ANSWER

There are many ways for trainees to answer questions, and some may be more comfortable for them than others. Use variety to keep interest high by providing several ways to answer during a training session.

Verbally—For many situations, quick verbal answers are time efficient. Verbal responses are a fast way to review material or solicit information. However, verbal answers are limited in the amount of involvement required, especially in a large group. Unless individuals are answering questions with a partner or in a small group, many may not especially benefit from the verbal answer of someone else.

Written—Written answers require a higher level of involvement by participants. They help reinforce learning and also give participants notes to take with them when the session is over. Sometimes, the process of writing responses helps participants "rehearse" for making verbal responses.

Signals—Invite participants to give a sign or signal such as raising a hand or standing up as a response. This method is limited to "yes" or "no" and "who can" or "who will" type questions. Answering questions by standing up or staying seated is a good way to incorporate movement in a lengthy session. When you want participants to answer with a signal, give the signal yourself to demonstrate what you want them to do. If you ask, "How many of you work with infants?" and you want them to raise their hands, raise your own to show them how you want them to respond.

Response Forms or Cards—Index cards, note pads, or forms can be used to get information from participants. Ask participants to tell how or what they do in a specific situation. Gather these forms early in a session and review them for information on what the participants still need to learn.

Agree or Disagree—Give participants cards that say AGREE on one side and DISAGREE on the other side. Participants hold up the card that tells how they feel about a statement when it is read. This is a variation of true and false questions.

Sign Language—Post signs around the room that answer a question you have posed. For example, if a question is, "How do you respond to an angry co-worker?" you might have several answers such as "Ignore her," "Tell her you understand she is angry," "Tell her she should not act like that," or "Ask her if there is anything you can do to help her." Have participants move to the area of the room where a sign reflects their feelings about a situation.

In the Bag—Have participants write their answers on cards and drop them in a bag that is passed around. The bag can relate to the training topic such as a doctor's bag for a session on health, a bag decorated with seashells and nature objects for a session on science, or a gift bag for a new baby for a session on child development.

Ways for Participants to Ask Questions

Asking for questions at the end of a large group session will likely get little or no response. Some participants may not want to appear ignorant and assume that everyone else knows the answers. They may be fearful of speaking up in front of a group or just not want attention focused on them. Adding gimmicks or other ways to make asking questions fun will stimulate more response. Sometimes providing a way for participants to ask questions anonymously is the best way to solicit questions. Adding an element of fun generates questions from some who otherwise might not join in. Sometimes offering a way participants can ask questions of the group rather than of the instructor smoothes the way.

Trainees must be made comfortable to ask questions. They need to recognize what they don't know and learn to ask questions as a way of seeking more information. Here are some ways to make it easier for them to ask questions:

Question Box (or Bag)—Have learners write their own questions about what they want to know about a topic. Ask them to place the questions in a decorated box or a gift bag. Let participants take turns drawing questions from the container. Other participants volunteer to offer answers to the questions. Expand on the suggestions that are given.

Tree Top—Draw a tree on poster board or on a flipchart page. Pass around cut-out construction paper leaves at the beginning of a session. Ask trainees to write a question on the leaf and tape it on a tree branch during a break. Then you or other participants can answer the questions during the session. As each question is answered or discussed, you or a trainee removes it from the tree. This activity can also be used for a quick review, with trainees writing one key point they learned on a leaf and then putting it on the tree.

Labels for Learning—Pass out computer labels or nametags. Ask learners to write a question related to the topic on each one. Then have them stick the label on a poster, flipchart page, or piece of butcher paper. Check off each question after it has been discussed. If a session is long, you might make several posters and have trainees post their questions by categories. This is a good way to use all those left-over computer labels on a sheet. You also can use sticky notes, but they may not stay on the posters or paper as well as labels do.

Prompters—If you are concerned that participants might be reluctant to speak up and ask questions in a large group, tape some questions under chairs. Ask participants to look under their chairs and read the question if they find one. Try offering a small prize to the first person who finds a question. This is a good way to get questions started.

Responding to Questions from Trainees

Repeating questions from the audience will help ensure that everyone hears them. If the room is large and a microphone is used, repeat the question into the microphone.

Repeating the question allows you a brief moment to think about the question before responding. Get into the habit of repeating questions whenever you work with a large group.

Thanking participants for their questions will encourage involvement. This courtesy demonstrates that you are interested in their questions. It tells them that you mean what you say about participation.

Have you ever attended training where the facilitator responded to most answers with "That's right," or "OK?" The participants will tire if the facilitator constantly responds in the same way to answers and comments or continually asks questions in the same manner. Additionally, responding in a way to encourage, not discourage, participants stimulates more questions. Here are some tips for responding to answers and comments from participants:

When Answers Are Appropriate:

- List the response on a flipchart or overhead transparency.
- Ask others to note it on their handout.
- Paraphrase or summarize the answer given.
- Probe for more information:
    "Can you give me an example of...?"
    "How did you react when that happened?"
    "Tell us some more about ..."
- Solicit additional responses:
    "Who else has a suggestion?"
    "What other ideas do you have?"
    "What are more ways we can..."
    "What does anyone else think?"

When Responses Are Incomplete or Unclear:

- Clarify by asking for more information.
    "What do you mean by...?"
    "Could you give me an example of...?"
    "Will you elaborate on that?"
- Ask them to state their response in another way.
- Ask for examples or descriptions.

When Answers Are Incorrect or Inappropriate:

- Avoid telling trainees they are wrong.
- Try to understand their point of view.
    "We used to think that, but now we know..."
    "That was once what many people thought, but now..."
    "I understand how you would think that, but..."
- Give more attention to appropriate answers.
- Focus on the topic when an off-topic remark is given.
    "Can you think of a way to..."
    "Let me rephrase the question. The question was..."
    "Tell us how that relates to..."
- Restate the question to provide an opportunity for another answer.

When You Get No Response:

- Rephrase the question to clarify it.
- Give an example.
- Allow enough time for a response.
- Ask yourself if the question was well planned and appropriate for the group.
- Ask yourself if the participants have the experiences to be able to answer.

TEACHING QUESTIONING TECHNIQUES

Understanding Open and Closed Questions—Here is an activity to help trainees understand the differences between open and closed questions. (An open question has many possible answers that are unique to the individual answering, whereas a closed question has only one answer.) The activity will help them become more skilled at asking open-ended questions. Divide trainees into groups of three and identify a person A, B, and C in each group. Person A will ask questions, person B will answer, and person C will be the recorder. Give each group a collection of small toys appropriate for the age group with which they work. Then proceed as follows:

- B chooses an object to examine.
- A asks B some of the following questions.
- B answers the questions as a child might.
- C records the questions and answers in writing.

The three then discuss whether the questions were open or closed. They examine the quality of the responses and the benefits of the two types of questions.

1. How can you use it?
2. Why did you choose that object?
3. Who wants to use it next?
4. What color is it?
5. Why do you think it's interesting?
6. What would you like to change about it?
7. What is it called?
8. Would you like to use it in the block area?
9. What can you do with it?
10. Can you think of another name for it?
11. Is it interesting?
12. Can you tell me something else about it?
13. Can you eat it?
14. If you could change anything about it, what would you change?
15. Can you describe it to me?
16. Can you roll it?
17. How can you use it?
18. Is it big or small?
19. How many pieces does it have?
20. What shape is it?

If you unexpectedly have too many people for the number of toys you have, make the groups larger and have members of the group take turns being A or B. Group members also can make some additional questions for the exercise.

Facilitation

Facilitation is the act or process of making something easier. A good facilitator understands group dynamics and knows how to get individuals working together as a unit. A good facilitator brings out the best in each individual and takes advantage of the interaction between individuals to compile an action plan or identify priorities needing attention. A facilitator serves as a catalyst to the group process. She is a role model in active involvement.

A good facilitator is a coach, a teacher, a change agent, and a guide. She is patient, proactive, and flexible. She values creativity and is able to work with different personalities. She has good skills in listening and questioning, in conflict resolution and creative problem solving. She can manage meetings and lead others. She has knowledge of group dynamics and the topic under consideration.

Roles of the Facilitator

Providing Information—The facilitator must be knowledgeable in the topic under consideration in order to make appropriate comments and offer information as needed. If not, participants will resent being in the session. It is, however, perfectly acceptable for the facilitator to say, "I don't know," when asked a question he is not prepared to answer. Adding, "Let me find out, and I'll get back to you about that," will raise her esteem and allow her to maintain credibility.

A good facilitator also knows when not to provide information. It can be difficult to remain quiet when you have information that someone else needs. Sometimes, however, the group needs to develop insight rather than just receive an answer. In such instances, the facilitator should not speak up. Asking the right questions to get participants to come up with their own answers is more effective than giving answers. In short, a good facilitator knows when to speak up and when to keep quiet.

Providing Resources and Materials—The facilitator can offer materials and resources for further information. Additional resources are helpful for those participants who prefer to study a topic in depth or who need a broader knowledge base. Suggesting books and other resources where participants can get additional information is an important function of facilitators.

Expanding on Knowledge—Guide and Goad—The facilitator must start with what trainees know and add to their skills and knowledge. She helps them seek information that they need and guides them in the process of higher level decision making. She continuously stimulates learners to question and to challenge themselves, and to see the "big picture" of long-term goals.

Offering Encouragement—A good facilitator lets participants know that their comments and ideas are valued. She makes an extra effort to get persons involved who may be reluctant to comment in a group. She serves not as a judge, but as a coach or mentor.

Keeping the Group Focused—Sometimes trainees become sidetracked with personal conversations during a group discussion. This can cause the group to digress from the most important aspect of the topic under discussion. The facilitator must tactfully intervene to keep them on task. Some helpful comments to prevent digressions are:

- "Our time is coming to an end, and we'll need to report soon. Let's move on to..."
- "I know we all have a lot to talk about, but our task today is..."
- "That is a very interesting topic, but it is more than we can address today. Perhaps we can include it next time."
- "I know that is an important problem, but since it doesn't apply to everyone, why don't we discuss it right after this session."
- "That will take more time than we have today. We need to address..."
- "Why don't we talk more about that at the break. Now, we need to..."

A good facilitator must keep the group focused on the objective of the group—not just by preventing digression, but also by continually analyzing the group process. The group must be able to see the real issue even when it is hidden by inconsequential information.

Monitoring the Schedule—Participants usually do not like feeling rushed. They generally dislike getting out late. Keeping track of the time is important. Additionally, a good facilitator will judge the time needed for each part of the planned activity and keep the group progressing toward a conclusion within the allotted time. The facilitator is essentially a meeting manager and will need to keep the meeting moving along. She will need to know when to let a discussion continue and when to call it to a halt. She will need to recognize when a discussion is waning and it is time to move to the next topic. She will know when it is time to begin to build consensus.

Clarifying—Sometimes a participant's comment may not be clear to the others. The facilitator can offer an example or additional information to ensure that everyone understands. She may restate the comments or ask for more information to ensure that all are clear on the ideas presented. She can ask the speaker to give examples or elaborate when a suggestion is unclear.

Summarizing—The facilitator will find it important to summarize information, not only at the end but during the discussion. Regular and frequent summaries will help the group stay focused and moving toward conclusion. It will help them recognize the progress they are making.

REACHING CONSENSUS

Reaching consensus is finding common ground. It is identifying the areas on which the members of the group can agree. Reaching consensus is not always an easy process, but it is often the desired end product of group work. The skilled facilitator will constantly seek to identify those issues or actions on which there is a general agreement. When there are diverse opinions about an issue or course of action, the facilitator must draw out the concerns. She must seek opportunities to negotiate in order for the group to feel they can support a specific activity. Sometimes these real concerns may be unexpressed or hidden. A member of the group concerned that the responsibility of completing a task might fall on him, for example, may oppose an action giving very different reasons. A member who fears change may not support an action that requires it, stating objection to the action on principle rather than giving the real reason. Also, a person may simply not understand what is being proposed, and may object without full understanding. The skilled facilitator must learn to read between the lines to create a way to build consensus.

Additional Facilitation Tips

As a facilitator, your role is to orchestrate the flow of comments and the participation of the learners. Here are some suggestions to summarize the facilitation role in training:

- Paraphrase frequently to help others understand or hear a comment.
- Verify your understanding or ask for further explanation.
- Ask for examples or more information.
- Compliment or reward an occasional comment to keep interest high.
- Elaborate when a comment is important or to suggest how a statement applies to the goal.
- Energize by adding humor or an interesting example.
- Mediate differences of opinion and relieve any tension that surfaces.
- Organize, categorize, and relate ideas for a global view.
- Summarize the major views of the group.

Effective Listening

In order to respond effectively to trainees, an instructor must be able to listen carefully to their comments. Active listening requires the trainer to pay attention not only to the words but also to the message that may not be expressed in the words. Here are some strategies to improve listening skills:

- Focus on what the person is saying and not on how you will respond.
- Paraphrase—restate the talker's ideas.
    "What I hear you saying is that ..."
    "Do you feel that ...?"
    "Could it be that ...?"
- Parrot—repeat key phrases as stated by the participant.
- Empathetic—reflect the feelings of the participant in a nonjudgmental way. Emphatic listening allows you to respond to participants and gives them an opening to offer more information. It lets them feel you understand their situation, and gives you a chance to find out what the specific barrier might be.

- For example, if a participant says, "I just don't see why we have to go outside when it is so hot," you might respond by saying, "You don't feel you should go outside when it is hot?"
- If a participant states, "I get so tired of parents being late all the time. I never can get home at a decent time," an emphatic response would be, "It sounds like you are needing more time at home. What are some ways you've tried to get parents to pick up their children on time?"
- If a participant says, "This just won't work at my center," you might respond by saying, "You feel easel painting will not work at your center?"
- If a participant asks, "Why should I go to all the trouble to organize the art area? The children just mess it up," you might respond with, "It sounds like you are really frustrated. Can we look at some ways that might help?"

Other listening and responding tools:

- Open doors for communication—"Tell me more about ..."
- Acknowledge nonverbally—Nod your head, make eye contact.
- Acknowledge with noncommittal expressions—"I see, Hum, Uh-huh, I understand."
- Do not grill the talker by asking interrogating questions—Interrogation is more of a tone-of-voice issue than what is said.

- Be a mirror—Think of yourself as a mirror, reflecting what the talker is saying or feeling.
- Do not blow off comments—Responses such as "You'll feel better about it tomorrow" or "Just forget about it" make light of the speaker's feelings.
- Do not preach—Avoid comments such as "You really should...," or "If only you would...".

Effective listening is an essential part of good training. A good listener both hears what is said and understands what is implied, or hidden, in a response. Effective listening stimulates interaction and helps trainees to feel that they are truly understood and valued.

Components of Effective Training

Setting the Stage for Learning

Paying attention to the physical and emotional environments is essential for training to be effective. The knowledgeable trainer will set the stage for learning to happen, rather than view himself as one who imparts knowledge.

The environment affects everyone. Look around you, and notice how you and others react in various settings. A gothic cathedral suggests quiet, reverent calmness; a skating rink brings to mind noisy, boisterous activity. Chairs in a circle convey a message that we expect interactions between participants; chairs set up in auditorium style create an expectation of lecture and passive listening.

The environment consists of the emotional climate as well as the physical arrangements. How participants feel about themselves, their relationships with the instructor and others, and the training itself will affect their learning.

The Physical Environment

Room Arrangement

Picture a large, community-wide planning event. Participants selected one of several concurrent sessions according to their interests. In one session, the room was the appropriate size for the twenty people in it. Chairs were in a circle, and interaction was excellent. Individuals, eager to share their ideas, interrupted each other with suggestions and comments in rapid succession. The facilitator barely could write fast enough to keep up with the brisk pace of the group's ideas. In another session, in a very large convention bay with chairs placed auditorium style, the facilitator was having great difficulty getting any comments or suggestions from the audience. The chairs were set far back from the lectern, creating an intimidating situation. This distance, coupled with the lecture-expected setup in the much-too-large room, stifled interaction. The difference between the two sessions was the room size and the arrangement of chairs. The first room favored the exchange of ideas, the other inhibited interchange. This incident documents how great an effect room arrangement has on participation.

How do you select the room arrangement that is right for the training that you want to conduct? Here are some suggestions:

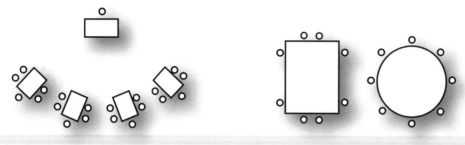

Fan-type Seating   **Conference Seating**

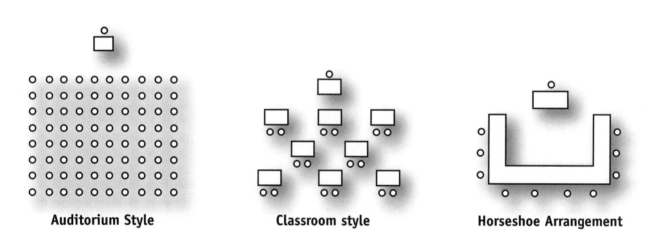

Auditorium Style   **Classroom style**   **Horseshoe Arrangement**

Selecting the Right Room Arrangement

Auditorium Style—Auditorium style is popular because it allows the most chairs in the smallest space. However, it is often a poor choice for training. This arrangement places the instructor in the front and everyone else facing him. The message given to participants is that they are to passively listen to the instructor. Auditorium-style seating makes it difficult for good interactions to take place among participants. Even when interactions happen, they frequently become exchanges between participants and instructor rather than between participants. To facilitate interaction, arrange the chairs in a circle ahead of time to let people know you expect interaction.

Classroom Style—Classroom style is similar to auditorium style except that tables are used and participants sit at the tables facing the instructor. The tables are an advantage if the training includes much writing or if participants need individual working space. However, the arrangement still has most of the same limitations of restricting interactions as auditorium style.

Horseshoe Arrangement—A horseshoe arrangement is often a good setup for a group of around twenty persons. If the group is larger, the sides of the horseshoe become too long to facilitate interaction, or they are too far apart for participants to talk easily with those on the other side. Participants should not be seated on the inside of the horseshoe because that puts their backs toward others and limits their ability to talk with the group and to see the instructor.

Conference Seating—Round tables effectively promote participation in small groups. The only disadvantage to round tables is that whole-group activities may be awkward since some persons will need to turn around to see when one person is talking to the whole group. Round tables take up much space and will require a larger room than might otherwise be needed. Sometimes, too, using audiovisual aids is hard with round tables because of the difficulty of everyone seeing the screen.

Fan-type Seating—The fan arrangement has three advantages: all participants can easily see the instructor and any audiovisual aids, the tables allow working with small groups, and the view of the room is relatively unobstructed. As with conference seating, it will take more room than some of the other arrangements.

Seminar Arrangement—This is very similar to auditorium style but usually means that the seats are bolted to the floor or hooked together, and cannot be moved around. Except for keynote speeches and motivational talks, seminar rooms are very restrictive and limited in their usefulness for most types of training.

Break-out Rooms—When several small groups are working on a project at the same time, it is convenient to have nearby rooms for some of the groups to work in. Having access to separate rooms reduces interference and distractions that occur when small group activities are conducted in one room.

Too Large and Too Small Rooms—If the room for the training is too large, it may be difficult for some to hear or there may be a sense of "nobody showed up for the session." It may be hard to provide a sense of togetherness and cooperative learning. When you must use a cavern of a room, try setting up at one end or in a corner. If the room is too small, participants may feel crowded and may not be able to hear in small groups because of noise problems. Try spreading into the hall or use partner activities. The key in room arrangement is to select an arrangement based on the plan for the training. Selecting the arrangement most conducive to the main activities of the training will help ensure its success.

ASSESSING THE PHYSICAL ENVIRONMENT

Plan ahead and always check out the site ahead of time. Keep records in a notebook or on a database for reference if you anticipate using the same facility in the future. Record the number of participants that rooms can hold with various setups. Note the availability and cost of audiovisual equipment, dry-erase boards and projection screens, how much you can adjust the lighting, and other information that will help you select the right place and be prepared.

THE EMOTIONAL ENVIRONMENT

ESTABLISHING THE EMOTIONAL CLIMATE

Just as the physical environment affects how individuals interact, the emotional climate will equally affect interactions. The facilitator is responsible for establishing much of the emotional climate of the training session. Here are some tips for a positive atmosphere:

Prepare Participants—Let participants know what to expect ahead of time. Knowing when the session will end, what credit will be given, and even where to park and enter the building will help them feel secure in what they will be facing. Participants often want to know ahead of time what the arrangements are for breaks or lunch and even what to wear.

Meeting and Greeting Trainees—The facilitator should arrive early enough to be ready and available to welcome participants when they arrive. Speaking to as many participants as possible and learning their names helps them feel wanted. It conveys a sense of being well organized and prepared. Talking to participants allows the facilitator to find out a little about them and what they want from the session. It helps the facilitator individualize and make training relevant.

Provide Guidance on Expected Behavior—Persons come to training settings from diverse backgrounds. Some will have had much experience in training environments; some will have had very little. Let them know what is expected by addressing these items:

- Do you expect them to participant? How?
- Are they welcome to eat in the room?
- What are the smoking policies?
- Will there be a break or do they leave at any time?
- Where are the restrooms and telephones?
- Is it all right to ask questions? How and when?

Creating Trust—Participants may be skeptical of you as a trainer in the beginning. They must learn that you are sincere and that you are not only knowledgeable in your field, but you care about them as well. Sometimes personal anecdotes will help them see you as genuine. Let them know about your experiences that are similar to their experiences. However, too many personal stories may turn trainees off to your message. Show that you respect them and value their opinions.

Protect Egos and Self-concept—Let trainees know that making mistakes is all right. Trainees often fear making a mistake or being embarrassed by not knowing an answer. Here are some tips for letting participants know it is all right to make an error:

- When you make a mistake, call attention to it in a light-hearted way.
- Let them know you do not have all the answers.

- Use face-saving techniques to respond to incorrect answers such as:

> "In some situations, it might work, but..."
> "You may not be aware of this new research that ..."
> "I thought so too, until I learned..."
> "Does anyone have another suggestion?"

ACTIVITIES TO ESTABLISH THE EMOTIONAL CLIMATE

Mistakes Are OK—To demonstrate that it need not be embarrassing to make mistakes, pass around pencils and liquid correcting fluid. Ask trainees to figure out why you are calling their attention to these two items and what the items have in common. Help them recognize that erasers and liquid correcting fluid exist because mistakes are made by many and can be corrected. Emphasize that for the training session, mistakes are understandable and OK.

Finding Answers—This activity is to show trainees that they may not have all the answers, but the important thing is that they know how and where to find answers. Hold up a dictionary, thesaurus, encyclopedia, atlas, or other reference books. Ask trainees to tell you why these books were published and how they are used. Several will tell you that these books are used to help us find the correct spelling of a word, the definitions of words, other words to use, information about a subject, or how to get places. Explain that books are sources of information, and that no one is expected to know everything. Tell them, "If someone knew all of this, we could just ask her, and would not have to buy the reference books." Lead them to understand that knowing where to get information is possible, but knowing everything is not possible, and no one is expected to know everything.

Hold up some early childhood books and child development materials in the same way. Emphasize that no one person knows everything, but every person has resources. Relate this to why they are attending training—to discover how to learn from resources, and the resources here are books, materials, and other participants. Emphasize that much of the value of training is to learn about sources of information to help us after the training ends.

Information Overload—Hold up a Sunday newspaper. Tell trainees there are reports that information and knowledge will double in the next hundred and fifty years, then double again in the next fifty years. There is more information in a typical Sunday newspaper today than the average person knew in the Middle Ages. Relate this information to how it is impossible for anyone to know everything. It therefore becomes even more important that one knows where and how to get information.

Junk Food for the Mind—To help participants recognize that negative feelings can be overcome, have them identify some negative phrases and words. Then write those negative phrases on empty junk food containers in large letters. After they have identified six to eight phrases, have them list some "healthy food" statements. Write these positive statements on empty containers of good food such as cans of vegetables and whole grain cereal boxes. Some examples of junk food sayings are: "I can't. Do I have to? You can't do it." Healthy food sayings are: "I can do this." "I will learn from this." "I am capable."

Supporting and Encouraging Efforts—Commenting and expressing appreciation for participation is encouraging to trainees. Some may be very reluctant to speak out and may not be confident in a group of other adults. Gimmicks and small rewards can sometimes help participants be sure you really do value their participation. Here are some small, humorous rewards that encourage participation:

- **Key chains**—"You've just identified a key to _____. Here's a key chain to put it on."
- **Small notepads**—"You've noted an important _____. Here's a notepad to write it on."
- **Play money**—"You've given us a million-dollar idea. Here's some money for it."
- **Small ruler**—"That's a good measure of progress."
- **Blue ribbon**—"That's an award-winning idea."
- **Small trophy**—"You've given us a world-class suggestion."

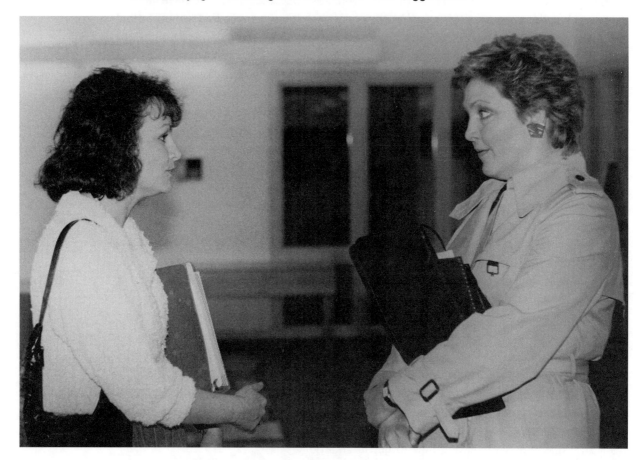

There's Nothing to Be Afraid of—Use this activity to help participants understand that fear is common and takes many forms. Put the phobias on a flipchart, overhead transparency, or individual handout. Ask them to match the name of the phobia in Column A with the Type of Fear in Column B. Phobia Match may be an individual, partner, or small group activity.

Phobia Match

Column A	Column B
1. Acrophobia	A. Fear of heights
2. Agoraphobia	B. Fear of open spaces
3. Ailurophobia	C. Fear of cats
4. Amaxophobia	D. Fear of driving and vehicles
5. Anthropophobia	E. Fear of people
6. Astraphobia	F. Fear of lightening
7. Brontophobia	G. Fear of thunder
8. Claustrophobia	H. Fear of closed spaces
9. Gephyrophobia	I. Fear of bridges
10. Hydrophobia	J. Fear of water
11. Mikrophobia	K. Fear of germs
12. Nyctophobia	L. Fear of darkness
13. Photophobia	M. Fear of light
14. Triskaidekaphobia	N. Fear of the number 13
15. Xenophobia	O. Fear of strangers

Answers:
1-A 2-B 3-C 4-D 5-E 6-F 7-G 8-H 9-I 10-J 11-K 12-L 13-M 14-N 15-O

Participants' Bill of Rights

Post the Participants' Bill of Rights in a prominent place in the training room or on a tent card. Publicly displaying such a statement makes clear the expectation to interact and share ideas courteously.

Participants' Bill of Rights for Training

Everyone has the right to:

have physical needs met
be listened to respectfully
expect courtesy and consideration
fully participate in the discussion and activities
work and take part free of distractions
learn and apply knowledge
make mistakes and profit from those mistakes
disagree in a inoffensive manner
share and receive resources and information for the group's mission

Statements such as these in the Bill of Rights help everyone understand what to expect and the rules for appropriate conduct. Other guidelines might be more specific, such as policies concerning eating and drinking during the training and freedom to take breaks at will.

MORE ENVIRONMENTAL TIPS

- Play music as participants gather before a session. Select tapes or compact discs for the mood you want to create: lively or restful, upbeat or slow.
- Wear clothes with pockets. Pockets are handy storage places for rewards, index cards, sticky notes, and other small items you will want to keep with you.
- Use a large watch to help stay on time if there is no clock in the room. Railroad watches add a nice touch and you can dramatically call attention to time limits.

UNDERSTANDING Adult LEARNERS

Adults can be coerced to attend training, even be required to be present for the full duration of a session. However, they cannot be forced to learn. Learning must come from motivation. How do you get adults to want to learn? Much of the success depends on an understanding of adults as learners and what it takes to make the learning meaningful for them. Only when they see the skills or material as important to them will they exert the energy and spend the time to learn.

How can one make the learning meaningful? Working with adult learners requires knowledge of how adults learn and skill in making the training relevant. The special skills and strategies needed in working with adult learners were described and popularized in a book titled, *The Adult Learner: A Neglected Species* by Malcolm Knowles. Knowles described the following assumptions about adults as learners (Zielinski, 1996).

- Adults usually favor self-direction.
- Adults' experiences are valuable resources for learning.
- Adults learn more from active experiences such as discussion or problem solving than from passive techniques such as lecture.
- Adults have specific learning needs arising from real-life events such as a change in employment.
- Adults are competency-based learners. They want to learn a skill that they can apply immediately.

As one looks at what is known about adult learners and what it takes to make training relevant, it is important to recognize these overriding principles that guide work with adults. You will note many similarities in how adults and children learn, but there are important differences as well.

Adult LEARNING Styles

We recognize a variety of learning styles in adults as well as children. Understanding that different persons need different activities for learning is a key to the effective training of both children and adults. What are some keys to training adults?

Use of All Senses—Some adults will learn primarily by what they hear; others mostly from what they see; and still others will need many opportunities to do the tasks described. Most will learn from a combination of all senses. Plan activities that involve several of the senses to help address the learning styles of the different adults who attend training.

Expressing Ideas to Others—Articulating an idea to another person helps one understand it. Teaching someone else how to perform a task gives one an opportunity to practice and refine one's own skill. Adults have much knowledge and many experiences to share. They want and need time to talk to each other about their experiences. Plan small group and partner activities to give adult trainees the opportunities they need to express their ideas.

Use of Experiences—Adults have a wealth of experiences on which to base learning. These experiences provide them with a framework on which to relate new training. Too, the experiences offer resources and examples for training. This history is important in designing training for adults.

Self-direction—Because adults favor self-direction, they will prefer choices in what tasks they do and how they do them. They will want to select tasks that are relevant for them and complete the tasks in a way that meets their personal training needs. Offer choices and allow for individual approaches to completing assignments.

Factors Affecting Adult Learning

How can you make training effective with adults? Here are some factors to keep in mind as you plan and conduct training:

Hands-on—Adults will want to be involved during training. In general, they would rather "do" than simply sit and watch. If you want to teach a new skill, include an opportunity to learn and practice the new skill. Even watching someone else perform a task in a demonstration will not be as effective as doing it oneself. It is relatively easy to recognize the importance of hands-on experiences in learning to use a computer or to play a piano. But hands-on learning is just as important in most other tasks adults must learn to perform. Although providing hands-on experiences takes more time and preparation, the results are well worth it in effectiveness and increased implementation.

Active Involvement—Without involvement, adults can tune out during a training session. Sitting passively opens the door to daydreaming or worrying about outside responsibilities. Adults have many experiences to draw upon and will desire involvement to share them. Many adults have few opportunities to talk with others about their work-related concerns or experiences. Consequently, they welcome the chance to interact with others who share similar jobs or needs.

Performance Feedback—Most adults want to know how they are doing. They need reassurance that their attempts are appropriate and not inconsistent with expectations. Coaching helps to keep them motivated and desiring to learn. Feedback through comments from the instructor and support through recognition of their efforts and performance are essential to effective training. Adults want and need ways to find out how they are doing.

Movement—Most adults are not used to sitting passively for long periods. They will need opportunities to move around either through instructor-planned activities or through their choice. In this day of sound bites on the evening news and the thirty-second commercial, adults have become conditioned to frequent changes. Consequently, it is helpful to change the type of activity often and schedule activities and breaks to allow for movement.

Repetition and Reinforcement—One rarely changes behavior or gains new knowledge after just one exposure to new information or new ways of doing things. Adults will need opportunities to repeat tasks or to have ideas repeated to reinforce learning and skills. Practice is important in their learning, but should not take the form of boring drill. Provide reinforcement by incorporating the same information or skill in several different ways through a variety of activities.

Special Concerns of Adult Learners

Adult learners come to the training situation with concerns and difficulties that may hinder their full participation in training and other staff development activities. An instructor of adults must take into consideration these needs and allow for them. Here are some of the concerns of adults to consider:

Family and Other Responsibilities—Adults have family responsibilities that may preoccupy their thoughts and interfere with their ability to concentrate during training. Concern about picking up a child after school or taking an elderly parent to the doctor may distract them from focusing on the task at hand. Adult learners may be making a mental shopping list rather than a list of what they want to learn. Adults are parents, caretakers of elderly parents, and responsible for and to others. They have mortgages, loan payments, and household expenses. These responsibilities and obligations may occupy adult trainees' thoughts and prevent them from focusing on the training content.

Time Limitations and Pressures—The responsibilities that adults have outside of work create time-related concerns. Trainees may worry about whether the session will end in time for them to get their child to a special activity. They may be concerned about household tasks they must do or the errands they must handle later. These family and home responsibilities often restrict how much time adults have to devote to training, especially when it is outside the usual workday. Being a full time employee and a caretaker of others limits the time and energy that is available for participation and follow-up activities.

Concerns about Performance—Adult learners may be very anxious about how they are perceived by their colleagues and others. They may have been out of a learning environment for many years and doubtful of their ability to meet expectations. They may be unsure of the procedures and worried about not knowing what to do. As a result, adult learners may be reluctant to participate due to fear of not being able to accomplish the required tasks. Although the fears may not always be articulated, they may show up in reluctance to attend training or participate in activities.

Fear of Failure—Everyone thrives on success. In our culture, failure is often viewed as undesirable. Failure can be embarrassing and harmful to self-esteem. Fear of failure will make it difficult for many trainees to fully benefit from the training. Trainees may fear changes outside of the training such as in their job responsibilities. Adult trainees may worry that they will not be able to succeed and complete the assigned tasks that they are required to do. Be sensitive to the many manifestations of fear and help alleviate them.

Fear of Embarrassment—No one likes to be embarrassed. Being unable to do what others can do is upsetting to most adults. Having co-workers or strangers see inept attempts can induce negative feelings toward training. Trainees may fear that they will be ridiculed by others if they cannot perform as expected. They may fear that they will be called upon to carry out a task they cannot do, or that they will not know answers to questions they may be asked. Adults may be afraid that others will think them silly or incapable.

Self-consciousness—Adults' self-esteem is often tied in with perceptions about their appearance or their abilities. They may be uneasy about their weight or how they look. They may not feel properly dressed or as capable as others in the group. They may think they do not express their ideas as well as others who are present. Adult trainees may not feel attractive, or be unnecessarily conscious of perceived or real disabilities.

Literacy and Language Barriers—Some adults come to the training situation with limited literacy. They may have reading difficulties that were not overcome or even recognized when they were in school, and they may have gone to great lengths to disguise their reading problems. Others may have learned English as a second language and may have some language barriers to learning. They may speak a dialect that is different from the majority and not understand all the idioms and expressions. If English is not the main language spoken, trainees may have difficulty in fully participating in activities. If literacy is a problem because of dyslexia or limited education, the adult may be very concerned about being required to read aloud.

Peer Pressures and Relationships—Depending on the makeup of the group, there may be relationships among attendees that affect participation. With supervisors present, trainees may be reluctant to express their opinions if their opinions differ from the supervisor. They may be afraid of disagreeing with their friends and co-workers and feel obligated to conform. There may be individuals present that they dislike. If trainees feel different from the group or have different ideas or interests, they might feel out of place. These relationships all affect how individuals behave and react in a learning setting.

Prior Negative Experiences—Some adults approach learning with a great deal of anxiety. Perhaps they did not do well in their formal schooling. Difficulty in reading or mathematics may have interfered with their ability to master formal school work. They may remember experiences that were unpleasant or embarrassing from their school days. If trainees have had negative educational experiences in the past, these memories may surface and make them reluctant to participate. Perhaps the negative experience has been from attending many training sessions that were boring or irrelevant. Trainees may remember passively sitting in hard chairs for long periods and equate training with dull, monotonous lectures. They may have experienced sessions filled with information they considered impractical.

Physical Comfort—Adults must be comfortable to avoid being distracted by temperature, light, noise, and other physical conditions. If the room is crowded or noisy, they may have trouble concentrating. Hunger pangs can distract them from learning. Adult learners will be concerned about ensuring there will be time to visit the restroom or make a telephone call. Adults seek comfort and react to comfortable surroundings. They will quickly notice if the chairs are too hard, or if the room is too cool or too warm for their comfort. Adjacent noise or irritating sounds may distract them. Even glare from a window or highly contrasting light may be uncomfortable. Suggest that participants bring a sweater for personal comfort. Planning for adaptation to temperatures is especially important when training is in hotels, since hotels must adjust temperatures for a large area. The room you use may be too cool for comfort, especially when the first participants arrive. Consider the location of a room selected for training in relation to other activities. If noise is coming from a sound system, hotel staff can often adjust it. If noise is from an adjoining room, try moving to the other side of your room to get away from it.

Health Issues—Adults may have various visual or hearing difficulties. The environment may make it difficult for them to hear or see well. They may have circulation or other problems that make it hard for them to sit for periods. Plan training to use all the senses and to allow for movement to address health concerns.

EVALUATING TRAINING

Unless you know how well you have done, you do not know what you need to do differently. To evaluate the progress you've made as a trainer, you must first evaluate the impact of the training that you conduct. Training evaluation is usually categorized into two types: formative and summative. Formative evaluation is conducted during the training. Formative evaluation allows one to check if issues that trainees previously identified as important to address have indeed been addressed. A trainer might include an activity designed to seek quick feedback from trainees on how they feel the session is progressing. Formative evaluation allows adaptation or revision on the spot to better meet the needs of the participants before the training ends.

Feedback and evaluation are helpful to the trainees as well as the trainers. When one considers that evaluation is time spent by trainees in reflective thinking, critical review, and analysis, the time required is well spent. Additionally, when trainers adapt their work to better meet participants' needs, training will be more effective. Asking participants what they think of the training is another way to demonstrate that you really care what they think and want to meet their needs.

Summative evaluation is generally conducted at the end of training to assess how well the training was done and what may need to change the next time a session is repeated. Summative evaluation is very helpful for adjusting content, activities, or procedures for the next group of participants, but usually comes too late to be helpful for the trainees participating in the session being evaluated. Here are some ways to conduct summative evaluations:

Ways to Evaluate Effectiveness

A widely accepted model for evaluating training effectiveness is based on the work of Donald L. Kirkpatrick, in Evaluating Training Programs: *The Four Levels*, who maintains that there are four ways, or levels, of evaluation. At the beginning level are those end-of-the-session reaction sheets distributed to participants that ask them to respond to what they liked or did not like about the training. Level 1 evaluation forms, often called "smile sheets," are the easiest and most common of the levels of evaluation. Level 2 evaluations are the various ways used to test what the trainees learned. Level 2 evaluations are often a type of pre- and post-test. Level 3 refers to the more difficult to conduct measurement of what behavior change occurred on the job. Level 3 evaluations will often consist of observations or other measurement of practice. Level 4 is the assessment of the impact on the business. Level 4 evaluations measure the financial and overall quality impact of the training. For early childhood education, we will consider the improvement of the program and how the training ultimately impacts the quality of services for children and parents in discussing Level 4 evaluations.

Smile Sheets: What Did They Like?

Smile sheets are those evaluation forms that are commonly used at the end of a training session that ask about what the trainees liked, what they felt they learned, and what they think should have been done differently. Evaluation forms may also include questions that call for reflective thinking to help individuals consider implementation and how they will use the new skills and knowledge at work.

These Level 1 evaluation forms have many limitations since they seek only trainees' reactions and opinions about the training. They tell us little about the real success of training, but they do tell us what is enjoyed about the activities. While this general reaction to the training may give us limited information about behavior changes, the forms do provide opportunities for trainees to think about the training and to recognize that their input is valued. Evaluation forms (see page 288-290 in the Appendix for examples) give us information about what trainees felt was missing or how engaged they felt. They can tell us about real-life problems that we failed to address. Unless trainees feel the session was useful, they may be unwilling to return for more. And if trainees do not enjoy the sessions, an opportunity to recruit them for more training is lost. Level 1 evaluation forms, or "smile sheets," have an important place in training, but should not be considered the best way to truly evaluate training effectiveness.

Assessing Knowledge: What Did They Learn?

Level 2 evaluations are those evaluations that determine what a trainee has actually learned as a result of the training. Level 2 evaluation may be an actual demonstration that trainees can perform the task, or it may be a paper-and-pencil test. The goal of Level 2 evaluation is to find out if trainees learned what you were teaching.

Well-written objectives are the first step in Level 2 evaluations. If the objectives are specific and measurable, including how the measurement will take place, then that identified means of measurement will often be the Level 2 evaluation. In designing training, first develop the objectives, then design the Level 2 evaluation.

Show You Know: Demonstration of Mastery—Demonstrations of skills by the learner are excellent ways to check mastery of skills. "Show You Know" is simply giving a name to a time in the training schedule to include demonstrations of abilities to perform tasks or use information. It is a system to incorporate an evaluation of changes in performance during a training session. "Show You Know" means that you incorporate a way that learners demonstrate to you how well they are able to implement the new skills to which they have been exposed. Cardiopulmonary resuscitation (CPR) training is an example of training that requires demonstration of mastery. CPR training includes a time for participants to demonstrate their ability to perform the required techniques.

Procedures for sanitary diaper changing and correct hand-washing are a few of the many skills that can easily be demonstrated even in a onetime session. Communicating with parents, reacting to an upset child, or handling a biting incident are skills that can be demonstrated through role-play. When planning training, ask yourself, "How will I know if they have learned what I want them to learn?" Whenever possible, allow time for demonstration of mastery.

Check Your Knowledge: Pre- and Post-Tests—Pre- and post-tests are common methods used for assessing learning in training situations. If participants may be intimidated by what they view as "tests," give them non-threatening names such as "Check You Knowledge" or "See What You Know" to help put trainees at ease. Pretests provide information about trainees' base level of knowledge. Post-tests provide a second level of knowledge to compare with the first. The comparison of the two is the measure of the results of the training.

Pre- and post-tests can be on separate forms distributed at the beginning and at the end of a session. Or if a single form is used, one can easily see what each individual learned from the training. Another advantage of using a single form is that it shows participants themselves what they learned. Still one more advantage is that the single form reduces the amount of paper used. An example of a single-page form for pre- and post-test is on page 291 of the Appendix.

Pre- and post-tests must be carefully designed to ensure they seek the required information. If the tests are too complex, participants may not take the time to read them carefully or may not think about their answers. If the forms are too easy, participants may not take the forms seriously. If the forms include too many types of questions, participants may become confused. About two types of questions seems to work best, especially for short-term or one-shot training sessions. True and False, short answer, multiple choice, or matching are some of the types of questions that work well on pre- and post-tests. See the section on Evaluation and Feedback Questions for examples of the types of questions that can assess learning.

Pre- and post-tests provide a better idea of what was successful than a smile sheet alone. They help you determine what activities worked and what information was unclear in order for you to do a better job next time. Pre- and post-tests are an important part of one's repertoire in ongoing efforts to see that the training is effective.

Always review post-tests with participants after they take them. Reviewing post-tests gives you an opportunity to clear up any misunderstandings and serves as an additional review. Reviewing tests gives you an idea of how confident participants are in their answers when you let them explain why they answered as they did.

Change in Performance: What Will They Do Differently?

Level 3 evaluation is much more difficult to conduct than Level 1 or Level 2. Level 3 is the measurement of actual behavior change on the job. Level 3 evaluation is important because unless changes are made on the job, the training has not been successful. There is no question that observed changes in performance will give a much better picture of training success. Ideally, a Level 3 evaluation will include observation on the job before training and again afterward. The disadvantage of Level 3 evaluation is that it can be time consuming and consequently expensive to conduct.

In a onetime workshop setting, it may be impossible to evaluate through observation at the degree desirable. However, there are ways to stimulate participants' thinking about how they will implement changes and to support change on the job. Checking for mastery will ensure a greater possibility that a change in behavior will occur. Allowing time at the end of the session for trainees to write what they will do differently will support changes in performance. Let them make a note of the best ideas of the session that they plan to use. Ask for implementation plans for when they return to the worksite. Here are ideas for more in-depth evaluation of mastery when it is not possible to observe changes on the job:

Follow-up Activities: Implementation Documentation—Assigning a follow-up activity that requires participants to submit evidence of implementation before receiving their training documentation can be a catalyst for change. Follow-up activities can help you evaluate how well trainees are implementing what they have learned and consequently how successful the training has been. Here is an example of a follow-up assignment for a session on integrating mathematics in the curriculum:

> By (date) submit the following assignment to (trainer's name and address)
>
> Select three books that relate to math concepts and read them to the children in your class. Choose books other than the ones we used in the workshop today. Report the names of the books, the author, and the copyright information. Write a paragraph summarizing how the children reacted to each story and what mathematical concepts you saw demonstrated by the children after you read the story.

Such an assignment will enhance trainees' use of the new information and serve as a review when they are back at work. Follow-up assignments have an added advantage of stimulating trainees' use of resources at their own site. Follow-up assignments require the trainees to think about the subject once again, review materials from the workshop, and reinforce the concepts they have learned.

Information from Supervisors—Sending a questionnaire or telephoning supervisors will often get information about how much change is occurring at work. Contact with supervisors will be most effective if the supervisors are clear about the training goals and content. Including them in the training design and in the training itself helps ensure that trainees will implement the new procedures. If the supervisors have not been included, contact will have less benefit since they may not know what to look for or be observing the changes in performance.

Follow-up Evaluations—Consider sending evaluation forms to trainees several weeks after the training to get information about what is useful on the job. You will likely get more information from trainees who complete the smile sheet evaluation forms a short time after the training. While the return in number of forms likely will be much less, the information may be more in-depth. After trainees have had time to think about the training once they are back on the job, they can be more accurate in assessing what is useful. Sending evaluation forms a week or two after training will give you a better picture of how behavior has changed on the job.

Bottom Line: What Are the Benefits to Children, Families, and Programs?

Level 4 evaluation attempts to measure a company's business results. In the early childhood field, measuring business results would be appropriate to many forms of directors' training in management and the business aspects of running a program. Evaluating how much time is saved, how much fee collections have increased, and how many more parents are satisfied are some measures of bottom-line financial impacts of training. Other measures might be reduction in staff turnover as a result of greater job satisfaction and successful experiences of employees.

While the financial benefits in the early childhood field are in reduced need for remedial education and fewer social problems, such benefits may be beyond trainers' ability to document without extensive research and effort. Because most of the training in early childhood is in actual work with children, relating the training to the financial aspects of a program is much more difficult. However, we can tie the benefits of caregiver training to parents' satisfaction with the program. And parental satisfaction is related to a program's ability to maintain full enrollment. For this section, however, the bottom line addressed will include how much the program has improved. A quality program is a bottom-line benefit for children and families.

Classroom Observations—Observing a trainee's classroom using a purchased or constructed rating scale is one of the most common means of Level 4 evaluation. Such observations give the instructor a better feeling for the environment in which the trainee works and the resources she has available. An observation before and another after training has taken place can measure the difference between what the trainee did before training and how well the trainee did afterward. A single observation will give some information, but will not measure progress. Unless the instructor knows what the trainee was doing before the training and what the trainee was doing afterward, she will not know if there was improvement.

Photos—When a session involves something visual such as room arrangement or improving an interest center, before and after photographs will be helpful. Let trainees bring photographs of a classroom as it is before training and after training has taken place to show how they have improved the environment as a result of the training.

Reunion Events—Reunion events held as a conclusion to training that took place over a period of time can be effective in assessing implementation. Reunion events can include displays of what has been done and might include scrapbooks, photographs of activities, or other ways to show off new activities. Reunion events also are helpful in building a support system to facilitate ongoing improvement.

Parent Questionnaires—Surveys of parent satisfaction can help assess their perception of program improvement. Parents can quickly complete questionnaires as they pick up their children at the end of the day. Parent questionnaires offer an opportunity to educate parents on the benefits of the change as well.

Interest Records—Comparing records of children's choices of activities before and after training can give you an idea of the effectiveness of training. Suppose an average of four children a day played with the blocks before the teacher attended a workshop on block play, and afterward an average of six did. That increase might represent an improvement in the trainees' ability to provide good block play experiences.

Incident Records—For some types of training, incident records can help with evaluation. If there has been an average of three minor injuries per month, and after training the number is reduced to two, one could consider that an improvement. Or, if discipline incidents before and after training decreased, that reduction could represent an improvement in the teacher's discipline and guidance techniques.

Evaluation and Feedback Questions

There are many ways for participants to communicate to you what they know. Select from these types to design questions for feedback, evaluation forms, or pre- and post-tests. As a rule, using no more than two or three types of questions is best. Changing the type of questions too often may confuse participants. Here are some types of questions to consider as you design questionnaires and tests:

Short-answer Questions—Include questions that participants can answer with a few words or in a few sentences. Short-answer questions are useful for a quick evaluation during training to see how well participants are mastering the material. These questions give you an idea of the literacy level of trainees when used for formative evaluations in order for you to adjust presentation techniques. Short-answer questions may require trainees to respond in phrases or in complete sentences, or to list information. Here are some examples of short answer questions:

1. When should you wash your hands?
2. What should you do if you suspect a child has been abused?
3. Tell two ways you encourage children to eat healthy foods.
4. Identify four ways to present stories to children other than reading a book to them.
5. What are some ways you can keep your playground safe?
6. Why is it important that children have time to be alone or with a few friends?
7. How can you communicate with parents who are unable to come to parent meetings and do not bring or pick up their children?
8. What are some of the ways to keep toys safe?
9. List some ways to keep your playground safe.
10. When should you inform parents about center policies and procedures?

Essay Questions—Longer questions are useful to evaluate how well trainees understand a more complicated issue. Answers to essay questions can consist of a paragraph or several pages. These questions have a disadvantage when working with participants who might find writing difficult, however. Essay questions can be time consuming to do during a training session. Essay questions make good outside assignments where trainees may take as long as they need to respond. The questions below are examples of essay questions.

1. How do you write anecdotal records, and how do they help you understand a child?
2. Explain what young children learn through play and why it is important to them.
3. How can we be an advocate for children and children's issues?
4. Discuss factors to consider in planning room arrangement.
5. Why is communication with parents important, and what are some ways to ensure that it happens?
6. Describe how you can prepare children for a field trip.

7. What are some characteristics of a professional and how do we support professionalism?
8. When are some good times to include music in the daily schedule, and why is it important that music be included throughout the day?
9. Discuss ways to help a new child adjust to your program.
10. Why are transitions difficult times, and how do you prevent discipline problems during transition times?

Fill-in-the-Blank Questions—Fill-in-the blank questions are actually statements that the participant completes by writing in a missing word or phrase. Fill-in-the-blank questions are useful in video viewer guides or as reading guides. Because these questions require a written response, they work well as reinforcement. The instructor must be cognizant that fill-in-the-blank questions may have several possible correct answers other than the one sought. This type of question seeks specific answers. Because fill-in-the blank questions require recall rather than recognition, they may be more difficult than some types such as matching or multiple choice. Sometimes a set of fill-in-the blank questions will include a listing of words from which to choose, which makes them easier to answer. When the choices of words are included, the questions may function more as a reinforcement since the correct answer may be deduced through a process of elimination. Here are examples of fill-in-the-blank questions with the words from which to select included:

1. When a child strings beads, he is developing _____ motor coordination.
2. If a toddler says "No," she is developing _____.
3. When a preschooler ties his shoelaces himself, he is learning _____ skills.
4. Preschoolers running outside are developing _____ motor skills.
5. When a baby smiles back at an adult, she is developing _____ skills.
6. Babbling is part of learning _____ for a baby.
7. When a child wants you to read the same story again and again, it is because she likes _____.
8. Toddlers who play side by side are participating in _____ play.
9. When a toilet-trained child starts having accidents, it is called _____.
10. Giving children time to figure things out for themselves helps develop _____ skills.

Choose from these words:

Matching—Matching gives the participant a choice of answers from which to choose the correct ones. Matching is useful, but once participants have completed some answers, they may guess at the remaining ones and get them correct just by chance. However, the

| Social | Fine Self-help | Gross | Autonomy |
| Regression | Language Parallel | Repetition | Cognitive |

experience provides reinforcement of concepts, even when the learner finds correct answers through the process of elimination. Matching works well when there are terms and definitions or parallel items that can be matched to the answers. These questions may be constructed to have the learner write in the matching number or letter or to draw a line between the matching items. Either way is effective. Here are two examples:

Planning

Write the letter of the definition beside the word that it defines:

Terms	Definitions
___ Daily Schedule	A. A specific program for children including philosophy, content areas, goals, and objectives.
___ Weekly Plan	B. A plan to organize the day that includes blocks of activities as well as transition periods for toileting, eating, and resting.
___ Curriculum	C. A written plan giving the activities for a week. The activities listed should be centered around the concepts and objectives being taught during that week's daily schedule.
___ Daily Plan	D. A detailed written plan for one day. It includes activities, time of the activity, a description of the activity, and any special equipment needed.
___ Objective	E. A statement describing a desired, observable behavior in each child as the result of learning activities. It includes the desired behavior, the circumstances or conditions, and the measure of successful performances.

Draw a line between the term on the left and the definition of the term on the right.

Terms	Definitions
Individualization	A short activity often used between activities or to assist in moving children from one area of the classroom or facility to another area.
Learning Activity	A plan or adaptation of activities for one person, based on that person's strengths and needs.

Curriculum Manual   A section or area of the classroom set up to support a specific part of the curriculum.

Learning Center   A book describing the way to implement the curriculum, including guidelines for planning and conducting learning experiences.

Transitional Activity   A single experience selected or planned for the children that includes goals, objectives, methods, materials needed, and an evaluation.

Multiple Choice Questions—Multiple choice is probably the most common type of question. Multiple choice questions require participants to choose from among several possible answers. Multiple choice questions may be difficult for the instructor to construct. Creating a clearly false answer is easy, but making answers that are somewhat possible yet incorrect can be difficult. This type of question calls for participants to select one or more answers from a list. Typically, multiple choice questions will have one or two clearly wrong answers, one or two almost right answers, and one best answer. Sometimes multiple choice questions will have an answer that includes one or more of the other possible answers. Here are examples of multiple choice questions:

1. _____ To handle a biting situation with a toddler, the teacher should:

    a) Bite the child who bit just enough to let the biter know what it feels like to be bitten.
    b) Comfort the child who was bitten, then punish the biter.
    c) Treat the bite, comfort the bitten child, show the biter with a frown that biting is not good.
    d) Comfort the bitten child, then call the parent of the biter to ask her to punish him when she picks him up.

2. _____ Which of the following menus contributes the most to a child's nutritional needs?

    a) Hamburger patty on half a bun, green beans, apple, salad, milk.
    b) Hamburger, potato chips, cookie, milk.
    c) Fish sticks, French fries, orange juice, peach slices.
    d) Hot dog on a bun, baked beans, carrot sticks, fruit drink.

3. _____ Emergent literacy should be supported by:

    a) Reading books to children often.
    b) Labeling items in the room.
    c) Drilling children on recognizing the alphabet.
    d) Both a) and b)

When discussing multiple choice questions with a group, discuss why certain answers are wrong and why one is the best answer. For example, in the first question above, a) is incorrect since it would be inappropriate to bite the child. Answer b) is incorrect since punishment is unlikely to address the reasons for the biting. Answer d) is incorrect since punishment will have little effect, and the toddler will not see any relationship between the biting incident and the punishment, especially hours following the incident.

In question 2, b) is clearly incorrect. Answer d) is close except for the fruit drink since fruit drink is not 100% fruit juice. Answer c) is almost acceptable but omits milk. However, a) is the best answer because it includes all components of the USDA requirements.

In the last question, c) is clearly incorrect, and both a) and b) are correct. The best answer to this question is d) because it includes both a) and b).

True and False Questions—True and false questions are statements that may or may not be true. The trainee identifies them as either true or false by writing in a blank or circling the words True or False beside the statement. These questions simply ask participants to identify if a statement is correct or incorrect. To stimulate analytical thinking, ask trainees to write a sentence telling why a statement is false or to explain why it is false if they are answering orally. True and false questions are more effective when participants are able to discuss their answers. Explaining why a statement is true or untrue helps the instructor in analyzing what the participant knows. For example, a participant may know that an action is not appropriate or that information is incorrect, but not know the appropriate action nor the correct information. Additionally, a participant has a 50/50 chance of getting each one correct just by guessing. Here are some examples of true and false questions:

Circle True if the statement is true. Circle False if the answer is false. If the sentence is false, tell why it is false.

1. True or False There is no need to have duplicate toys for toddlers since they need to learn to share.

2. True or False Talking to infants helps them learn language.

3. True or False Unit blocks build important math concepts.

4. True or False There is no need to plan, since play is important for young children.

5. True or False The teacher should never suggest possibilities for play because it will interfere with children's creativity.

6. True or False It is valuable for children to try out their ideas even when you know they will not work.

7. True or False Although they like it, water play encourages young children to become over-stimulated and should be avoided.

8. True or False Writing down the stories that children tell helps them learn the purpose of writing.

9. True or False Infants should not go outside since they might get sunburned.

10. True or False It is best to sit or stoop down to talk to a child.

The first statement is false. However, a portion of it may confuse some trainees since they will see learning to share as a positive action. The second statement is fairly obviously true. The fourth statement is partially true (play is important for young children) but is false because it says there is no need to plan. The fifth is false because of the word "never" and the sixth begs a "why" answer. The ninth statement is a common misperception that many will mistakenly view as true. Discussing these questions will help participants understand the subtlety in them and recognize circumstances under which the actions are and are not appropriate.

Summaries—Although not questions, summaries are useful following videos and reading assignments. Summaries help you assess what information the learners got from the assignment and also help the learner organize her thoughts. In summaries, learners simply write a short description of what they have seen, read, learned, or done. Here are some examples of using summaries to assist or evaluate learning:

1. Summarize the article, *Let's Go Outdoors*, in your own words. Describe the author's main reason that children should play outdoors and the suggestions she gives to promote outdoor play.
2. After viewing the video, *Partnership with Parents*, summarize the key points and tell how they apply to your program.
3. Find an article about communicating with parents and summarize it in no more than three paragraphs.
4. Describe the activities you observed when you visited the Early Childhood Center. Include in your description how the teacher introduced the activity and interacted with the children during the activities.
5. Summarize what you learned from the projects on inclusion of children with special needs that you recently completed.

Evaluating on the Go

It is often helpful to have a system for checking how participants are feeling about the progress as the training unfolds during sessions. Getting information before the session ends allows the instructor to adjust activities or content to better meet the needs of trainees. It lets trainees know that you value their input and want to meet their needs.

Fast Feedback Forms

See pages 292 and 293 in the appendix for two examples of fast feedback forms.

Activities for Feedback During Training

In addition to forms, activities can provide feedback concerning how the participants are reacting to the session. These feedback activities help the instructor recognize participants' unmet needs, then adjust the training and individualize to better meet those needs. Here are some quick ways to get feedback from a group:

Training Temperature—To get quick feedback on how well the training is addressing the needs of trainees, have them set a cardboard thermometer to show how "hot" the training is. Let them color in the thermometer at logical points during the session.

Take a Stand—Place the numbers one to ten on the floor. Ask participants to stand near the number that best represents their understanding of a specific concept. This activity not only gives the instructor a quick view of how people feel about their mastery of the learning, but offers a chance for participants to move around. For fun, write the numbers on footprint cutouts.

Three Goals—Have participants write three goals at the beginning of a session. Several times during the session, ask them to review their goals and decide if they have met them. If participants did not meet goals, ask what more can be done to help them. Take time at the end of the session to let participants write what they learned.

One, Two, Three—To quickly assess trainees' mastery of information, ask them to summarize the main three points of the session. Have them write the information on index cards for you to review at the break.

Priorities—List key concepts from the training on cards. Have participants sort the cards in order of importance based on their priorities. This activity is a good way to see what is most important to the participants. List the main priorities on a flip chart and periodically ask participants if the topics have been covered to their satisfaction. Check off items in the list as participants feel satisfied with the coverage.

Receipt Book—Ask participants to write a receipt for the information or suggestion that helped them the most. This activity is a good way to get some feedback on small group discussions or to quickly evaluate what was most helpful. Sales books and receipt books are available inexpensively from office supply stores.

Sales Book—Have participants write their questions on a sales slip at the beginning of the session. They list the questions for which they want to "buy" an answer from you or others. After the session, have them write another sales slip, making a few comments about the usefulness of the information they bought.

CHAPTER 6

TROUBLESHOOTING

An effective trainer must recognize and adapt to a variety of situations and participants. She must be able to adjust to numerous personalities and training settings. She must be thoroughly prepared and ready to adjust the content to better meet the individual participant's needs. Also, she must have a plan to assist in the implementation of the training at the work site.

PARTICIPATION AND PERSONALITY ISSUES

Knowing participants' names and calling them by name will prevent many problems. Make large name tags so that you can see names during the session and use names frequently.

Other problems can be prevented by setting guidelines at the beginning of a session. However, experienced trainers will recognize the following personality issues that present special challenges to them and may call for intervention.

RELUCTANT PARTICIPANTS

Reluctant participants may have been required to attend the training when they would have preferred to do something else. They may have had previous negative experiences. Involve them often, especially in the beginning. Make the training interesting, fun, and relevant.

Tips For the Reluctant Participant:

- Ask what they expect to get out of the class.
- Emphasize the benefits of the training.
- Ask open-ended questions to get them involved immediately.
- Give them some responsibility and express appreciation for their efforts.
- Give them recognition when they participate.
- Ensure early success in activities.
- Call them by their name often.
- Help them be part of the group.
- Keep a sense of humor and make the training fun.

Another type of reluctant participant is the shy, quiet trainee who does not like to have attention focused on her. This person may hesitate to take part and want to watch from the sidelines uninvolved. The shy participant may need support and encouragement in any attempts to reach out, however small. This person may participate best in individual and partner activities. Sometimes, too, this participant may understand much more than she expresses. The trainer will want to be sure not to overlook the shy, quiet participant.

Here are some activities designed to get trainees involved, participating, and volunteering in a fun way:

Exploration—Give participants some playdough, art materials, or construction toys to explore. Ask them to see what they can do with them. Ask them to talk to each other about what they did with the materials. Ask them to share ideas that they tried and how they might use exploration with their children.

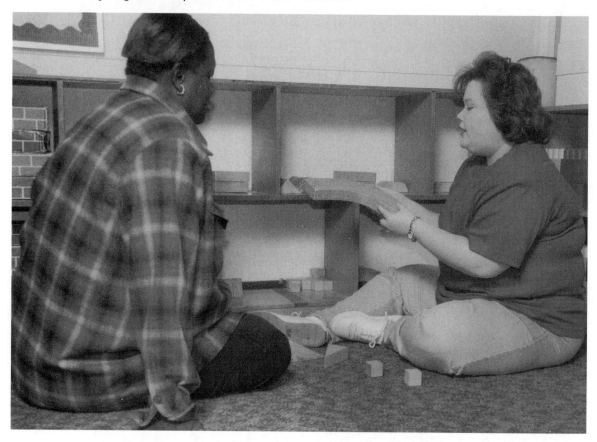

Nursery Rhymes—Start well-known nursery rhymes and ask trainees to fill in missing words. Get them involved in chanting the rhymes with you. Or ask them questions such as "What did Jack and Jill go up the hill to get?"

Me, Myself, and I—Ask participants to tell three things they want to learn in the training. Relate what they request to the content of the workshop.

Bouncing Ideas—Use a small rubber ball and bounce it to several trainees. Relate bouncing the ball to how we learn by participating. Then ask them not to catch the ball. Point out how the game stops if the balls are not bounced back, and that the same is true of ideas if we do not all participate.

Low Literacy Levels

For trainees with low literacy levels, be sure you present information in other ways than reading assignments. Summarize instructions verbally and give directions both in writing and orally. Use pictures and graphics to help trainees use clues to written material. Provide many hands-on experiences. Let them watch others before you expect them to perform a task. Ask for volunteers when you want someone to read aloud to avoid embarrassing anyone.

In designing handouts, be sure to leave much white space to keep handouts from appearing intimidating. Check the grade level if your word processing program has that capability. If the reading level is too high, shorten sentences and use smaller words until it is the right level for the group.

Side Conversations

Two people engaging in a private conversation can be disconcerting to the trainer and interfere with the group process. The side conversationalists may be reluctant participants who are required to attend and who are not interested in the training. They may have other events or issues on their minds. They may be with friends whom they seldom get to see or they may be immature. Here are some ideas to try when side conversations become distracting:

- **I Can't Hear You**—ask the pair to share their comments with the whole group.
- **Divide and Conquer**—use a partner activity and pair each with another person.
- **Stand by Me**—move over and stand beside the talkers.
- **Can We Talk?**—let the talkers know at the break that you and others are finding the interruptions a problem.
- **Social Hour**—allow a longer break or set a designated time to provide for social conversation.

Distractions and Latecomers

These are the participants who let their cell phones ring or their pagers buzz during the session. They may eat snacks in a noisy way or cause commotion when they enter the room late or leave for a break. Distracters may decide to move a chair while you are making a key point. They shuffle paper, look in their purse for items, and drop things. Distracters can be helped by offering guidance in appropriate behavior. Discuss ground rules before and during the training. Latecomers are a common problem in training and can be distracting to those who are there and ready to start on time. Close the door when you begin your session and start with an exciting or high-energy activity. Let latecomers recognize that they have missed something interesting and fun. It is important to consistently start on time when holding a series of sessions or a class. If you do not start on time, then participants will not come on time in the future, and you will establish a cycle that is hard to break. If you must help the latecomers catch up, do so at break if possible or during some other activities. Taking time to repeat what latecomers missed is irritating to those who arrived on time. Another type of distracter is the person who does not stay focused on the topic and has his own agenda that he wants discussed. He often tries to involve others in his personal cause or issue. Here are some techniques to deal with distracters who have difficulty staying focused on the topic:

Tangent Tokens—Have a few Tangent Tokens to give out to call attention when persons digress from the topic. The Tangent Tokens may be poker chips, milk caps, foreign coins, doubloons, or other round objects. These Tangent Tokens can be a humorous way to call attention to the need to stay on task.

Soap Box—When a participant has a strong opinion or digresses from the topic, pass her a soap box to hold while she elaborates on her opinion briefly. Then put the soap box aside to focus on the topic under discussion. The soap box adds humor to sessions and allows for a participant to be heard, but not to the extent that it is disruptive to the discussion.

Staying Focused—Give a magnifying glass to a participant and ask him to help the group to stay on topic. Demonstrate how you can move the glass forward or backward to bring the image into focus. Every time he feels the group is digressing from the topic, he should hold up the magnifying glass and call attention to it. The magnifying glass serves as a reminder to stay on task.

ANTAGONISTIC PARTICIPANTS

They are often the "They made me come and I didn't want to" participants. They may have a low self-esteem that makes it difficult for them to feel comfortable in a training setting. The antagonistic attitude may be a cover-up for insecurities. Or the attitude may just be learned behavior that has worked for them in the past. Involving the antagonistic participants in the training and giving them recognition when they behave appropriately will often help. Sometimes, the situation may require a private talk during a break.

Addressing the problem directly may be the best approach at times. A statement such as, "That sounded very aggressive to me. Was it intended that way?" may help change the behavior.

Try the following steps to confront an antagonistic or harassing participant:

"I need your help..." State that you desire and need their cooperation.
"The situation is..." Describe what you have experienced.
"The difficulty this creates is..." Describe the problem for you and the other participants.
"In the future ..." State what you want to happen now.

Negative Participants

The negative person may be a reluctant participant. Her negative comments may indicate that she did not want to attend the session. Or she may be pessimistic overall. Limit the negative person's time to comment through the structure of the activities to reduce her influence on the group. The activities and suggestions that apply to showoffs will be useful in limiting the influence of the negative trainee.

Tips For Trainees with Negative Attitudes:

- Get them involved in the training, early and often.
- Call them by name frequently.
- Give them responsibility for a task.
- Put them with a positive group and those with a more positive attitude.
- Recognize their experience and contributions.
- Reward performance improvement.
- Have a humor board. Designate one bulletin board for cartoons, jokes, funny sayings, or humorous articles.

Showoffs, Know-it-alls, and Dominators

These participants are the excessive talkers who may be overly enthusiastic or may like being the center of attention. They may have a personal cause or agenda. Sometimes they know, or think they know, more than the leader. Make use of scheduled responses when you have someone who wants to monopolize the time. Structuring the system for responses and comments to make sure that everyone gets a turn will help keep these participants from monopolizing the training session. Several ways to get everyone involved and reduce the influence of the showoff are:

Talking Stick—Pass around a stick. (A rain stick is good.) Only the person with the stick may talk.

Jot it Down—Ask participants to write down their ideas, comments, or questions. Then react to them.

Two Cents Worth—Everyone gets two pennies and must give one to the facilitator whenever they talk. This gives everyone at least two chances to comment.

Take a Number—Have participants take a number randomly or pass them out at the beginning or during a break. Then have them respond in numerical order by lowest first or highest first.

Time's Up—Use a simple timer or have someone time comments with a stopwatch.

Microphone—Pass around a toy microphone. Only the person with the mike may talk.

Alphabetical Order—Ask participants to comment or share ideas in alphabetical order by their first or last name.

Give Them a Job—Give the "showoff" a task. If they are seeking recognition, this may meet their needs.

Pair Up—Divide into pairs and give partners some time to talk to each other.

Personality Clashes

When two participants bring outside controversies into the learning setting, it can be disruptive for others. This is a time to divide and conquer. When dealing with more than a simple disagreement in methods, organize a small group or partner activity that will separate the two sparring parties.

When there are tensions among the participants, others in the group will often be uncomfortable. How does the trainer diffuse tension? Taking a break after there has been a confrontation may help cool things down. Sometimes using team-building exercises or specific activities designed to help participants appreciate each other's talents will help. Here are some activities to help participants learn to appreciate each other and to get along:

Appreciating Diversity—Pair up partners and pass around boxes of "multicultural" crayons. Ask each participant to take one. Ask partners to use the crayons to list the differences between them—hair color, education, experiences, birthplace, or anything else. After a few minutes, stop and identify the partners with the longest list. Have one partner read the list to the class. Give them each a box of multicultural crayons or other multicultural materials as a prize.

The Straw that Broke...—Give partners or small groups a bunch of drinking straws and a roll of masking tape. Ask them to build a free-standing structure by taping straws together, but not taping anything to tables, the floor, or the walls. Since one person will have great difficulty building without the help of another, they will soon see the need to assist each other and work together. Give a prize to the team with the tallest structure. Help them understand that this activity could not be completed without helping each other.

Sometimes simply separating those attendees who are not getting along or who engage in side conversations will resolve the problem. Reducing opportunities for direct interaction with each other is the goal in these strategies. Below are some specific ways to referee when participants do not work together well or whose attitudes are negative:

Separating Problem Participants—Here is a tip for splitting up people familiar to the presenter as "problem" attendees—perhaps because they talk or make annoying comments during presentations. This method requires access to social security numbers, birth dates, or other numerical data. Add up the digits in the social security numbers of the difficult students before the class or during a break. Find a pattern that will divide them. For example, ask everyone with an even total (3+9+5+6+2+3+2+9+9=48) to sit on one side of the room, odd on the other. Or divide them by the last digit (odd or even) in their social security numbers, their birthdates, or their telephone numbers.

Assigned Seats—If potential conflicts are anticipated or just to separate trainees who came together, put name tags on the chairs or tent cards with names on them on the table. Place the names to separate people who work at the same location, who are from the same town, or who may not work well together. Ask participants to find their place by looking for their names.

Guiding Groups—Divide groups according to known or controlled criteria, such as stickers or other issued items, places assigned, or colors of clothing worn. Use methods of dividing to guide the small group composition and separate negative participants or those who do not work well with each other.

Attention Issues

Distracted trainees who are mentally removed from the activities at hand have little if any chance to improve. Keeping trainees focused on the content, especially when training occurs at the end of a workday or in the afternoon immediately following lunch, can be difficult. Here are suggestions to help keep participants' attention:

Getting and Keeping Attention

The average attention span of an adult learner is approximately forty-five minutes. If sessions are longer than one hour, use some of these ideas to increase retention and keep attention levels high:

- Keep individual training parts to a maximum of forty minutes. Schedule breaks or question and answer time throughout each part, not just at the end.
- Vary strategies by using several presentation techniques such as small group discussion, demonstrations, partner activities, and individual study time.
- Be creative with your audiovisual aids. Use several formats, such as overheads, white boards, videos or slides, flip charts, and demonstrations.
- Provide frequent feedback based on formative evaluations. Frequent feedback allows the learners to assess their own progress in a non-threatening manner.
- Allow ample opportunity for participants to tell you what they are or are not getting from the session. Adults like to be involved in the decision-making process.

Preventing Inattention After Lunch

People are more apt to feel sluggish right after lunch, particularly if they have had a large meal. Fatigue begins to set in and it becomes harder to focus on the training activities. Energy levels may be lower as the day wears on. The time of the day immediately after lunch requires extra planning to hold everyone's attention.

- Schedule activities that require physical interaction and movement such as hands-on and high-participation activities.
- Use humorous and fun activities such as games.
- Change the format of the training such as moving into small groups or pairs.
- Have a new leader for variety.
- Have movement-in-place activities.
- Use props and other attention-getting devices.
- Avoid turning out the lights for videos or other audiovisual equipment.
- Keep your own energy level high.

FACILITATING TRANSFER OF LEARNING TO THE WORK SITE

"Why don't they do what I taught them?" is an often-asked question from trainers as well as administrators. Sometimes training does not "take" as we want it to. Change is hard, and it is often slow. Habits developed over years cannot be changed in a few hours or even a few days. Some experts report that most people translate only ten percent of what they learn into action. How can we increase the percentage and help ensure that people implement what they have learned? Here are some tips:

Baby Steps or Giant Steps?—Try a multi-phase program designed to help trainees apply skills as they learn parts. Learning in small steps will help prevent participants from feeling overwhelmed by too much, too soon. A series of workshops and ongoing classes offer opportunities to set progressive goals and to build on previously mastered skills.

Where Ya Goin'?—Trainees must be able visualize what they will be able to accomplish at the end of the training and how they will accomplish it. Without a realistic goal, they will become discouraged. Visualization, goal-setting, and selecting objectives can help trainees see what they will accomplish in training. Make certain that trainees have clear objectives they wish to accomplish.

How Ya Gonna Get There?—After trainees understand what they will be able to do at the end of training, discuss some of the ways to reach the goals that trainees have set for themselves. Then follow up with an experience to visualize how they will reach the destination and accomplish their goal. Self-assessments, action plans, and timelines can serve as a roadmap for where trainees are going. Ask them to view themselves taking the steps necessary to reach their goal. The steps will be their road map to their destination.

Jot It Down—Provide many opportunities for taking notes. Written material can be reviewed at a later time to reinforce training. Writing information helps the learning process.

WHY TRAINING FAILS

There are various factors why training fails and why learned skills are not implemented. Significant others at the workplace or home may not support the change. These influential others may be smugly or cynically telling themselves, "Just wait awhile. They'll see those changes won't work, and then we can get back to normal." Others may be subconsciously working to get them to conform to the old ways. Often there is a gap between those who have been trained and those who have not. Those who have not been trained will likely not understand the enthusiasm of the newly trained staff and even resent their motivation and excitement. Bringing new ideas into an environment that does not nurture the changes will doom it to some level of failure.

To help offset possible negative influences at the work site, have participants analyze the support they will have on the job and what things they can implement without support. If trainees will not have support for all of the changes, encourage them to implement those they can while building support for the others.

Sometimes, individuals fresh from training try to do too much too soon and become overwhelmed. It is better to succeed at implementing three new ideas that to fail trying to implement twenty. The trainer's role is to keep the trainee's goals within a reasonable range.

Lack of enough repetition is another reason training fails. Some reports are that content covered only once has less than a ten percent chance of being retained for thirty days. Yet, content covered six times has a better than ninety percent chance of being retained. Consequently, including repetition and reviews throughout the training is helpful.

Lack of feedback on their efforts is another reason trainees give up when they are back at work. Perhaps they were enthusiastic about a new art activity they learned, but when they tried it, the children got paint everywhere. If they do not have someone to help them assess what went wrong, trainees may give up without knowing the one tip that would have helped them. Follow-up assistance and support once trainees are back at the work site can reduce training failure.

Often when trainees return to work, they have responsibilities that accumulated in their absence. A substitute may not have completed paperwork, or a situation arose which others could not handle. Taking care of mail, planning activities, and generally catching up will take trainees' attention away from the new skills. Such accumulated tasks may make persons rely on old habits rather than taking the extra time to implement new, less familiar ways of working.

Another factor contributing to failure may be that the trainee perceives that the training was impractical or irrelevant. If a trainee never fully recognized the value of the training, it will be unlikely that she will practice the skills, even though she could perform during the training. Resistance to training may carry through even after the training ends if not successfully overcome during the training.

Making Reviews and Summaries Frequent and Fun

People need supervised practice to form new habits. This practice must be built into the training design. Games and puzzles are excellent ways to incorporate reviews into training. Games often allow participants to use information they have learned to solve problems. Word puzzles such as crosswords or Word Find are good ways to review terminology. Word puzzles have another advantage in that they can be taken to the work site to serve as follow-up reminders.

Incorporate reviews by using the same information in a variety of ways. A participant may complete a worksheet, participate in a partner activity, and play a game that all include the same concept. Information may be introduced through a worksheet, then shared and expanded later in a partner activity, and used still later in a small group game. Include a place for trainees to write what they are going to do at the work site on an evaluation form or in an implementation plan. Thus, the participants will be exposed to the same information several times throughout the training.

Review techniques can take many forms. However, when the trainer announces, "Let's review," participants may tune out immediately. They likely will consider reviews boring or may feel they do not need it. Participants may assume that they no longer need to pay attention since they have already heard the information. Announcing the activity without indicating that it is a review will reduce or eliminate the tune-out hazard.

Review and Reinforcement Techniques

Because participants must use information to master it, building in review activities is important to any training activity. Review time at the end of a session serves as a transition from the training to the job. Review activities provide participants with an opportunity to see for themselves what they have learned. Here are some guidelines for reviewing information:

- Conduct reviews as individual activities, with partners, or as small or whole group activities.
- Reviews may be a brief or a longer application or use of information.
- Space reviews throughout the training session, not just at the end.
- Reviews may be hands-on such as having trainees demonstrate a procedure or use information to solve a problem.
- Use reviews for fun and to add humor.
- Choose an active process, and reviews can add opportunities for movement and interaction.

Review and Reinforcement Activities

Musical Review—Pass out large sticky notes and a pencil to each participant. Ask each participant to write an important idea from the session on a sticky note and put it on the wall. If the group is small, have them write two or three ideas, each on a separate note. Play music and let participants walk around the room until the music stops. Have each participant read the nearest note aloud. Then each participant removes the idea read from the wall. Repeat the exercise until all ideas are read. This activity not only offers a way to review, but gives participants a chance to move around.

Awards Ceremony—Hold an awards ceremony to celebrate and discuss the most important course ideas and suggestions. Give each participant a ballot for nominating a winner in several of these categories:

- Most original suggestion
- Most practical suggestion
- Best comment made in class by a participant
- Most useful idea
- Best activity during the session
- Most fun activity during the session
- Best idea to try

Announce this activity at the beginning of the session so participants will be alert to ideas and make notes about the ones they want to select. For fun, make the ballots cutouts of blue ribbons or small trophies. After choosing, hold a brief discussion about the winners. Give a small trophy or blue ribbon to the participants who suggested the award-winning ideas.

Egg Toss—Number slips of paper according to the class size—for example one through ten in a class of ten participants. Insert the slips of paper inside plastic eggs. Number the same amount of small prizes correspondingly. Near the end of the session, ask each participant to list five questions and answers related to the course material. They may use their notes, handouts, or other reference material for accuracy. Give all the participants an egg and have them sit in a circle. Have a volunteer ask one of her questions then toss her egg to another person. If the recipient answers correctly, he keeps that egg and tosses his egg to another person, asking one of his questions. If a participant answers incorrectly, the egg returns to its original owner, who then throws it to someone else while asking the same question. Continue the process until someone answers correctly and keeps the egg. After all trainees have had a turn to toss their eggs, ask them to open their eggs, and they win the prize that matches the number inside. You also can write the number on the eggs rather than on the slips of paper.

Ad Campaign—Divide into small groups and give each group a flip chart and markers. Ask each group to pick something it has learned from the session. The group then creates a magazine or newspaper advertisement promoting the importance of what was learned or the benefits of implementing a new procedure. The groups may use text, cut-out pictures, or drawings to make their ads. They may use construction paper rather than flip chart pages, if they prefer to work on their own.

Wall of Wisdom—This exercise helps trainees share training tips and keeps people focused on applications. Ask trainees to write their biggest course-related problems on index cards and to keep the cards with them during the course. When a trainee learns something that helps solve one of the problems, he adds the solution to the card and posts the card on a designated "Wall of Wisdom." During the session, ask trainees to share the problem and the solution. The "Wall of Wisdom" also may be a large sheet of paper that trainees write on directly.

Creative Review—Divide trainees into groups to find a creative way to present a review of material covered. Have art supplies and resources for the topic available. To get them started, offer a few possible ways to show the content of the training. Suggest making a poster, performing a skit, setting the steps of a procedure to a nursery rhyme, singing information to the tune of a popular song, etc. Emphasize that they should be as creative as possible and that almost anything goes. The activity will not only offer a way to review content, but will add humor, interaction, and problem-solving opportunities to the session.

High Score—Divide trainees into three groups and designate them as Group A, Group B, and Group C. Have each group write two questions based on the information presented, using handouts, notes, or other resources. Then have the group put away the reference materials. Instruct Group A to ask Group B a question. Tell trainees to make their group's answer as complete as possible. Have Group C evaluate Group B's answer, using a rating scale of one to five (one is lowest, five is highest). Ask Group C to explain how Group B's answer could improve if the score is less than five. Then let Group B ask a question of Group C and have Group A evaluate the response and suggest improvement. Repeat until all three groups have asked their questions. Give small prizes to the group that scores highest. For a longer review, simply have the groups write more questions.

Taking Flight—Have each trainee write questions, important facts, or key points from the training on a piece of paper. Fold the paper to make airplanes. Then let the trainees throw the paper airplanes toward a hula hoop held up by a volunteer. The first one to get a plane inside the hoop wins a prize. Then unfold the airplanes, read the questions, and ask for volunteers to answer. For fun, give everyone a pilot's license afterward. The activity can stop here or be extended by having each participant get an airplane, read the question, and ask a volunteer to answer. Taking Flight also can be an icebreaker if trainees write their name and some information about themselves. Each trainee picks up someone else's plane, reads the information, and gets to know that person. The activity can be a needs-assessment tool if, at the beginning of a session, trainees write questions they want answered.

Circle Repetition—Ask trainees to sit in a circle. The first person states one bit of information about the content of the workshop. The second person repeats the first statement and adds another bit of information. Continue around the circle until the information is too much to remember or everyone has had a turn. This activity provides repetition in a fun way. It is most useful when training includes definitions or many short facts to learn.

Photo Review—Pass around photographs for discussion starters. For example, use photos of unsafe playground conditions or poorly arranged classrooms to discuss playground safety or room arrangement. For issues where the situation may be unclear, write a caption to go with the photograph. Write a description of what is happening in the photo. For example, if a photo is an adult talking to a child, describe what has happened and write what the adult is saying. Have partners or small groups critique the situations in the photos, describe the problems depicted, and discuss appropriate responses. Do not use anyone's classroom or playground as a negative example. Set up the classroom yourself for demonstration purposes and be sure trainees know that you set up the situation to depict problems. Let them know that the photos are for illustration, not actually the way the playground or classroom looked. Sometimes public playgrounds or backyard play equipment will provide opportunities to illustrate unsafe conditions. For black-and-white photos, copy the photographs on a copier to have sets for each group. If the copier is adjustable, set it to make the copies lighter than usual for better quality. Prints also can be put through a scanner to make several copies. Scanners work well with color or black-and-white prints. Another way to have enough copies is to take two or more photos of any situation you wish to depict, then ask for double prints.

Collage—Make a collage as a review activity. Have participants cut pictures from catalogs that remind them of content from the session. Afterward, they may take a few minutes to explain their collage to the rest of the group. The collage may be an individual, partner, or small group activity. If it is an individual activity, trainees can take it with them; if it is a partner or small group activity, it facilitates interaction.

Give One, Get One—This review activity requires participants to write down five key points from the session. Then, equipped with a list of participants in the session, each person approaches another person on the list and shares one key point with the other person. They then check off that person's name and continue until they have given and received a key point from each person in the group. In a large class, divide into smaller groups for this activity or it will take too long, and participants will lose interest.

Tic-Tac-Toe Memory Test—To review terminology or definitions, list and number the terms to review on an overhead transparency, flip chart, or poster. Have a list of the definitions handy for reference. Give trainees paper Tic-Tac-Toe grids. Have them write numbers randomly in each square of the grid. They should use the numbers from the list of terms. For example, if you have twelve terms, they should select from the numbers one through twelve. They will need at least nine terms or will need to use some numbers twice. Call out the definitions randomly, one at a time. Trainees must match the definition to the numbered term on the lists and cross the corresponding number off their Tic-Tac-Toe grid. When someone crosses off three numbers in a straight or diagonal line, that player is eligible to try for a prize. The trainee must correctly define each of the terms that correspond to the numbers crossed off her grid. An incorrect match of definition and term means the game continues. Play several times to give the group experience with all of the terms. A variation is to use more terms and a Bingo grid with a FREE space and have trainees get five across, down, or diagonally.

Card and Board Games for Review—To review and reinforce learning, card games and board games provide opportunities to discuss and apply knowledge. Card games for review can be a simple as drawing a card with a question or situation on it and discussing the answer or appropriate response with a partner or others in a group. Write one question on each card and turn them upside down between the players. Let players draw one at a time, then answer the question or react to the situation described. For board games, use any of the board games described pages 108-119. Or use a playing board and let players answer a question before they move their playing piece.

The Value of Overlearning

We know that a person forgets much of what is learned. As time goes by, participants may slip into old habits or "forget" what they knew when they left a training session. Consequently, overlearning (practicing past the level of mastery) is an important reinforcement tool. Studies have shown that overlearning can improve one's ability to use new skills and knowledge and to apply new concepts to more complex tasks. Overlearning builds confidence in the trainee and increases the chances that the trainee will perform as expected on the job. Overlearning helps trainees decrease their response time, learn to perform without hesitation, and increase their ability to use information correctly.

Overlearning requires much review and reinforcement. Overlearning is the practice that forms habits that are performed almost without thought. For overlearning to occur, a concept to be mastered must be repeated and presented in a variety of ways. The concept may be a topic for a small group discussion and also included as questions on a worksheet. It may be discussed in the overview at the beginning of the session and also presented as a game activity.

We know that individuals must use information for the information to become a part of their repertoire. Since our goal is to form new habits of working, facilitating overlearning is an important skill for a trainer; accordingly, opportunities to practice a skill are important components of training.

Memory Aids

Using Associations—When trainees fully understand the general principles behind what they are learning, they are more likely to apply the new skills. Analogies help trainees understand general principles. Associations help trainees remember key information by giving them something with which to link new information. Associations can be objects that emphasize ideas visually and make them easy to remember. Here are some possibilities:

Tool Box—Present a toy tool box with the tools labeled to represent the techniques you are presenting. For example, in a workshop on discipline, have tools labeled redirection, active listening, ignoring, praise for appropriate behavior, etc. As each technique is discussed, use the tool as a visual aid to hold trainees' attention and help them remember the technique. The activity emphasizes that the techniques are tools that you use to solve a problem, not an end in themselves.

Keys—Write key ideas or points to remember on infant toy keys or on keys made from poster board or construction paper. Use the keys as memory aids. A variation is to write the terms on keys cut from colored transparency sheets and show them on an overhead projector.

First-aid Kit—Label some common first-aid item containers with the skills or steps that address a problem. For example, to "fix" a biting problem, vitamin bottles might be labeled with prevention techniques and a bottle of antiseptic spray might represent treating the injury. An adhesive bandage box could remind trainees what to do about the child who bit, and a thermometer box might represent assessing the situation. A prescription pad could symbolize the importance of recording information and communicating with parents.

Using Acronyms—Acronyms are words formed from the first letter of several other words. Acronyms are useful memory aids, especially for steps in a process or procedures. For example, FACE UP to Biting can stand for using the following steps to address biting issues with toddlers:

FACE UP TO BITING
F ocus on the bitten child
A ttend to the wound
C omfort the bitten child
E valuate the cause and circumstances
U nderstand the developmental aspects of biting
P revent some of the causes of biting:
      Duplicate toys
      Supervision
      Teach the words

Here are other examples of acronyms that link learning how to plan with a theme of dental health:

Put **TEETH** in Your Plans

pick a	**T**heme
	Evaluate resources
Select	**E**xperiences
	Teach—set up, interact
enjoy	**H**appy children

Here is a way to teach dental health:

B R U S H

B ooks, pictures
R esources—toys, equipment, supplies, scrounged materials on the topic
U nits—planned activities
S ongs, music, and movement activities
H appy children, happy teachers, happy parents

Supervised Practice—Give trainees opportunities to ask questions and to experiment with new skills and behaviors in a safe environment. Supervised practice gives trainees the chance to gain confidence while learning. It gives the trainer a chance to evaluate mastery and adapt or reinforce instruction. It is the time to provide constructive feedback that focuses on the trainee's specific needs. Supervised practice provides an opportunity to help trainees make a direct connection between the training and their job responsibilities. It gives the trainer an opening to demonstrate that the new methods are easier, faster, better, or otherwise beneficial to the trainee.

Giving Feedback—Feedback is essential as trainees try out new skills. Feedback is more than just telling trainees how well they are doing. Here are suggestions for providing feedback during supervised practice:

- Observe actual performance closely.
- Describe what you see while it is fresh on your mind.
- Be as specific and objective as possible.
- Focus your comments on what you observed, why it is important, and what needs to happen for improvement.
- Ask questions to assess trainee's understanding.
- Ask for the trainee's view of his progress and of your comments.
- Provide feedback even to trainees who do not seem to want it.
- Suggest the next step—what does the trainee need to do to continue to improve?

Sometimes it is difficult for a trainer to give constructive criticism, and sometimes it is hard for a trainee to receive criticism. Finding a way to take the sting out of criticism is important in soothing egos and preventing hurt feelings and anxiety. Here are suggestions for steps to follow in constructive criticism:

1. Ask the trainee for two areas in which he felt he did well. Allowing him to critique himself first eliminates the risk that he will simply repeat the comments you make.
2. Give two areas you observed as strengths. State some specifics about why the actions or ways of doing the task were good.
3. Ask for two areas in which the trainee felt he could improve. Because trainees are frequently excessively critical of their performance, limiting this request to two will keep the trainee focused. Probing as to how he thinks he might improve will help him think about needed changes.
4. Give two areas that need improvement. Phrases such as "Here is a suggestion," "Another way is to...," or "You will find it helpful to..." are some tactful ways to word feedback comments.

Handouts and Job Aids

Handouts and job aids can be references when participants return to the job or attempt new tasks without the help of an instructor. Handouts and job aids must be clear and understandable and designed to be useful outside the training situation. Poor, hard-to-read, or unattractive copies are unlikely to be used or even kept after the session. Information or instructions that are not easy to understand are less likely to be used.

Design handouts with the expectation that participants will keep them as a reference. Include enough information to be helpful, but not so much that participants will set them aside. Put your name, address, and telephone number on handouts to make it convenient for participants to contact you with questions that come up later.

A job aid is anything that helps workers implement what they have learned. Job aids serve as a reference and reminder for how and when to do a task, and under what circumstances. Charts showing the proper way to diaper, signs reminding employees to wash their hands, check lists of the steps required to complete a form, and help screens on computers are examples of job aids. Job aids help persons successfully learn new tasks by reminding them of the proper steps at the time they need to know.

When a task is new and must be learned, or when a task is done infrequently, job aids are an important means of assisting the learning process. They can serve to reinforce learning. They remind trainees about key points and help them to keep applying new skills. Job aids may be instructions on an index card, a tent card with information, a sticker, or a poster. Even a sticky note stuck on a computer with instructions is an example of a job aid.

A list of steps to take, a checklist of what to do, and a chart of how to perform a task are all examples of job aids. Job aids should be brief and placed in the location where the task will be carried out. A diaper-changing chart should be above a diapering table; instructions for preparing snacks should be near the snack supplies; an evacuation chart should be posted in a very prominent location. Job aids provide a transition between more detailed manuals or instructions and the trainee's ability to perform a task from memory.

List of Steps as a Job Aid

Following is an example of a job aid that reminds personnel of van operation procedures.

• •

Instructions for Using Van

Before leaving:
1. Write down the odometer reading. Fill in the destination, time, and your name in the blanks provided.
2. Check the gasoline gauge.
3. If you need gas, request a purchase order from the secretary.
4. Everyone must wear seatbelts.
5. Upon arrival at your destination, record the odometer reading again.

Upon return:
1. Record the odometer reading.
2. Report any problems or difficulties to the director.
3. If the gas gauge is less than 1/4 tank, report it to the director.

Do not remove these instructions or the odometer log from the van.

• •

Checklists as Job Aids—Checklists can take many forms. They can help trainees evaluate their performance and whether they have met their goals. They can help trainees remember the specific steps to a process they are learning until the steps become a habit. Here is a sample checklist for closing a classroom at the end of the day:

• •

Closing Checklist

___ Be sure all trash cans are emptied and no open food is left in the room.
___ Verify that all children have been signed out and note any problems.
___ Complete attendance records, incident reports, and sickness or accident reports and take to office.
___ Notify the director of any incidents, accidents, or any concerns expressed by parents.
___ Flush toilets, check supplies of toilet paper, tissue, and paper towels.
___ Return any audiovisual equipment to the storage unit.
___ Lock supply cabinets.
___ Have lesson plans on clipboard and gather all materials and supplies for the next day.
___ Straighten shelves and place new materials out for the next day.
___ Sign out and have a good evening!

●●

It is easy to create checklists and charts to use as job aids. Simply list the things that need to be done and follow these tips:

- List the specific steps in the order that they should be taken.
- Keep the wording simple and clear.
- Actually checking off the steps as they are taken may be necessary for complex tasks or when trainees are first implementing a new skill.
- Include information about time requirements such as when tasks should be done.
- Be clear about how trainees are to document that the tasks are done—initialing, signing, or dating it.

Charts as Job Aids—Charts such as those that show the steps in administering CPR, charts listing common first-aid procedures, and information about communicable diseases are good uses of charts as job aids. Here are some guidelines to make charts effective in helping transfer of learning:

- Keep the wording simple.
- Catchy phrases add interest, but must not detract from the message.
- Use illustrations to clarify information.
- Place charts near the areas where they are likely to be used.
- Make the words and illustrations large enough to be seen from the location where the chart will be viewed.

Other useful charts to make during training are ones that show the learning that occurs when children are in various interest centers. These charts can be reminders for staff as well as parents about the value of blocks, dramatic play, art, and other regular activities. Here is a sample chart to remind trainees of the value of play. Charts like this in interest areas also help educate parents on the purpose of activities.

225

> **Through play, children learn:**
>
> Cooperation
> Language
> Problem-solving
> Coordination
> Math and science
> Roles and responsibilities

Preventing Relapse

Trainers and administrators alike are disappointed when participants leave a training setting and then do not implement what they learned. For training to be successful, there must be a partnership between the trainee who recognizes the need for new skills and information, the trainer who designs and delivers the training, and the director who supports the learning and application on the job. This three-part training partnership is essential to see that training is effectively implemented. Besides the lack of a strong training partnership, some of the most common reasons that trainees do not implement what they learn are:

- Co-workers may not support the new behaviors. Co-workers may even pressure the trainee to return to old behaviors.
- Trainees may doubt their ability to use the new skills when they are away from the training environment.
- There is a backlog of work at the work site that they must complete, causing the trainee to rely on the easiest, quickest, and well-known method.
- Trainees may not have had enough experience with the new skills and have not fully mastered them.
- Support in the form of materials, supplies, or encouragement may be lacking from administration.
- Trainees may wait too long to attempt new behavior and forget what they learned.

Some techniques that can be helpful in preventing relapse are:

- Recognize that some relapse may be unavoidable, then work to minimize it through planning.
- Provide numerous activities to facilitate transfer such as overlearning.
- Anticipate the problem areas likely to cause relapse.
- Evaluate and assist the trainees' skills in contending with negative pressure and understanding of co-workers' attitudes.
- Enlist the support and assistance of the trainees' supervisors.
- Provide ongoing support when lapses are likely to occur.
- Include a peer-coaching component or buddy system to involve co-workers.
- Provide follow-up support on the job when possible.
- Make the training event very visible and provide recognition to those who attended.

ACTIVITIES TO FACILITATE TRANSFER OF LEARNING

Specific activities can help trainees make the transition to implement new skills on the job. Many of the review and reinforcement activities also help with transfer.

Brick Wall—Have participants identify barriers to accomplishing a task. For example, if the topic is planning, participants may say they cannot plan adequately because of a lack of time, skills, or resources. As each barrier is identified, the participant naming the barrier uses a cardboard brick to build a wall. Write the barrier on a sticky note or on an index card and attach it to the brick with masking tape. Continue identifying barriers until a wall is constructed. Then ask participants for ways to break down the barriers. Each participant who offers a suggestion about how to remove or overcome a barrier gets to take down a brick.

Graffiti Board—Post a large sheet of butcher paper on the wall. The paper should be large enough that several people can get to it at a time. Before they leave, ask participants to write one thing they are going to do differently. If the group is large, allow participants to write after they finish other activities to prevent a rush at the end of the session. Or you can post several sheets around the room to spread out the writers.

Make Your Mark—To make a commitment to change, have trainees make a hand print on a banner labeled, "Make Your Mark!" Ask them to write their name, the date, and what they are going to do differently under their hand print. Have several shallow pans of tempera paint to make prints and plenty of paper towels for cleaning hands.

Watered Down—How Change Influences Others—To help trainees understand the dynamics of making changes, show them a half-full glass of water. Dip a colored marker in the water until the water becomes tinted. Relate to how change is gradual and how one person (the marker) can influence others (the water that becomes tinted). Then pour the glass into a pitcher of water to dilute the color. Relate to how training or progress can have an effect on others but also can be diluted by those who have not had the same experience. Others (the water in the pitcher) may not accept the changes and dilute the effect of training (the colored water in the glass). Ask for suggestions on implementing new techniques in the workplace and in building support so that the new learning will not be diluted.

Mental Wizards—Ask participants to make mental notes of key points they want to remember during the presentation and to remember how many they made. Then ask them to make written notes of the key points they selected. The writing task itself will reinforce learning and facilitate recall. Spend a few minutes periodically during the session and again at the end of the session having participants recall the key points. Ask them to repeat the procedure one hour after the session ends, again three hours later, and once more the next day. Spaced repetition and recall will help participants retain what they have learned.

Olympics—Olympics is a good review technique to stimulate participation. Divide participants into teams. Keep score as follows: Each time a team member answers a question correctly or volunteers, the team gets a point. Have a scorekeeper who records the points and the reason they were awarded to the team. At the end, review the scores and summarize the information the teams contributed. Give Olympic-style medals to the winning team.

Visualization—Allow time for trainees to visualize what it will be like as they apply new skills. Ask them to imagine how it looks, sounds, and feels. Visualization will help them see the benefit of changing and make a commitment to use the new skills. What they can imagine, they can do!

Affirmations—An affirmation is a statement that describes a result. Affirmation is used successfully as a technique for such desired changes as losing weight, improving self-esteem, and maintaining positive attitudes. Affirmation is, in essence, telling yourself repeatedly what you plan to do. Ask trainees to repeat the affirmation at least five to six times a day for the next month. To help them remember, make job aids or reminders to post in conspicuous places. Ask them to post the reminders by the telephone, the computer, a bulletin board, or any place that they see many times a day.

Affirmation statements should be positive—what is to be done, not what is not to be done. For example, "I will eat at least four servings of fruits and vegetables a day" rather than "I will not eat sweets." Many find it helpful to specify how much or when. Here are some examples:

> I will complete my lesson plans every Friday by 3 p.m.
> I will hold a conversation with every child, every day.
> I will tactfully remind my assistant of the goals for her work at least weekly.
> I will write a personal note to each parent, each week.
> I will use at least thirty minutes of naptime to plan and prepare.
> I will arrive at work at least fifteen minutes early to be calm and at ease.
> I will reduce stress by exercising at least three times a week for at least twenty minutes.

Group Action Plans—Have trainees make a group plan for applying new skills once they return to the job. Trainees can select the skills that they collectively need, exchange ideas on how to implement them, and list ways to overcome barriers. A group plan entails making a commitment to the group and will increase the likelihood that the changes will occur.

Bubbles of Opportunities—Blow bubbles, using a purchased solution or your own. If the group is large, have several volunteers blowing bubbles as well. Ask participants to catch as many bubbles as they can. Relate catching the bubbles to pursuing ideas or courses of action. One cannot do everything, so we must choose goals that are possible. Some ideas, like some of the bubbles, may be out of reach. If you choose one or two achievable goals and

6 CUPS WATER

1 CUP DISHWASHING LIQUID

2 TABLESPOONS CORN SYRUP

pursue them, they are easily within your grasp. Some opportunities, like the bubbles, may be quickly lost. Use the experience at the end of a session and ask, "Which of the ideas presented today are you going to pursue?"

Simple Bubble Recipe
1 cup (250 mL) hand dishwashing liquid (use a brand that
    produces a lot of suds)
2 tablespoons (30 mL) corn syrup
6 cups (1.5 L) of water

Contracts and Letters—Written contracts can help stimulate trainees to commit to change. Signing one's name on the dotted line supports commitment. Contracts describe explicit expectations and should spell out the specifics of performance to help ensure commitment. Contracts for trainees should include what they will do and when. Ask trainees to read the contract carefully before they sign. If trainees are writing the terms of the contract, have them spend enough time to think thoroughly about what they will commit to doing. The goals they set must be realistic as well as challenging.

Mailing contracts and letters to trainees following a session accomplishes several tasks. When trainees receive a letter or a copy of a contract in the mail several weeks after the training, they are immediately reminded of the training and what they planned to do differently. Receiving a letter or contract with a personal note from the instructor helps trainees see the instructor as caring and interested in their progress. Carbonless paper used for contracts allows the trainer to keep a copy and the participant to have one as a reminder to take home. Here are several types of contracts:

Contract with Myself—Pass around the form on page 294 in the Appendix and ask participants to review it. Discuss the factors that might prevent them from implementing the changes they have learned. Ask trainees to make a commitment to the changes that are within their control and to work to address factors that may hinder implementation. Remind them that the goals they set for themselves in the contract must be reasonable and attainable. Then give each one an envelope in which to place the contract. Ask trainees to address the envelope to themselves. Tell them that they will get the contract from you in a few weeks, and they should use the contract to check to see how well they are doing. A reminder to oneself is often accepted better than a reminder from someone else.

Letter to the Instructor—At the end of a session, distribute the form on page 295 in the Appendix and discuss its purpose. Ask trainees to send the form back to you by a date two to three weeks following the session to help you evaluate your work. Remind them to be candid and frank and share their insights and the discouragement they might feel. Then give them an envelope addressed to you in which to place the form when they complete it several weeks following the session.

Letter to the Parents—Writing a letter to the parents of the children with whom they work is a good way for trainees to build support for change. Helping the parents understand the value of training is important to support a trainee's efforts to improve. It is a good technique for educating the parents about the appropriateness of the changes that are happening. A sample letter to parents is on page 296 in the Appendix.

Action Plans—Action planning is another way of assisting with transfer of learning and implementation of new skills. An action plan is a document generated by setting goals, identifying activities to reach those goals, and establishing a timeline for reaching them. When the plan involves more than one person, identify the person responsible for each component of the plan. Action planning is a good strategy to use when training involves staff who work together. Here is a sample plan for a program that wants to improve their policies and procedures for arranging for substitutes.

ACTION PLAN

Outcomes (Goals)	Activities	Deadline	People
Develop a written procedure for arranging for substitutes.	Gather resource materials related to substitutes and substitute policies. Distribute copies of useful articles or information to staff.	September 15	Mary Johnson
	Gather all memos and existing written materials related to substitutes and distribute copies to staff.	September 15	Ed Hernandez
	Hold a staff meeting to review written materials and resources, brainstorm ideas, and select Substitute Committee to draft procedures and distribute to other staff members.	September 29	LaTonja Williams to notify and facilitate
	Draft a document for review by other staff.	October 14	Substitute Committee
	Finalize document.	November 1	Substitute Committee
	Hold staff meeting so everyone understands any new procedures and has a copy.	November 8	LaTonja Williams to notify and facilitate
	Evaluate document to revise if needed.	December 1	Substitute Committee

After the Workshop: Follow-up Activities

Following up after the training can help participants use the information or new skills on the job. When participants return to the work site, they sometimes encounter unexpected problems or they find that they did not fully understand something. By planning follow-up activities, the instructor can help with the transfer of learning. Remember to set a deadline for follow-up activities and give the directions in writing.

Response Cards or Forms—Giving participants addressed envelopes and forms to complete and mail later will help them implement what they learned. Response cards may be printed postcards or blank cards given out with a request for trainees to write a few comments about how they are implementing the new skills. Response forms can be questionnaires or evaluations that participants return a few days after the training. The value of response cards and forms is that they remind trainees of what they learned and the need to apply it on the job. Another benefit is that the act of completing the card or form requires the trainee to think about the training. Using such follow-up techniques will also help evaluate the effectiveness of the training.

Consider summarizing the responses from the trainees in a newsletter and sending the information to all trainees along with additional material. Success stories from others can be a support and stimulus to further improvement and can reduce relapse. Seeing one's name in print or receiving recognition for progress can be a good motivater for continued improvement.

Telephone Calls—About two weeks after the training, take time to call the participants. Sometimes trainees have questions after they get back to the job, but will not take the time to contact the instructor. They often will ask questions if you initiate the contact and give them an easy opportunity. The telephone call can serve as a means of evaluating your own effectiveness and assessing additional training needs. It also demonstrates that you care about trainees' progress.

Letters to Participants—A letter sent to participants two to three weeks after the training can be a reminder of what they learned. The letter can provide new information or answer any questions that went unanswered during the training. With word-processing programs, even individual letters can be printed quickly. Letters sent after training help trainees recognize that the trainer cares about their progress and how they are doing.

Even a form letter is helpful in reminding trainees of what they learned when individual letters are not possible. To save time, have participants address envelopes or postcards to themselves during the training to make it easy to send them follow-up notes or information.

Points for Performance—Allocate points for specific actions that you want to take place on the job. Ask trainees to achieve a certain number of points by a specific date, at which time they will report by telephone or by postcard.

Here is a sample Points for Performance assignment for a session on Creative Art:

Dear Trainees:

During the next two weeks, give yourself points according to the following chart. Please try to accumulate at least 100 points by (insert date). Please contact me by telephone at (insert telephone number) within one week following the due date to tell me your total points. At that time, I also will wish to talk to you about how you are doing in improving your art program. Please feel free to contact me if you have any questions about this assignment or your work in creative art.

Sincerely,

(signature)

Points	Activity
1 point	Displaying a child's artwork.
1 point	Talking to a child about his or her art.
1 point	Sending artwork home with a child
2 points	Talking to a parent about a child's artwork
2 points	Explaining to a co-worker the value of children's art
2 points	Incorporating some recycled materials into your art program you have not used before
3 points	Trying some art materials you have never used before
3 points	Explaining developmental stages of art to a co-worker
3 points	Helping a co-worker learn to do an art activity you learned at this workshop
4 points	Writing an anecdotal record about a child's art
4 points	Trying one of the new art activities you learned in this session
4 points	Trying a new art activity that you found from a resource book
5 points	Writing a parent letter or newsletter article about children's art
5 points	Speaking at a parent meeting about the value of children's art
5 points	Leading a staff meeting discussing children's art

Building a Supportive Environment

Part of the training success will depend on creating an environment for change. Trainees must have support as they work to learn new tasks and implement new behaviors. This support can come in many forms.

Help participants feel success as they take steps toward changing how they perform tasks. This likely will mean that supervisors and managers must be involved in support roles. Administrators must recognize and encourage trainees' attempts to implement new ways of doing things. Many a participant has returned to work full of new ideas, only to be devastated by "That's too messy!" "It won't work here," or "That's not the way we do it." Without understanding and support at the work site, there will be limited progress in changing behavior. Involve administrators in the actual training activity whenever possible so they fully understand the changes needed. Have several persons from the same site attend training together to provide support for each other back on the job. Here are some additional suggestions for building a supportive environment for change:

Support Groups—Organizing a group of trainees to meet and discuss progress can keep trainees moving forward in implementing new skills. Ongoing meetings offer opportunities to reinforce new skills and concepts. Give participants time during the training to arrange meetings. Let them know they can call upon you for additional information and help. Provide for an exchange of addresses and telephone numbers to support the effort. For best results, try to make the support groups include five to eight people. Fewer than five places a heavy burden on each participant in terms of contribution and energy, and the group may fizzle if a few are absent. Groups larger than eight may not feel they have enough time for full participation. Some may feel intimidated in a larger group and not be as open and candid with their comments.

The instructor may be a part of the group as a participant, an observer, or a resource person. The instructor should seek to play a lesser role as time goes by, and the group takes on its own direction. If the instructor is not able to attend the meetings regularly, an occasional visit is helpful to the group.

The group may not need a formal organization, but a small amount of structure can help keep a focus. Preparing some topics or questions for the first few meetings will help fledging groups. The following guidelines may be helpful as a support group organizes:

• The purpose of the group is to support and help each other.
• The discussion in the group is confidential so the members can be candid.
• Members do not judge, criticize, or evaluate each other.
• Each person makes it a priority to attend.
• The group meets on a regular schedule set well in advance.

Provide Recognition Systems—Recognition systems such as friendly competition, displays of work, or reunion events help with retention and reduce relapse. Having others notice the new skills and abilities will reinforce the continued use of the skills. Certificates, plaques, and ribbons are easy ways to provide recognition of achievement.

Reunion Events—When trainees have been together for a period of time, they develop friendships and form bonds with each other. Reunion events held several weeks after training ends provide opportunities for networking and becoming reacquainted. Alumni reunion events can be a celebration such as a party or dinner or even another training session specifically designed to follow up on earlier training. These events offer a time for trainees to share their common experiences, receive recognition, and get additional help.

Transfer Partnership Notebook—A transfer partnership notebook is a loose-leaf binder in which to insert handouts and other training material. The notebook should contain an activity sheet in the front that documents that the trainee's supervisor has reviewed the training material and provided support for implementing the changes to be made. A regular review of the training notebook can keep the information and skills fresh, increasing the impact the training will make. The notebook can include additional materials on the topic that the trainee has found. A transfer partnership notebook can be organized in many ways, but the essential component is that the trainee and the supervisor review the information in it.

Administration Support—Request that administrators support trainees as they work to implement new skills. Ask that trainees be allowed to share with others what they have learned. Teaching others reinforces learning by the one doing the teaching as well as providing information to the learner. Ask that the administrator provide support to trainees by allowing them to:

- Share what they learned at a staff meeting.
- Show information through a bulletin board.
- Put an article in a newsletter or write a parent letter about the training.
- Teach others at work what they learned.
- Make a display about the new activities.

Providing Materials and Supplies

If trainees do not have what they need to put new procedures in place, progress will be limited. Even if trainees get materials they need several weeks after training, the information will not be fresh by then and motivation may be gone. Give participants sample forms, copies of articles, and other resources to facilitate implementation. Provide access to videos you use in training for review at their leisure or to share with other staff. If there is no ready source of materials, give trainees ideas for free or inexpensive substitutes. Provide lists of suggested books, videos, tapes, and records related to the training that they can check out from their library. Let them know how easy it is to get materials from their local library and what items are available.

Logistical Matters: Whatever Can Go Wrong, Will

It is the nightmare of all facilitators. The video essential to the presentation cannot be used because the VCR will not work properly. An activity that has always been very popular bombs this time for no apparent reason. The audience is not the size expected, and much of the plan must be scrapped. An essential box of props did not arrive at the training site as promised, and they are needed for trainees to understand the concepts presented. When disaster strikes, keep a sense of humor and proceed to Plan B. The following suggestions will help you adapt and adjust when the best-laid plans go awry:

Workshop First-aid Kit and Emergency Plan

A workshop first-aid kit has saved many a training session. Keep a supply of essentials available in a tote bag or a box to grab up and go on a moment's notice. Tape, scissors, name tags, pens and pencils, dry-erase markers and erasers, chalk and an eraser, index cards, sticky notes, and an extension cord with a three-pronged adapter will all come in handy eventually. Other useful items are stickers or other small items that can be rewards for participation and short quotations or inspirational readings to use as fillers. A supply of transparency sheets with markers allows you to change the way you present information if you need to adapt with little notice. If you often travel to training by car, keep a flip chart pad and easel and a dry-erase board with markers in the trunk.

Every trainer needs a few tricks that are fun and adaptable to many groups and various situations. This bag of tricks should include all materials for quick activities to use on the spur of the moment. Team-building experiences often work to get a group focused if they lack unity or to get them back on track if they have lost cohesiveness. Asking participants to write their most pressing problem on an index card that you can review will often give you insight into the real needs of participants. Put the materials for your bag of tricks into your workshop first-aid kit so you will always be prepared.

You may be asked to fill in for someone who had to cancel suddenly or who asked to conduct an extra session when attendance is more than expected. Keep your training materials in close proximity to each other. Invariably, time is limited, and you may have little time to look for items. Tote boxes are great for storing all the materials for a session together.

When shipping items to a training site, take along your original handouts and the most important items just in case your shipment does not arrive on time. As a precaution, ship your materials to arrive before you leave home so that if you find they did not arrive, you can put more materials in an extra suitcase. Twenty-four-hour copy services make it possible to produce new handouts at any time of day or night. If your material may need revising after you arrive at the training location, take a computer disk with your data and information on it. If you need to rework your presentation at a borrowed or rented computer, you will have what you need on the disk. Keep information about where to purchase supplies or where business services are available for the areas you travel to frequently.

Preventing and Coping with Training Disasters

Every trainer will eventually be faced with a disaster. Regardless of the preparation, there will be communication breakdowns and unexpected emergencies that call for resourcefulness and adaptability. Here are ways to prevent and cope with disasters in the training arena:

Arrive early—The room may not be set up as you requested. There may be few or no electrical outlets where you need them. You may need to adjust lighting or arrange for a display table. Arrive well ahead of time to make needed changes and still be set up and ready to greet trainees as they arrive. Nothing gets a trainer off to a worse start than to come rushing in at the last minute or not be ready when participants get there. Arriving early helps you to feel in control and frees you to adjust as needed.

Flexibility and Resourcefulness—Training requires numerous skills. A good trainer must have knowledge and many experiences to draw upon, especially when a session is not going as well as it should. A good trainer must be able to adapt to the audience and react to the group. Being flexible is essential. Be ready to change a small group activity into a partner activity if necessary. Be prepared to shorten or lengthen activities or to substitute another activity when things are not going well.

When you are aware of a problem ahead of time, this is your chance to show creativity and problem-solving skills. Look around the meeting room and see what you can substitute for missing items or use to create a new activity. Look into your bag of tricks and see what you have. Adapt, adapt, and adapt again.

Group Size Is Not What You Expected—Someone forgot to tell you that an extra fifteen people are attending your session! You had planned for four small groups, but now that will not work with the extra attendees. What can you do? Do you have materials for six groups instead? Can you adapt the activity to a whole group experience? Do you have enough materials to make it a partner activity? Is there a way you can make more materials?

You expected twenty-five, but only four are here and it is already time to start. A very large group can be difficult to work with, but a very small group may be hard to motivate. Having a small group will likely mean that your planned activities do not take as long because the discussion is shorter or trainees do not participate as much. What can you do additionally that is worthwhile? How can you get trainees to participate? How can you take advantage of the small size and personalize the session?

Tips for Very Small Groups—Provide structured response and comment time to get everyone to talk. Suggestions for structured responses are in Participation and Personality Issues in this chapter on page 207. Bring the participants close together. A few people spread out in a large room is a barrier to communication and interaction. Take advantage of the opportunity to individualize the session by finding out more about the attendees through icebreaker or other activities to better address their needs. Ask participants to write their names in large print on their nametags or on name tent cards so that you can call them by name.

Tips for Very Large Groups—Be sure the sound is adequate. A large group that cannot hear compounds the difficulty. Recognize that participation is more difficult. Participants are often reluctant to speak up in a very large group. Divide into smaller groups or use individual or partner activities.

Audiovisual Equipment Doesn't Work—When audiovisual equipment will not work and cannot be replaced in time for the session, it pays to have posters, overhead transparencies, handouts, or other materials with much of the same information. While these may not be as effective as the planned video, it does allow one to cover the content in spite of the mishap. Having other materials to reinforce the information is a good practice even if there is no equipment problem since reinforcement and repetition are important.

The Plan Just Isn't Working—The best-laid plans sometimes go astray. Sometimes an activity just does not work with a group, even if it has worked very well before. The dynamics of each group make a difference in how the group reacts to any activity. What can you do? Have a few alternative activities that you can use. Take time to brainstorm with the group about their needs. Ask them for suggestions on appropriate learning activities or give them a choice. When they suggest an activity or have choices, they will usually participate better. Feel free to cut short an activity that is not working and move on to the next one.

Participants Are Not Responsive—There are many reasons why a trainer may not get the expected responses. Perhaps the trainees were required to attend and are resisting the directive. There may be concerns such as rumors of layoffs that bother them. There may be stress caused from recent expansion or new services. They may not see the value in the training or feel they already know enough about the topic. It may be that they simply had something else they wanted or needed to do. Whatever the reasons, several things may help:

Mixing Up—Divide and Conquer—When people work together, they tend to have had similar experiences at the work site. As a result, they may not interact with each other and the interchange of ideas may not be as good as when participants are from different work settings. Suggestions for separating those who work together are given in Chapter 2 on page 50.

Involve Participants More—Hands-on and Small Group Activities—Asking questions and listening to concerns will sometimes open up discussion. Pull out an activity that involves everyone in hands-on or small groups.

Move Around—Circulating and walking around the room will often stimulate participation. Speaking individually with trainees may help. Call them by name often so they cannot be anonymous or lost in the group.

I Can—To get a volunteer, randomly pass out cards with the statements shown here. To target a particular trainee for participation, be sure he gets card number seven. "I Can" is a good way to select a spokesperson for a small group activity, too. The activity adds humor when participants realize how they have been selected. State the instructions that call for a volunteer, then ask for those with cards to read their cards in numerical order:

1—That is a wonderful idea
2—I like it, too
3—Let's do it now
4—We need a volunteer
5—Who would be a good person to do it?
6—Yes, I wonder who feels they can do it?
7—I can

Getting Them Back from Breaks—Another type of distracter is the straggler who returns from breaks after the designated time or who continues personal discussions after the session reconvenes. Here are tips for getting trainees back in their seats and ready to continue:

Holiday Noisemakers—Enlist the help of several enthusiastic assistants. Use New Year's Eve or Halloween noisemakers to announce that the break is ending. At the appropriate time, each assistant goes to a group of participants and blows or shakes the noisemakers. Usually the fun will be enough to nudge stragglers back. This is an especially useful method when a large group spreads out over a wide area. The technique relieves the instructor from having to herd the group back into the training room. The instructor can be ready and waiting to greet trainees when they enter.

Timer—Use a simple kitchen timer set to go off at the time break is to end. The timer removes the human element and provides an objective means to designate that the time has ended. Timers are equally useful to designate the time that small group activities will end. For small group activities, set the timer for five minutes before time is up to give the groups time to wrap up and to demonstrate how to handle transitions.

Door Prizes—Announce before the break that you will draw for a door prize five minutes before the scheduled starting time. Then draw names at the appointed time, requiring winners to be present. Drawing for door prizes early is particularly good for ongoing classes where it is easy for persons to be increasingly late returning from break or getting to the class at the beginning.

Save the Day with Humor

Whatever the training disaster, humor is often the way to get participants to respond and ignore the unexpected difficulties. Use an activity that is fun and funny. Humor can help a group gel and change the mood of the room even when there are problems. Keep a supply of generic humorous activities on hand and readily available. Here are a few:

Great Truths Children Learn

Print the following statements on index cards or pieces of construction paper. Distribute them to participants to read aloud. Let the groups make up some of their own.

- You can't bathe cats in the bathtub.
- If your mother says "no," go ask your grandmother.
- If your brother hits you, don't hit back. They always catch the second person.
- No matter how long you work at it, you can't put toothpaste back in the tube.
- Ice cream will make your skinned knee quit hurting.
- You can't hide spinach in a glass of milk.
- When your sister is mad at you, don't let her brush your hair.

- Only Superman may wear his underwear on the outside.
- Never ask your two-year-old brother to hold a ripe tomato.
- If it follows you home, you get to keep it.
- You can't trust dogs to watch your hamburger.
- The side of the car you are not on will have the best scenery.
- Don't sneeze when someone is cutting your hair.
- Puppies still have bad breath even if you give them a breath mint.
- Don't ask, "Are we there yet?" more than once every five miles.
- Never hold a vacuum cleaner and a cat at the same time.
- Spaghetti sticks to the wall.

Hypothetical Questions
Use these questions in the same way as Great Truths.

- Why do we call it "rush hour" when your car can hardly move?
- If we plant a tree, can we tree a plant?
- If a store is open 24 hours a day, 365 days a year, why do they need locks on the doors?
- Why do we call them bathing suits when we don't take a bath in them?
- Milk cartons say, "Open Here" but have you ever seen one that says, "Open Somewhere Else?"
- Why does sour cream have a "use by" date?
- If it's a circular drive, how do you get in and out of it?
- Who turns out the light inside the refrigerator?
- Why is it when you deliver something by car it's called a shipment, and when you deliver something by boat it's called cargo?
- Why do we still refer to a phone "dial" when there isn't one?
- How do "Don't Walk on the Grass" signs get there if no one can walk on the grass?
- If toast always lands butter-side down and cats always land on their feet, what would happen if you strapped the buttered toast on the back of the cat and dropped them both?
- Why do we call it a field trip when we never go to a field?
- If olive oil comes from olives, corn oil from corn, and sunflower oil from sunflowers, where do we get baby oil?
- Has anyone ever forgotten how to ride a bicycle?
- Why do they call it a "garage sale" when the garage is not for sale?

Survival Kits—To help maintain a sense of humor, ask participants what they would put in a survival kit. Give them a few ideas to get them started, identifying what one must know and skills needed that nobody tells you about.

Directors' Survival Kit
- How to use a plumber's helper "Why can't they remember to put the paper towels in the trash can?"
- How to say, "It's time to pay your fee" in fifty-two different ways so you don't sound like a recording every week.
- How to select the right nut, bolt, screw, nail, washer, tape, hook to repair the

wagon, door hinge, doll bed, chair, water table, truck, easel.

- How to select and use the right pliers, screwdriver, hammer, wrench to do above.
- At least ten ways to "make the hurt go away" for all those skinned knees, scrapes, bruises, and insect bites that are a necessary part of active play.

Infant Caregivers' Survival Kit
- At least five ways to remove formula stains—one for each day of the week.
- How to hold two infants at a time.
- Four ways to play Peek-a-Boo.
- Hundreds of ways to reassure mothers of newly enrolled infants that you are competent.

Time-saving Tips

The busy trainer rarely has enough time for all the preparation that is essential to effective training. Active training for adults is dependent on resources and materials. There are handouts to prepare, games and materials to create, props and supplies to locate. All of these take time. How does one make the most of the preparation time that one has? Here are some suggestions:

Organizing Materials

Many hours are wasted looking for things that have been misplaced or misfiled. If you cannot find items you cannot use them—and training will suffer. Organize materials for easy and quick retrieval, then always take the time to return them to their designated storage places. Time spent organizing and storing will be returned in time saved preparing; it will also reduce frustration. Whatever the reason you have limited time, organization will help you meet the challenges.

Organizing materials will reduce time spent searching for or re-creating materials. Making copies of a handout requires far less time than remaking the handout and then making copies. Using games you have already developed will eliminate time needed to make new ones. The more training you do, the more difficult the organizing task becomes, but at the same time the more necessary it is. Whichever way you organize your materials, the essential measure of effectiveness is that the system must work for you.

Filing and Finding

Where is that handout original I made last month? The one that took me two hours to create? If I cannot find it, either as a hardcopy or on my computer, it will take another two hours to redo it, and my workshop starts in three! Every trainer has felt similar frustration.

If you did not file it, you will not be able to find it when you need it. Sort those stacks of materials sitting on desks and tables. Organize and put them in appropriate files on a regular basis. Visit a local office supply store for ideas to help organize materials. Use colored folders or file folder labels to categorize materials. The key is that you develop and use a consistent system.

Simplify, combine, and eliminate forms, reports, letters, and memos to the extent possible. Make it a goal to have one copy that you can find. Keep only what you need and will use. It is far better to have three good resources that you will use for a topic than a dozen that you cannot find.

When possible, copy items front and back. This simple procedure cuts the storage space for two-page items in half. Edit or reduce handouts to avoid having an extra page with just a few lines on it. Change the margins, font size, or reword text to avoid an extra page when possible. For organizing paper items, here are some suggestions:

Organize by Topic—One folder for a general topic such as Dramatic Play will work fine when there are few printed materials to store. As more materials are collected, it may be desirable to break down the general category into subcategories with separate folders. Devise a system similar to this example for organizing materials by topic:

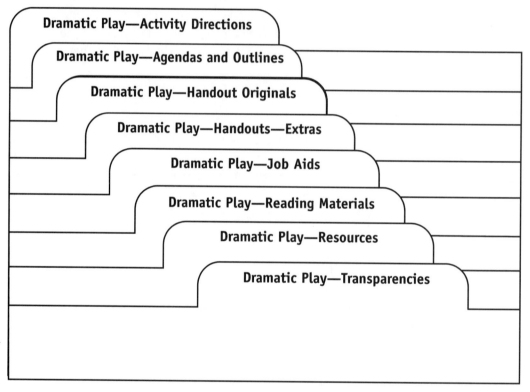

Dramatic Play—Activity Directions

Dramatic Play—Agendas and Outlines

Dramatic Play—Handout Originals

Dramatic Play—Handouts—Extras

Dramatic Play—Job Aids

Dramatic Play—Reading Materials

Dramatic Play—Resources

Dramatic Play—Transparencies

Such a system will help you quickly find all the materials you need for a topic if filed alphabetically by the general category, then by subcategories. This topic approach to filing will keep materials likely to be used together stored together and easy to find.

Organize by Item—Sometimes it is easier to put like items together regardless of the topics. For example, you may wish to keep all handout originals together in one folder or notebook and all transparencies together in another place. This system may work best if you often use the same materials for several different purposes. A transparency that is used as an icebreaker could be stored with transparencies or with icebreaker materials since it may not relate to a specific topic.

When It's Not Where It Should Be—You know you have a specific paper item, but it is not in the usual place or where you think it should be. Here are some tips to help locate the missing piece of paper:

- Check the folders in front of and behind its usual place. It is easy to misfile paper in an adjoining folder.

- Think back to the last time you used the item and what else you were working on at the time. If you used it with other materials, it may have been put with them. Paper clips often catch on other loose papers.

- Check between folders and in the bottom of the drawer. Small papers sometimes fall to the bottom if put between folders.

Look in any stacks of unfiled materials.
Take advantage of the opportunity to clean out files. As you look for the lost item, eliminate duplicate items or outdated materials. Reducing the amount of paper you must look through makes it easier to find what you need.

Extra Handouts—For the trainer who typically has many extra handouts or forms, files may not work for extra handouts. Cabinets with drawers or open sections are available to store larger amounts of paper than can be accommodated in file folders. The cabinets are usually referred to as literature organizers. Label the drawers or sections with a coding system. Use a letter for the sections across the top to designate the column location and a number for the drawer or section row.

With the aid of a computer table or database, you can develop a system to easily find where the extra handouts are stored. The table can be sorted alphabetically by the title of the handout, printed and posted at the cabinet for reference. Just look alphabetically for the name of the handout to find the column and row where it is stored. For example, All About Discipline handouts would be in the second row across (B) and the third drawer or section down (3). Here is an example of how a table to find handouts stored in a cabinet might look:

Row and Number	Name of Handout
B-3	All About Discipline
B-2	Being a Professional
B-1	Field Trips
A-3	Healthy Child Care
A-4	Infant Social Development
C-2	Opening a Family Child Care Home

A-5	Partnership with Parents
C-4	Physical Development of Toddlers
B-4	Portfolio Assessment
C-3	Recognizing Child Abuse
C-1	Records to Keep
A-2	Room Arrangement for Toddlers
B-5	Safety in the Classroom
A-1	Understanding Child Development
C-5	Working with Families

Always use exactly the same name when referring to handouts to prevent mix-ups. When working with a large number of different handouts, it will be very easy to confuse similar titles such as Partnership with Parent, Parent Relationships, Parent Partnerships, Working with Parents, etc. Always give a handout a title, and consistently use the exact title to refer to the handout to reduce confusion over references to specific handouts.

Original Copies of Handouts—Always make new handouts from an original to maintain quality. There will be more spots, more misalignment, and other distractions when you make copies from copies. To locate the original to make copies requires that originals be kept in an accessible place and protected, such as in protective pages in a notebook. Mark the original with a highlighter that will not copy to help ensure that the original is not accidentally used as a handout.

STORING TRANSPARENCIES

Transparencies and items that are too large for file folders may be stored in accordion files. These are heavy paper file holders divided into sections that can be labeled by topic. Accordion folders are a workable system to keep all transparencies together when they are used for several different topics. Take the time to label the divisions within the accordion files to quickly find what you want.

STORING POSTERS

Posters may be hung flat on a skirt hanger or rolled and stored in cardboard tubes or divided containers. If posters are rolled, they tend to curl and will be more difficult to hang or display when needed. Hangers that dry cleaners use for draperies are large enough to hold some posters by draping them across the bottom of the hanger. Posters may also be draped over racks. If the posters are on regular poster board, store them in the box that poster board comes in when purchased in quantity.

To find a poster when you have many, write a title on the edge of the poster. Write the title either on the side or the top, depending on which is easier to see with the storage system you select. Having the title on the side or top will make it much easier to find a specific poster. Create a coding system by topic and attach a label with the code. For example, if there are three posters for music activities, they might be labeled as:

Code	Poster Title
M-1	Activities to Encourage Music
M-2	Making Rhythm Instruments
M-3	Using Music Throughout the Day

By creating a table or database on a computer, the coding system can expand, but it is easy to alphabetize the titles as new ones are added.

Storing Bulky Materials

Props and large items that will not fit in a file cabinet present challenging storage problems. Stackable plastic boxes or heavy cardboard boxes work well if you purchase or locate enough boxes that are alike. Take time to label the boxes to find what you need without hunting through all of them.

Create a list of the items in each box on a computer program to make it easy to find items. For example, if you do not remember where you put the small truck that you use for several different purposes, search your computer list to find "truck." Boxes containing a large number of items may be numbered or coded to correspond with the computer list. A system like this allows you to change the contents easily, adding to, removing, or reorganizing the materials in each box while still being able to locate items quickly. Here are some other tips for storing bulky items:

- If the boxes are clear, you have the extra advantage of being able to see what is in them.
- Post a list near or on the boxes for easy reference.
- If the boxes are large, handles make them easier to transport.
- Consider the weight of the boxes. If there are many books, for instance, dividing them into two boxes may be better than having one that is too heavy to lift.
- Determine how easy it is to remove the lids. Some have attached lids that may be an advantage.
- Consider how the boxes will stack in limited space.

Magazines and Professional Journals

Keeping up with resources such as magazines and professional journals presents another challenge. Looking for specific items or articles can be extremely time-consuming. If you save magazines for ideas, photocopy the table of contents from each one and put the copies in a notebook. Write notes about ways to use the articles. Then, when looking for that article on portfolios that you read six months ago, you can find it easily. Just peruse the table of contents of all the publications you have. The contents page usually has the issue date or volume and number to make it easy to locate the issue that you need. Of course, keeping your periodicals arranged in order is essential. When indexes are available, save those as essential aids in finding what you need.

To keep your magazines and journals in order, purchase cardboard or plastic holders designed for that purpose. If the volume number, date, or issue number is not on the spine, write that information where it is easily visible such as just inside the edge of the back cover. This will help you find a certain issue without removing the periodicals from the holder.

Improving Presentation Skills and Presence

Because training involves being in front of a group, many of the principles of public speaking apply to training as well, especially if the training is conducted with large groups. Talking in front of a group of peers or strangers can be frightening for many. However, there is help for overcoming these fears and improving presentation skills.

Overcoming Stage Fright—Even the best trainers experience occasional uneasiness. Concerns about skills in communicating or being effective will surface at inopportune times. Concerns about the participants themselves and how they will react will make a trainer uneasy, particularly with a new group. Will they respond? Will they be difficult to work with? Will they be hostile or non-cooperative? Will they like the activities? Will I remember how to do the activities? Will I remember what I need to say and do? All of these are questions that worry trainers to some degree at times.

Preparation, practice, and experience are helpful in building confidence. For even more confidence in stage presence, training in public speaking helps. Consider taking a public speaking course at a local college or joining an organization such as Toastmasters to build speaking skills. Network with other trainers through organizations such as the American Society for Training and Development.

Dress Appropriately—An effective, capable presenter must be comfortable. But, comfortable clothing does not mean blue jeans and t-shirts. Clothing should not bind or restrict movement. Shoes should enable the presenter to move around easily without risk of tripping or stumbling. Jewelry may be distracting if it is large, dangling, or if it is noisy such as some bracelets are. However, a large watch helps you stay on schedule in rooms where there is no clock.

Some authorities suggest that a trainer should dress as well as what they expect the best-dressed participants to wear. Dressing more expensively than most of the participants may make participants view the trainer as "ivory tower" and not one experienced in the trenches. Dressing in expensive clothes may cause participants to discount the information and ideas presented as not being realistic. Underdressing may be interpreted as unprofessional or showing lack of adequate consideration of the event.

Take a look in a full-length mirror before heading out to train. A visible lingerie strap, the edge of a petticoat hanging below a dress, a hem that has pulled loose, a tie or shirt with a stain will be distracting to trainees.

Relating to the Audience—Trainees want the person leading them to know more than they do. They want the instructor to have experience and be able to offer worthwhile and practical advice for the problems they experience at work. Trainees want to know that the instructor cares about them, especially in ongoing classes where the group will be together over time. They want to know that the instructor understands their needs and wants to help them. They will not care how much the instructor knows until they know the instructor cares!

When the instructor can use personal experiences to make a point or can select anecdotes from his experience, the trainees will more likely relate to him as one of them. They will be less likely to see him as a person with grandiose ideas that they view as impractical. Sharing examples of problems faced and how you found a solution is helpful in building credibility. Be cautious that you are not viewed as bragging or wanting to talk about yourself too much, however.

Demonstrate early in the training that you enjoy being with the trainees. The instructor who rushes in and rushes out does not convey an interest in the trainees or the training process. Arrive in time to greet and talk to individuals. Let them know you will be around at breaks or after the session to answer questions and talk to them further.

Learn the trainees' names and use them during the session. Use large name tags to be able to call trainees by name if they are unknown. Make a note to remember something about each one to use in conversation during the session.

Do not use a lectern as a barrier between you and the audience. Walk away from it as often as possible and interact with participants whenever possible. Circulating helps relieve the "you" and "them" attitudes and helps trainees view you as a guide rather than a lecturer.

Trainees frequently state that they prefer instructors who really understand the problems they face on a daily basis. Another study shows that people attending training relate to and like trainers most who:

- Are available before and after the session and during breaks to discuss issues and answer questions.
- Encourage participation and make use of the trainees' experiences.
- Use a variety of methods rather than just lecture.
- Use effective aids properly.
- Are masters of their subject, but can communicate it at a level trainees understand.

Maintaining Eye Contact—Looking directly at trainees helps you judge their responses and helps keep their attention. If the group is small, look at, not past, the person being addressed. If the group is large, scan the audience often, looking directly at some of the participants as frequently as possible. Knowing your material and planning carefully frees you to look at the audience as you would in social conversation. Even if you plan to read a short passage or some directions for activities, know them well enough that you can look up from the paper often.

Looking directly at a person demonstrates that you care about them and will help establish a bond with them. You will know how they are reacting to your message from what you see in their faces—are they frowning, looking puzzled, or nodding agreement? Trainees will be more likely to view you as sincere, honest, friendly, and credible when you frequently look them in the eye.

Have a large enough watch or a clock somewhere in the room so that checking the time is not obvious. If you use a watch, place it on the lectern. This way, you will be better able to maintain eye contact.

Be Prepared—Overprepare. Practice how you are going to say things and explain concepts. Practice giving instructions and directions. Run through your audiovisual materials. Check and double-check to see that you have everything you need. Know your material well enough that you can work from brief notes. Even when repeating training that you have conducted many times before, take time to review. Being overprepared will help you have the confidence to project a poised, competent image.

Be Available—Trainees like to have the instructor as a resource. Make yourself accessible before the session, during breaks, and for a time after the session to help create positive relationships. Be sure your name, address, and telephone number are on several handouts or on some of the materials to leave with trainees. Let participants know they can call you and talk about any questions that come up as they implement new skills. It will help them see you as an approachable and available person. Giving trainees information to contact you demonstrates that you care about their success in using what you have taught them.

LEARNING TO GIVE PRESENTATIONS

Americans rank public speaking as their number-one fear. Yet top executives rank the ability to communicate as a major key to success in business. Make your next training presentation a real winner with these tips:

Work backward. Develop the closing first to guarantee a strong finish. Memorize it and skip to it if you run short of time in your session.

Begin with a bang. State a startling statistic, ask a provocative question, or tell a personal experience that relates to the topic. Your audience will size you up in the first few minutes and decide whether what you are saying is worthwhile and something they need to know.

Use visual aids to focus attention. Your trainees are more likely to pay attention and understand if you give them something to look at that illustrates the concept.

Think in threes for strong impact. Many great speeches have a three-part list. "I came, I saw, I conquered." "Of the people, by the people, for the people."

Think in contrasts. "To be or not to be...;" "One small step for man, one giant leap for mankind."

Sometimes, even very experienced presenters are uneasy about an upcoming session. Here are some tips to help get over pre-presentation jitters:

- Memorize the first few minutes of your presentation so you can start strong without hesitation.
- Plan the first few words for each key point you plan to make. Create "cheat sheets" on index cards if necessary.
- Practice telling any stories or examples you plan to include.
- Rehearse, rehearse, and rehearse again!
- Arrive early to check on the room and be ready.
- Be available to greet your audience as they arrive.
- To release tension, breathe deeply, press palms together, or sit in a chair and lift up on the seat.
- Take a course in public speaking to gain confidence and continue to improve.

ELIMINATE DISTRACTIONS

We have all had high school teachers or college professors who had predictable mannerisms that were very distracting. We remember counting the times an instructor said "you know" or pulled on his collar or repeated some trite phrase. Old habits are hard to break, and it may take the aid of a public speaking class or a group such as Toastmasters to eliminate them. However, the time spent overcoming such mannerisms is worth it, since such distractions can make a presentation much less effective.

Distractions caused by your actions can hinder your success as a trainer. A careful, objective evaluation of your presentation techniques is the first step in eliminating any annoying mannerisms. As difficult as it is to watch or hear oneself, video and audio tapes that you thoroughly analyze will help you see areas that need improvement.

Videotape an occasional session as a trainer. Many of us develop unconscious habits and mannerisms that will detract from stage presence. Have a more experienced trainer critique a presentation to help identify ways to improve. Become a critic of others. Watch other trainers and speakers with an objective view to what they could do to improve.

Voice Quality—How You Say It

Vocal quality can have a profound effect on the image you create. A monotone voice or a voice that is too loud or too soft, or too high pitched or whiny will make it difficult for participants to listen. Listening to yourself with a tape recorder will help identify any problems with voice quality. Public speaking classes or organizations can help eliminate habits such as saying "uh" often.

Raise your voice and be evangelical about an issue from time to time. Occasionally drop your voice for emphasis. A whisper can be a great attention-getter!

Take time to learn to use a microphone for those times when your voice does not project well enough for the room and audience size. Practice will help you judge just how far away you should be from the microphone. Learn the fine art of manipulating a hand-held mike while walking around the room.

Stand while speaking. Standing adds power to words and keeps the audience's attention. Standing allows a speaker to project an image of confidence and makes it easier to use visual aids.

Gestures and Other Body Language

Gestures can emphasize a point and help hold participants' attention. Gestures help create a sense of enthusiasm and animation. They can convey feelings and emotions. They can dramatize, clarify, and support your ideas. Gestures are visual aids and attention-getters. Even more importantly, gestures channel and dissipate nervous tension and help you appear relaxed. Using gestures effectively is a skill, and skill requires practice. Practice gestures until they become comfortable and natural.

Gesturing helps you be at ease and makes your presentation more interesting to watch. Here are some tips for effective gestures:

- Vary your gestures. Use different hands and change what you do with them.
- Use gestures to emphasize physical characteristics such as direction or size.
- Hold gestures a bit longer than you might in normal conversation. Jerky or rapid gestures can make you seem nervous and uncomfortable.
- Show the importance of a point or issue by hitting your fist in your open palm.
- Open arms signify openness to your audience; arms held down can mean suppression or secrecy; and holding arms outward may connote a halting or nega-

tive meaning.

- Prompt your audience by demonstrating the action you want them to take such as raising a hand or clapping.
- Use a clenched fist to show power or determination to take action.
- Compare and contrast by moving your hands together to show similarities. Move them in opposite directions to emphasize differences.
- Fold your arms across your chest when you want to depict determination or strength.
- Hold up a finger as you make a point. As you summarize or state points, hold up the corresponding numbers of fingers.
- Show unity by clasping your hands together in front.
- Match facial expressions to your message to appear sincere.

    Demonstrate happiness with a big smile.

    Show distaste for something by a frown.

    Raise your eyebrows to show surprise.

    Depict determination with a serious look.

    Show sadness by turning your mouth down slightly and lowering your eyes or head.

Distracting Mannerisms

Some gestures or physical actions are especially distracting or inhibit communication. Actions to avoid or minimize are:

- Turning your back to the audience.
- Keeping your hands in your pockets.
- Jiggling pocket change; adjusting your hair, clothes or glasses.
- Swaying, rocking, or pacing while you talk.
- Nervous habits such as twirling a bracelet, twisting a collar, or licking your lips.
- Hugging the lectern.
- Any gesture repeated too often.
- Staying stiffly behind the lectern.
- Turning your head or eyes from side to side repeatedly or rapidly.

Giving the Right Non-verbal Message

Non-verbal communication, including gestures, eye contact, facial expressions, and posture, account for some of your message. Be your best visual aid:

- Dress appropriately for your audience and setting.
- Stand up straight—remember what your mother taught you about good posture.
- Move around with enthusiasm.
- Look participants in the eye.
- Smile and exude confidence.
- Enjoy the experience; you have knowledge to share and the participants want to hear what you have to say.

Using Notes

Notes can take many forms. Overhead transparencies or posters can list key points and become an outline that reminds you of what comes next. When you have taken the time to practice, the notes serve as brief reminders. Reminders can be slides, props, or pictures that illustrate points. Worksheets or handouts placed where they are easily visible and in the order they will be used serve as reminders of planned activities. When training materials themselves serve as notes or reminders, one can maintain more eye contact with the trainees.

Write reminders where they will be needed. Put notes directly on the top copy of a stack of handouts that will be discussed. Purchase specially designed frames for transparencies that have space for writing.

If you need traditional notes to ensure that you do not forget some important points, use index cards whenever possible to avoid having stacks of paper at a lectern. Writing out what you plan to say is good in the planning stage, but may make a session seem memorized and forced if you rely heavily on such a written text during the session.

Keeping It Simple—Abraham Lincoln's Gettysburg Address is famous for its simplicity and eloquence, yet it is only 262 words long. Two hundred and two of the words have only one syllable. Clarity and persuasiveness does not mean complicated. Simplify your language and use short words if they convey the meaning adequately. Use words that are proven persuaders such as: you, save, new, results, easy, health, safety, love, proven, guarantee. Here are some substitutes for words or phrases that may be too long or overused:

For This . . .	Try This . . .
accommodate	serve
advise	tell
at this point in time	now
component	part
conceptualize	imagine
conclusion	end
currently	now
eliminate	cut out
expedite	rush
facilitate	make easy

finalize	finish
in the near future	soon
incorporate	include
indicate	say
inquire	ask
interface	talk with
numerous	many
operational	working
parameters	limits
procure	get
solicit	seek
subsequent	next
utilization	use
verification	proof
viable	possible

Simplifying does not mean that speech should be dull or lack interest. On the contrary, removing jargon and clichés, using vivid words economically, and speaking in the active voice will make language stronger. Use descriptive, precise words to convey clear meaning. For example, one might write or say, "Lashonda picked up her soft doll and hugged it gently. 'This is my baby,' she said," describes what happened descriptively, precisely, and in the active voice. It is much clearer than, "The doll was picked up and held by Lashonda who expressed the concept that the doll was her baby."

Training No-nos

Certain kinds of conduct in training will alienate participants generally and will be met with dislike. All deserve attention when you are trying to improve your presentation skills. Some of these training no-nos are:

- Getting off to a slow start.
- Sitting down while presenting—it makes one seem tired.
- Not modeling what you are teaching or expecting from participants such as being late from breaks, etc.
- Talking over the heads of or down to the participants.

- Speaking in jargon—using too much technical language or unknown terminology.
- Burying the meaning by spending too much time on irrelevant or trivial information.
- Not being sensitive to the comfort of the participants—failing to notice or take action concerning temperature, noise, or difficult participants.
- Being wordy—not using enough visual material other than text.
- Using illegible or difficult-to-see materials.
- Being verbose—using large words when simple ones will do.
- Speaking in a monotone or talking too low for them to hear you well.
- Including too many personal stories.
- Chewing gum or eating while presenting.
- Using an attendee as a negative example or embarrassing an attendee.
- Making assumptions—assuming how the audience feels and what participants want.
- Running on too long in giving instructions or information.
- Keeping participants past the announced ending time.
- Leaping in thought and presenting information out of order. For example, teaching diaper-changing steps without first discussing gathering the supplies.

Appendix

Contents

Training Definitions

Action Plan—A written plan that designates what is to be done, when, and by whom.

Adult Learning—The body of knowledge that addresses how adults learn and what most adults need for training to be effective.

Agenda—The schedule for the day. Usually includes routine matters and the order of activities to be conducted in the training session.

Application—The process of using information, usually in an effective way.

Audiovisual Materials—Items such as video tapes and overhead transparencies that are used in training.

Audiovisual Equipment—Electronic equipment that is used in training such as VCR's, televisions, overhead projectors, slide projectors.

Auditory Learners—Persons who learn best through what they hear.

Brainstorming—An activity in which many ideas or suggestions are generated without regard to feasibility.

Closure Activities—Experiences planned specifically to come at the end of a training session that are designed to signify that a session is over.

Coaching—A process of critiquing, supporting, and encouraging a person to attempt new skills.

Concurrent Session—Training sessions happening at the same time usually in the same facility that require participants to choose which one they will attend.

Conference—A training session that lasts for several days, usually bringing together members of an organization or selected group.

Debate—A presentation of conflicting views by two people or two groups. Debates usually have a pro and con aspect.

Demonstration—A situation where one person or group shows how to complete a task to others. Demonstrations also may illustrate a concept or make a point.

Displays—An arrangement of materials, usually for participants to view during breaks.

Door Prizes—Gifts given at the end of a training session usually through a random or chance-based selection process.

Dry-erase Boards—A slick, white board that functions similar to a chalk board except that it uses specially designed markers. Dry-erase boards are often called white boards.

Environment—The facility and emotional climate that surrounds a training activity.

Evaluation—A process of assessing the impact and effectiveness of training.

Facilitation—The process of working with a small group to assist them in setting priorities or in making decisions.

Feedback—Information received by a person that comes from another person and follows an event or activity. Usually designed to help individuals improve their skills.

Field Experience—An activity at a location other than the training site.

Flip Charts—Tablets of large pages of paper intended for viewing by groups.

Follow-up Assignments—Activities that are completed several days or weeks after training. Sometimes required before credit is issued.

Game—An individual or group activity that often involves competition. Games usually provide an opportunity to practice skills and actions or to use information that has been learned.

Handouts—Printed sheets of paper, brochures, or other printed materials given out during a training session for participants to take with them.

Housekeeping Details—The routine tasks and information that trainees need to know or do, such as procedures, schedules, announcements, and locations of things they may need.

Icebreaker—An activity designed to introduce participants or to serve as an introduction to a training session.

Individual Activity—Any activity that involves only one person. Completing a worksheet, reading an article, making something alone are examples of individual activities.

Interactive—Describes the process of communication and interchange among participants and instructor during training.

Interest Groups—Often used interchangeably with concurrent sessions.

Interview—An activity in which one participant seeks information from another by asking questions.

Job Aid—An item that trainees may take with them to help them remember what they have learned.

Journaling—The process of keeping a written record on a regular basis of thoughts, ideas, activities, or reactions.

Learning Station—A self-contained set-up of an activity designed for participants to learn through their own exploration with little interaction with the instructor.

Learning Styles—Refers to how an individual learns best: Auditory, Visual, or Kinesthetic.

Lecture—An organized, usually formal talk designed to present information to a group. A lecture may include visual aids.

Needs Assessment—A means of finding out what training is needed by seeking information from persons who will be affected by the training.

Objectives—Specific, measurable statements describing what participants are expected to be able to do following a training session.

Opening Activities—Activities intended to set a clear opening to a training event. Opening activities may be the same as icebreakers.

Outline of Content—A listing in outline form of information or facts that will be covered in a training session.

Over-learning—The process of learning a skill past the point of mastery.

Pace—The speed at which activities are conducted during training, such as how often a new activity is introduced.

Panel—A group of three or more people who present information or discuss their views on a topic or problem. Usually a panel consists of persons with varied backgrounds who bring specific expertise to the discussion. A panel is typically less formal than a lecture.

Partner Activity—Any activity that requires two people such as interviews or debates.

Planning Aid—A system or form to bring structure to the process of planning training.

Pre- and Post-test—A test that is given before training is conducted and again after training is completed. These tests seek to measure what participants learned. Often known as Level 2 evaluations.

Projects—Activities that involve a complete task that usually produces a product.

Props—Objects or items that are used during training, usually as accessories or to physically illustrate a principle or make a point.

Questioning Techniques—The variety of ways in which questions are asked or answered.

Questionnaire—A printed list of questions or requests for information, usually designed to assess needs or gather information from a selected group.

Recorder—The person selected to make notes or summarize information or decisions made by a small group.

Reflective Practice—Thinking about one's experiences or actions. Reflective thinking is usually an individual activity, but may be part of a partner or small group activity.

Registration—The process of indicating that one plans to attend a training session. Also the process of signing in and documenting one's presence at a training session.

Reinforcement—The process of assisting learning through a means that supports the use of the information or skills.

Relapse—The act of reverting to old methods rather than using newly learned skills and techniques.

Repetition—The process of covering material more than once.

Retreat—A training usually lasting for several days in a location removed from the work site. Retreats are typically for team building or long-range planning.

Review—A summary of material previously introduced.

Role-play—The dramatization of a situation or problem. May be a spontaneous demonstration of actions based on assumed roles or may be scripted in whole or in part.

Scenario—A description of a situation or event.

Script—Written statements, usually for role-play, that tell participants what to say.

Seminar—A type of training that usually involves several different instructors.

Slides—Photographs that can be projected on a screen.

Small Group Discussion or Activity—A group of four to eight people with an exchange of ideas focused on a specific issue or topic. Often a recorder or spokesperson will report to a whole group. Small group discussions may have guiding questions, but are relatively unstructured. Small group activities include a task to accomplish or a product to develop.

Smile Sheets—Forms distributed at the conclusion of training that seek to assess how participants felt about the training. Often known as Level 1 evaluations.

Spokesperson—The person selected by a small group to represent them in reporting their activities to the whole group.

Summary—The process of reviewing information and selecting the key elements.

Supervised Practice—An opportunity to practice a new skill while given assistance by another.

Tent Cards—Small, folded cards with information, usually placed on tables during training.

Training Session—A training experience where a group of participants come together for a specific period of time.

Transfer of Learning—The process of applying what has been learned in a training session to the work site.

Transparencies—Clear sheets to use with an overhead projector.

Viewer Guides—Printed material that guides the experience of viewers by suggesting what to watch for or requires that they use the information in the video or other audiovisual items.

Visual Learners—Persons who learn best through what they see.

Whole Group Activity—Any activity that includes all attendees at a specific training event, such as lectures.

Worksheet—A type of handout that requires participants to write and add information to what is printed on the papers.

Workshop—A type of training session that is usually less than one day and involves hands-on experiences for participants.

References

Arch, D. *Tricks for Trainers, Vol. II.* Edina, MN: Resources for Organizations, Inc., 1993.

Baird, L. S., C. E. Schneier, and D. Laird, eds. *The Training and Development Sourcebook.* Amherst, MA: Human Resource Development Press, 1983.

Brandt, R. C. *Flip Charts: How To Draw Them and How To Use Them.* San Francisco: Jossey-Bass, Inc., 1986.

Carter, M. and D. Curtis. *Training Teachers: A Harvest of Theory and Practice.* St. Paul: Redleaf Press, 1994.

Dean, G. J. *Designing Instruction for Adult Learners.* Malabar, FL: Krieger Publishing Co., 1994.

Frank, D. *Terrific Training Materials: High Impact Graphic Design for Workbooks, Handouts, Instructor Guides, and Job Aids.* Amherst, MA: HRD Press, 1996.

Johnson, D. and B. Carnes. *Making Training Stick: A Collection of Techniques to Follow Up, Follow Through and Reinforce Training.* Edina, MN: Creative Training Techniques International, Inc., 1988.

Jolles, R. L. *How to Run Seminars and Workshops: Presentation Skills for Consultants, Trainers, and Teachers.* New York: John Wiley and Sons, Inc., 1993.

Jones, E., ed. *Growing Teachers: Partnerships in Staff Development.* Washington, D.C.: National Association for the Education of Young Children, 1993.

McKeachie, W. J. *Teaching Tips: Strategies, Research, and Theory for College and University Teachers.* Lexington, MA: D. C. Heath and Company, 1994.

Newstrom, J. W. and E. E. Scannell. *Games Trainers Play: Experiential Learning Exercises*. New York: McGraw-Hill, 1980.

O'Sullivan, B. *Staff Orientation In Early Childhood Programs*. St. Paul, MN: Redleaf Press, 1987.

Petit, A. *Secrets to Enliven Learning: How to Develop Extraordinary Self-Directed Training Materials*. San Diego: Pfeiffer and Company, 1994.

Pike, R. with C. Busse. *101 Games for Trainers*. Minneapolis: Lakewood Books, 1995.

Pike, R. with C. Busse. *101 More Games for Trainers*. Minneapolis: Lakewood Books, 1995.

Sork, T. J., ed. *Designing and Implementing Effective Workshops*. San Francisco: Jossey-Bass, Inc., 1984.

Tertell, E. A., S. M. Klein, and J. L. Jewett, eds. *When Teachers Reflect: Journeys Toward Effective, Inclusive Practice*. Washington, D. C.: National Association for the Education of Young Children, 1998.

Thiagarajan, W. *Lecture Games*. Amherst, MA: HRD Press, 1994.

Zielinski, D. ed. *Adult Learning in Your Classroom*. Minneapolis: Lakewood Publications, p. 73.

Zielinski, D., ed. *Delivering Training: Mastery in the Classroom*. Minneapolis: Lakewood Publications, 1996.

Zielinski, D., ed. *Making Training Pay Off on the Job*. Minneapolis: Lakewood Publications, 1996.

Zielinski, D., ed. *The Best of Creative Training Techniques*. Minneapolis: Lakewood Publications, 1996.

Zielinski, D., ed. *The Training Mix: Choosing and Using Media and Methods*. Minneapolis: Lakewood Publications, 1996.

Publications

Training Magazine
Lakewood Publications
50 S. Ninth St.
Minneapolis, MN 55402
Phone: (612) 333-0471

Creative Training Techniques Newsletter
Lakewood Publications
50 S. Ninth St.
Minneapolis, MN 55402
Phone: (800) 328-4329

Organizations

American Society for Training and Development
1640 King Street
P.O. Box 1443
Alexandria, VA 22313-2043
(703) 683-8100
www.astd.org

Resources for Organizations
7600 West 78th Street
Edina, MN 55430
(612) 829-1954

Toastmasters International
P.O. Box 9052
Mission Viejo, CA 92690
(800) 9WE-SPEAK
www.toastmasters.org

Training Needs Assessment Questionnaire

As you know, a committee made up of center employees is planning the training for the upcoming year. Please take a moment and answer the following questions to help us design the training to better meet everyone's needs. We value your input. Please be as specific as possible in answering all of the questions.

Please number in order of preference. These suggestions are the committee's ideas, but we welcome other suggestions.

I would most prefer to attend training on the following topic:
___ Guidance and Discipline
___ Working with Parents
___ New Activities for Learning
___ Improving the Classroom Environment
___ Other Suggestions

_____

_____

What specific questions or concerns do you have about the topics you chose?

_____

_____

_____

_____

What do you want to learn from training in the topics you selected?

_____

_____

_____

_____

List your personal strengths and areas you wish to improve:

I feel that I am good at:

_____

_____

_____

_____

I want help with:

_____

_____

_____

_____

I would like to be able to implement the following new skills after training:

_____

_____

_____

_____

I prefer training at the following times:

   ___ Saturday morning   ___ Monday evening   ___ Wednesday evening
   ___ Saturday afternoon ___ Tuesday evening   ___ Thursday evening

_____

Signature (optional)   Date

Thank you for taking the time to complete this questionnaire. Please feel free to discuss any additional ideas with the members of the committee at any time. If you have any questions or wish to discuss other ideas, please contact _____ at _____.

Please place this completed questionnaire in the box beside the sign-in sheets in the office by _____.

Training Activity Outline Form

Learning Objective—Following the training, the learner will be able to:

_____

Actions that must be taken to accomplish the objective:

_____
_____
_____
_____
_____
_____

Knowledge that the learners will need to take these actions:

_____
_____
_____
_____
_____
_____

Sequence of content—List the training content in the order in which it can best be presented in training.

1. _____
2. _____
3. _____
4. _____
5. _____

Sample Training Activity Outline Form for Selecting Books for Young Children

Learning objective:
Following the training, the learner will select at least five appropriate children's books from among 25 books, some of which are inappropriate. The learner will be able to describe the features that make the selected books appropriate choices.

Actions that must be taken to accomplish the objective:
Following small group discussions, trainees will be given 30 minutes to choose 5 appropriate books. Trainees will describe the basis of their selection to the class.

Knowledge that the learners will need to take these actions:

What constitutes a good children's book?
  Good illustrations
  Understandable language
  Good story content
  Related to children's experiences
  Age-appropriate

What are ways to identify good children's books?
  Caldecott Award books
  Classic children's literature
  Recommendations of experts
  Using criteria listed above

What constitutes an inappropriate book?
  Too long or too much text on a page
  Stereotypic or cartoon characters
  Too abstract for the age of the children
  Talks down to children
  Poor or confusing illustrations
  Contrived stories
  Not based on children's experiences
  Includes violence or other aspects inappropriate for children

Sequence of content—List the training content in the order in which it can best be presented:
Following an overview of some aspects of good children's books, trainees will work in small groups and complete the following tasks:

1. Read and discuss the handout.
2. Look at ten Caldecott Award books and discuss common features that make them good choices for children.
3. As a group, select five examples of good children's books.
4. As a group, find two examples of inappropriate books. Identify why they are inappropriate for young children.
5. Select five books you would use with children. Describe to your group why these are good books for children.

Interview

Pass out the following interview sheets. Participants complete the sheets by interviewing someone next to them. Then they introduce the person they interviewed to the group. For variation they could move around and meet someone new.

Tell the Person Next to You

What did you do that you are most proud of during this past year?

What was your biggest challenge? How did you meet it?

What was your biggest disappointment? How did you handle it?

What would you do differently if you had a chance to do something again?

Another version of the same activity

Tell the Person Next to You

What did you find to be most stimulating during the past and caused you to grow the most?

What are you looking forward to in the year ahead?

What worries you the most about the coming year?

What would you want to say about your work one year from today?

Sample Journal Assignment

1. During this class, please keep a journal of your experiences, thoughts, ideas, and learning related to this course and working with young children. You will not be graded on your entries. The purpose of the journal is to get to know you better in order to guide your learning and professional development.
2. You may evaluate class activities, materials and information, your work, or make suggestions to improve the class experience for you or others. Please be as specific as possible with your suggestions.
3. Make entries in your journal in the way that works best for you. The entries may be a written narrative, lists, questions, drawings, or a summary of resources. Use the method that is appropriate for the information and one that effectively communicates what you want to convey.
4. You will receive a weekly topic for your journal. Please address that topic, but add other comments or questions as you think of them. You will have time during class to write. As you leave class following a journal assignment, leave your journals on the table in the back of the room.

Your first assignment:

Write your name and telephone number on your journal.

Tell what you want to learn from this class and why you want to teach young children.

Consider your long-term goals. How will taking this class influence what you want to be doing ten years from now?

Other assignments will depend on the subject, content, and goals of the class. Assignments should be relatively open-ended to allow trainees to follow their interests and make the writing relevant to their individual experiences. Here are some suggestions for journal assignments related to working with young children:

- Describe an experience reading to a child.
- Tell about a time you were around someone who was very angry. Describe how you felt.
- Observe an infant and describe what the infant does.
- Finish one of the following statements:
    When I was a child, I enjoyed...
    As a child, I liked adults who...
    When I started school, I felt...
    Once I had to leave someone I cared a lot about, and I felt...
    When I was a child, I really disliked...
- Write about a time you were scared.
- Describe a favorite play activity you had as a child.
- Observe parents with children in a public place. Describe how you feel about the way they interact with their child.
- Tell about a favorite teacher and why he or she was your favorite.
- Describe a relative other than your parents or grandparents who made you feel special.
- Give an illustration of a time you felt really frustrated because you did not have the ability to do something you wanted to do.
- Tell about your experience with young children outside this class.
- Discuss what you feel you do best with young children and what age you most like to be around.

Anecdotal Records Crossword

There are some important components to include in every anecdotal record. After you complete your crossword puzzle, discuss with your partner some examples of these components.

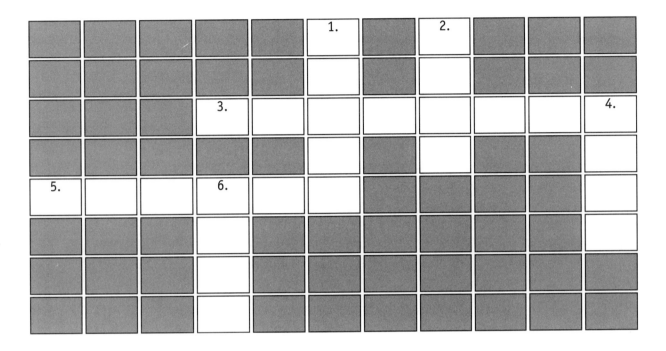

Across

3. The place where the event occured
5. The exact words that the child says

Down

1. Not opinions or judgments
2. The day the behavior was observed
4. Who was being observed
6. The _____ of day the event occured

Choose from these words:

Date
Facts
Location
Name
Quotes
Time

Word Scramble on Props for the Housekeeping Center

Unscramble the following words to identify some common props for the housekeeping center. Write the words in the blanks beside the scrambled words.

1. ODSLL DNALLOD DBE

   — — — — —   — — —   — — — —   — — —

2. BELTA NDA ARISCH

   — — — — —   — — —   — — — — — —

3. TOPS, NAPS AND SHEIDS

   — — — —   — — — —   — — —   — — — — — —

4. VETOS, KINS, AND GERRIFORATER

   — — — — —   — — — —   — — —   — — — — — — — — — — — —

5. NORI NDA NORINGI ROADB

   — — — —   — — —   — — — — — — —   — — — — —

6. SREDS-PU SLOHETC

   — — — — - — —   — — — — — — — —

7. FOSA DAN RAICH

   — — — —   — — —   — — — — —

Answers to Word Scramble:
1. dolls and doll bed
2. table and chairs
3. pots, pans, and dishes
4. stove, sink, and refrigerator
5. iron and ironing board
6. dress-up clothes
7. sofa and chair

Word Jumble for Interest Centers

1. An active interest center

    — — —◯— —

2. A quiet interest center

    — — — — — —◯

3. An interest center that should be near water

    — —◯—

4. This interest center supports literacy

    ◯—◯— — —

5. A great place for dramatic play

    — — — — — — — — — —
    ◯—— —

6. A place for rhythm instruments

    — — —◯—◯—

7. You'll find the puzzles in this interest center

    —◯— — — — — — — —
    ◯— — — —

8. A center for discovery

    — — —◯— — —

Unscramble the circled letters to discover a key word.

Answers to Word Jumble
blocks
library
art
writing
housekeeping
music
manipulatives
science

Key word; creativity

Interview Your Partner
Evaluating Your Class Schedule

Take a few minutes to think about how you would answer the questions below. Then take turns asking each other the questions. Jot down your partner's responses to the questions.

What is the hardest time of the day for you?

_____

_____

When do you feel rushed?

_____

_____

When do you think you need more help?

_____

_____

When is the most difficult time for the children?

_____

_____

What are some ways you would like to change your schedule?

_____

_____

What aspect of your schedule works very well for you?

_____

_____

What tip would you give a new co-worker about scheduling?

_____

_____

_____

What mistakes would you help a new worker seek to avoid?

_____

_____

_____

Here is an example of a guide sheet for debates. After participants have completed Part 1, instruct them to complete Part 2.

Debate Guide
Should You Give Material Rewards?

Part 1
One of you selects position A below, and the other selects position B. Use this form to make notes about what you want to say. Then discuss your point of view with your partner.

A. Material rewards reinforce good behavior.

_____

_____

_____

_____

B. Rewards encourage children to expect "payment for being good."

_____

_____

_____

_____

Part 2
With your partner, develop guidelines for when material rewards should or should not be used.

_____

_____

_____

_____

With your partner, identify non-material rewards:

_____

_____

_____

_____

Sample Partner Worksheet

Art Supplies

Work with your partner to make a list of art supplies appropriate for 3-5 year-olds. Put a **P** beside each item that you must purchase and an **S** beside materials that you can scrounge. Agree on the purchased materials that are essential to meet the goals of your program and mark them with a star.

Partner Worksheet

Encouraging Social Development

Work with your partner to list materials, methods, and activities that encourage social development in young children. Describe how or why the things you listed encourage social development.

Materials, Methods, Activities   Why or how these encourage social development

_____

_____

_____

_____

_____

_____

_____

_____

Partner Worksheet

Administration

Marketing Your Program

Discuss these questions with your partner:

What is marketing?

Why do you need to market your program?

When should you market your program?

What do you consider your most effective marketing techniques?

List three free ways to market your program:

1. _____

2. _____

3. _____

List three inexpensive ways:

1. _____

2. _____

3. _____

List three expensive ways:

1. _____

2. _____

3. _____

Doll Patern

What Do We Want Children to Do During Transitions?

Describe the behaviors and attributes you want children to display during a specific transition time. Examples of difficult transition times are when children are going outdoors or coming in, moving from group time to interest centers, picking up toys and materials, or preparing for lunch. Think about these questions, then write your thoughts in the space below.

What does it look like?
What does it sound like?
What does it feel like?
What can you do to make it happen?

It looks like:

It sounds like:

It feels like:

I need to do this:

Good Story Sources

Chicken Soup for the Soul: 101 Stories to Open the Heart and Rekindle the Spirit by Jack Canfield and Mark V. Hanson
Chicken Soup for the Soul: A Second Helping by Jack Cantfield and Mark V. Hinson
All I Really Need to Know I Learned in Kindergarten by Robert Fulghum
It Was on Fire When I Lay Down on It by Robert Fulghum

Title	Concepts or Topic
I Won't Go Without a Daddy by Muriel Stanek	How to help children adjust to a separation or divorce
Will I Have a Friend? by Miriam Cohen	Children worry about new experiences and need help with transitions to new settings
The Tenth Good Thing about Barney by Judith Viorst	A child's adjustment to losing a classmate
Goodnight Moon by Margaret Wise Brown	How to help children with transitions
Alexander and the Terrible, Horrible, Very Bad Day by Judith Viorst	Children need understanding when things are not going right for them
There's a Nightmare in My Closet by Mercer Mayer	Children's fears
The Carrot Seed by Ruth Krauss	How we too often react negatively to children's efforts and determination

Viewer Guide

The Whole Child: A Caregiver's Guide to the First Five Years
Developing Social Competence in Young Children: Getting Along Together?

As you watch the video, decide if the following questions are true or false. Write your answer in the blank provided. Be prepared to explain your answer or give examples from the video.

_____ When we say "please" and "thank you" we are teaching children how to be polite.

_____ We do not need to do what we want children to do because they should be expected to do what we say.

_____ Active teaching means lavishing praise on children.

_____ We can help children learn empathy for others by reminding them of their experiences in similar situations.

_____ Negotiation is an important skill, but it is too complex for young children to learn.

Select the best answer and write the letter in the blank. Be prepared to discuss why you selected the answer that you chose.

_____ Ways caregivers should NOT use to help children learn to share are:

a) tell them that they should always share and not to be selfish.
b) make sure there is enough equipment and materials to go around.
c) comment on generous behavior or when a child shares.
d) allow children to use items until they are ready to pass them on to another.
e) point out that another child is waiting for an item.

_____ Caregivers can teach children to be fair by:

a) explaining rules and how they apply.
b) emphasizing cooperation rather than competition.
c) helping children learn to bargain with each other.
d) both a) and b).
e) a), b) and c).

_____ A good way to reinforce desirable behavior is to:

a) punish children consistently when they misbehave.
b) ask them to copy other children who are following the rules.
c) point out that it feels good to help others.
d) do not allow them to do what they want until they do what you want them to do.

Example of an Interactive Worksheet

Reading or Math Readiness Comparison

Locate a reading or math readiness workbook designed for 4- or 5-year-olds. List the readiness skills in the workbook. Beside each skill, describe a way for children to develop that skill using real materials and experiences.

SKILL   ALTERNATE

1._____   _____

2._____   _____

3._____   _____

4._____   _____

5._____   _____

6._____   _____

7._____   _____

8._____   _____

9._____   _____

10._____   _____

11._____   _____

Example of an Interactive Worksheet

What Do you Put in Portfolios?

Developmental Checklists

Anecdotal Records

Interest Records

Photographs

Samples of Children's Work

_____

_____

_____

_____

_____

Example of an Action Sheet

Directors' Training

Thinking about issues ahead of time helps you plan how you will react to situations and events when they occur. The situations given below are the types of issues that directors must respond to regularly. Write the action you feel is appropriate in each situation. Be prepared to share your ideas with others.

What will you do if . . .?

A ten-year-old brother comes into the center to get his two-year-old sister. Sometimes he even carries her to their mother's car.

Mrs. Wallace brings four-year-old Jeremy with a honey bun several mornings a week. Eating it has become a problem since the other children want one too.

A mother needs to enroll her child to start Monday. It is Friday afternoon, and she cannot get the required health record by Monday morning. You have two vacancies and NEED TO ENROLL this child.

A father asks for the names of children in his four-year-old son's class to invite them to a birthday party. He asks you to give the invitations out since there is not enough time to mail them.

A three-year-old is having trouble adjusting. Her mother thinks if she can bring the family puppy to school, it would help her feel at home in this new setting.

A woman you do not know arrives to get three-year-old Samantha. The woman appears intoxicated, but her name is on the authorized pick-up list.

Four-year-old Darien is in a preschool program for the first time. His mother wants you to stop him from dressing up in those "ladies' clothes," something he does frequently.

Example of a Self-evaluation Sheet or Checklist

Evaluation of Outdoor Play Area

For each of the following, put a check in the HAVE column if it exists at your site. If it does not, put a check in the NEED column.

HAVE   NEED

HAVE	NEED	
		Adequate space—at least 75 square feet per child
		Attractive, clean, free of litter
		Variety of terrain (slope, level, etc.)
		Variety of surfaces (grassy, dirt, hard area for riding tricycles.)
		Fenced or protected with securely closed gate
		Convenient storage for small outdoor equipment
		Open area for running and group activities
		Clear traffic patterns
		Free of supervision barriers
		Sunny and shady areas
		Adequate drainage, no standing water
		Cushioned surface under all climbing equipment
		Trees, shrubs, plants, space for a children's garden
		Free of roots and other tripping hazards
		Covered sand box with a variety of accessories
		Water play available and sanitary
		Variety of climbing equipment available
		Wheel toys for riding, pushing, pulling, and accessories to support their use in dramatic play
		Multi-purpose equipment for a variety of activities
		Place for child to be alone or with a few friends
		Adequate small equipment, such as balls, hoops, parachutes, riding toys
		Items to promote small group activities, such as construction materials, dramatic play props

Example of a Reading Guide

Media Violence and Children

Read the brochure, *Media Violence and Children* (National Association for the Education of Young Children, Washington, D.C., 1994). According to the brochure, repeated viewing of television violence by young children leads to their becoming:

1. More aggressive toward others
2. Less sensitive to the suffering of others
3. More fearful of the world around them

Some of the subtle effects of overexposure to television violence are:

1. Media violence can harm social development
2. Violent programming presents limited models of language use
3. Viewing television violence limits children's imaginations

The brochure gives you seven suggestions for what you and parents can do to reduce the violence to which children are exposed through the media. List those steps here:

1.

2.

3.

4.

5.

6.

7.

Which of the action steps are you already taking?

Which of the steps will you implement now?

Often, children are exposed to violence in video games and through other technology. What are some guidelines in using computers or videos with young children? Write them on the back of this sheet and be prepared to discuss them in your small group.

Example of a Checklist and Decision Sheet

Aggressive Behaviors

When an aggressive incident occurs, remember the following steps in guiding the child:

1. Accept the child's feelings through verbalizations.
2. Set limits for the child so the child does not continue to develop unacceptable behavior patterns.
3. Provide release for negative feelings at the moment they occur through the use of materials appropriate for the release of tension and aggression such as:

    Pounding benches
    Playdough
    Tearing paper
    Physical activity

4. Encourage and support the child while in the process of releasing the aggression.
5. Help the child to understand what is an acceptable way to deal with aggression and what is not. "You may hit the playdough, but not your friend; you may tear the newspaper, but not a book."
6. Focus on the future, not on the past. Do not rehash the incident, nag, or cajole.

List some examples of aggressive behavior on the left. On the right, write in what to say and how to react to the behavior:

Behavior	Reaction
1.	
2.	
3.	
4.	
5.	

Example of a Recall Sheet

Early Impressions

What do you remember about your first day of school?

_____

_____

_____

What do you remember most from your first year of school?

_____

_____

_____

What do you remember about your teacher?

_____

_____

_____

Positive: _____

_____

_____

_____

Negative: _____

_____

_____

_____

Think about what was important enough to you that you still remember today. Why were those things important?

Example of a Script Starter
Role Play Scenario

How Children Learn

Ms. Jackson, mother of a three-year-old girl:

"Well, Mrs. Smitherman, I just don't want Leslie to be behind when she goes to school. The children in your class seem to spend a lot of time playing. When will she start learning?"

Mrs. Smitherman, Leslie's teacher:

"Ms. Jackson, the children are learning a lot through playing. Just today, Leslie . . ."

Mr. Jacobi, father of a four-year-old girl:

"I'm really worried about Madison. She hasn't learned phonics yet, and I'm afraid she won't be ready for school. Can't you use flash cards or something? What about that phonics program I hear advertised so much?"

Miss Elaine, Madison's teacher:

"I understand your concern. Let me show you some of the activities Madison has done. Here is a ..."

Shirley, mother of a three-year-old boy:

"Betty, I really like the program here, and Quinton has a good time every day. I am concerned though, that he can only count to ten. His cousin goes to ABC Center and can already count to fifty."

Betty, director of the program where Quinton is enrolled:

"Shirley, I would like to share this brochure with you about how children learn math. It says . . ."

Tent Card Template

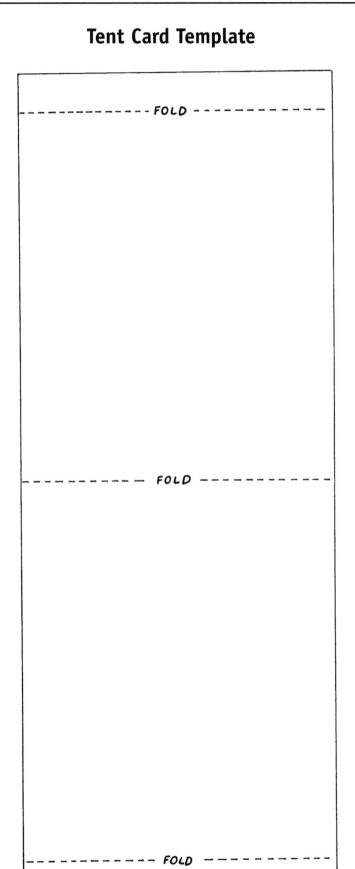

Training Evaluation Form

(Insert name of sponsoring organization) is pleased to make this training session available today. We are asking for your comments on this program to improve professional development and to better meet your needs. Please answer the following questions and turn this form in at the end of the session.

Name of Session: _____   **Date:** _____

Name of Facilitator: _____   **Location:** _____

1. Did the facilitator explain the goal or what was to be accomplished?

    Yes _____   No _____

2. Did the session fulfill the goal that the facilitator expressed?

    Yes _____   No _____

3. How much of the information presented can you use?

    All _____   75% _____   50% _____   Very little None _____

4. Please rate the following components of this session:

Organization of presentation	excellent ____	good ____	fair ____	poor ____
Facilitator's knowledge of material	excellent ____	good ____	fair ____	poor ____
Facilitator's style of presentation	excellent ____	good ____	fair ____	poor ____
Facilitator's ability to answer questions	excellent ____	good ____	fair ____	poor ____
Facilitator's ability to relate to audience	excellent ____	good ____	fair ____	poor ____
Overall rating of facilitator	excellent ____	good ____	fair ____	poor ____
Usefulness of handouts	excellent ____	good ____	fair ____	poor ____
Usefulness of video or audio-visual aids	excellent ____	good ____	fair ____	poor ____
Usefulness of hands-on activity	excellent ____	good ____	fair ____	poor ____
Overall rating of facilitator	excellent ____	good ____	fair ____	poor ____
Comfort of facility	excellent ____	good ____	fair ____	poor ____

Please complete the following:

I liked:

I wished:

The most important thing I got from this session was:

Other comments that would be helpful to us (use the back if necessary):

Thank you for your responses. All of your comments are important to us in planning meaningful professional development events that meet your needs.

Evaluation Form

Date _____   Instructor _____

　　　　　　　Session Title _____

Please circle the number that best describes your rating of this session with 5 being the highest rating and 1 being the lowest rating:

	Low				High
Overall, how do you rate this presentation?	1	2	3	4	5
The instructor was	1	2	3	4	5
The content was	1	2	3	4	5
The handouts were	1	2	3	4	5
The facilities were	1	2	3	4	5
The visual aids were	1	2	3	4	5
The goals of the training were	1	2	3	4	5
The pace of the session was	1	2	3	4	5
The instructor's enthusiasm was	1	2	3	4	5
The instructor's knowledge of the topic was	1	2	3	4	5

What aspect of the workshop was the most helpful to you?

If you could change anything about this session, what would you change?

What other topics you would like offered?

Parent Meeting Evaluation Form

Date _____ Topic _____

We would appreciate your taking a few minutes to fill out this evaluation form. We are very interested in your reaction to the parent meetings. Any comments or suggestions you have will be valuable in helping us assess the effectiveness of the programs. Your comments help us plan future meetings.

What is your overall assessment of this parent meeting?

Poor   Fair   Good   Excellent

What is your assessment of the instructor's ability to communicate the content of the meeting?

Poor   Fair   Good   Excellent

Were your expectations of the meeting met?

Yes   No

What features of the meeting did you like best?

What features of the meeting did you like least?

What would you recommend be done to improve the parent meetings?

What other topics would you suggest?

Thank you for your help in completing this evaluation form.

Example of a Single Page Form for Pre- and Post-test

Check Your Knowledge

Unit Blocks in the Classroom

At the beginning of the workshop, please write your answer on the left in the Before column. Then put your sheet away. We will answer the questions again at the end of the session in the After box on the right.

Before	Mark the following True or False	After

_____ Blocks are too expensive for small centers.   _____

_____ Blocks are important learning materials for children of all ages.   _____

_____ Children learn math skills such as shapes and sizes from playing with blocks.   _____

_____ Because blocks are so interesting to children, supervision is not necessary.   _____

_____ Children should always be expected to build something in the block area.   _____

_____ Since block constructions must be cleaned up, there is no way to keep a record of children's work.   _____

_____ Accessories for block play may include cars, trucks, signs, animals, and people.   _____

_____ Unit blocks are proportional (related) in shape and size.   _____

_____ To properly set up a block area, you should have a rug and shelves marked to show where the blocks go.   _____

_____ To introduce blocks to children, the teacher needs only to tell children the rules and what the blocks are called.   _____

_____ The only way to get children to clean up is to require that they do it.   _____

_____ Block play contributes to social development.   _____

_____ Building with symmetry means that the child uses only blocks that are alike.   _____

_____ Children should always be required to put away the blocks at the end of the day.   _____

• •

Please complete this section at the end of the workshop. Use the back of the sheet if you like.

How have your ideas about how to use blocks changed as a result of this workshop?

Now that you have attended this workshop, what will you do differently to enrich block play in your classroom?

Fast Feedback Form

Check-Up Time

Please take a few minutes to complete this form and place it on the registration table during the break. Let me know your reactions to the training to this point. Please write comments in the square beside the factor being rated and under the heading that best describes your reaction until now. Thanks for your input.

Category	Far Better Than I Dreamed	Better Than Expected	I'm OK with Everything So Far	It Needs Some Improvement	I'm Disappointed
Organization of Training					
Pace of the Activities					
Content of the Training					
Opportunities to Learn from Others					
Practical Material I Can Use on the Job					

Please write any additional comments on the back of this sheet.

Fast Feedback Form

Directions: Place an X along the line that describes your reaction to the training thus far.

1. How is the training progressing?

      Too slow for me   Could be faster for me   Fine so far   Too fast for me

_____

2. Is the organization of the training meeting your needs?

      Very little   Could be more relevant   I'm happy with it   Just what I needed

_____

3. Are you getting information you can use?

      Not much   Could be better   I can use some of it   I can use most of it

_____

4. Give me any suggestions that will help me help you!

5. Do you have any questions or problems you would like to have addressed?

6. What information would you like to share with the group?

Contract with Myself

I commit to making these changes in my work with children as a result of the training session that I have attended today. I fully pledge to do everything within my power to improve my work by taking the following steps:

1._____

_____

_____

_____

2._____

_____

_____

_____

3._____

_____

_____

_____

4._____

_____

_____

_____

_____   _____

Signature   Date

Sample Letter to My Instructor

To:

I attended a training session about (put the topic here) on (put the date of training here). Here is some information that I would like to share with you about my work following the training:

I have changed my work in the following ways:

1._____

2._____

3._____

4._____

I have not been able to put these skills and changes in place:

1._____

2._____

3._____

4._____

I suggest the following changes in the training to make it more helpful to attendees like me:

1._____

2._____

3._____

4._____

_____   _____

Signature   Date

Sample Letter to Parents

To Parents of Children in My Classroom:

I attended a training session about (put the topic here) on (put the date of training here). During the session, I became convinced that I could improve my work with children by changing how I conduct some of my class activities. Here is some information that I would like to share with you about my work following the training:

I have changed my work with your children in the following ways:

1._____

2._____

3._____

4._____

I made these changes because: (list several reasons the changes are good for children)

1._____

2._____

3._____

4._____

I will be happy to discuss with you the importance of these changes and how your children are responding and learning through the new methods. Please take a few minutes when you pick up your child to let me tell you more about these exciting changes.

Your child's teacher,

_____   _____

Signature   Date

Word Find
Equipment for toddlers

```
P W K Q T W D I R Y C Y L W C I L P N A H P R I R
T A U C K U D E N O H P E L E T Y O T E J B E N Y
E C T Y C I N H L J U R B X B K X P U Q A Y S F V
X L J Q K L H L D S Y L N A F R W O M E B L O M N
G I G H G N D N H F F M H T I D B R S R A L H G M
X W T E B B G P E C J D Q A S A I P V M T N C N I
Q H F F I Q U M K M D R H I X V T U I I J B A O D
Z G Z E B L R S B Q F C X M S B I N E O O C E U W
A W M Q L E L I I N G C K Q Q S A I H D P N K Z O
H P D T I Q H A F N D S N J G D O F G V S J Z A B
C Q O J O U Z A T Z S X M R E H O G I F C Z A P J
G Y J 1 J J A K S R N M O F C S O K J P J C R S Q
S Q V R I R C Q O T E P F X Y I K O S K A E S T Q
O K J A M O L C B N S U E S W F P O H R T J D Y S
P D P T R B M M J Q T P E U E C E B O R P O A O F
V Z H X V T R I P S I U C B H X U D O B R J E U M
U T G Z E I H R Q M N Z S Q B S N S C A D M B F U
D W W C S X A R S R G Z Z V I Y E Y R H X R P M P
I D X G F B Q O F Z B L C L D P Y H Z P D O A M W
S L H G I H S R F M L E M X A U W Z R R F B N O F
L K D G K Y L S U D O S E H O Z Z C U Z N W S S B
T G R Q N V V D Y Q C X S W W M C B A L L S A F N
O H S A M S D H K L K M D V Z P Z P L E L I U D S
C Q Q T U Y K D F C S A S K W L C R O P M M V H W
B D Q Z R U A Y O F S Y O T G N I D I R V Q C V X
```

Find the words below and circle them in the grid above. They may read left to right, right to left, up and down, of: diagonally in any direction. Two-word answers will have no space between the words and hyphens will be omitted.

BALLS
NESTING BLOCKS
RIDING TOYS
SNAP BEADS

BOARD BOOKS
PUSH PULL TOYS
ROCKING CHAIR
STUFFED ANIMALS

MIRRORS
PUZZLES
SHAPE SORTER
TOY TELEPHONE

Word Find
Scheduling Considerations

```
K G N V A J J A C S R E B Y N I T Q A L B K S X T
V O H N L E A L A D S O A A O P Z Q Y J A S J J R
D D N U R C N N V P E V U E G A W H P T A A W Z A
F X L D G C V R Q D N H S T C C F F B N T Y Z P N
Y O T R C G T A E H E E S T I E U P V E S Z B F S
I X Z N K N A Z C E G T I U L N F A I C G J D O X
C K Q Y R I O O H A W V A B R A E U Y H F E S S T
B E H E S T E W G C I P A I U N Q S O J T U R X I
Z J U A X E M X H T O T B X T T U V W A H G T W O
J E Y V B L Q V I O C N J Q E I J M I A Z S L V N
S D L E H I F E C I L Q S U C S N T E O E S W M S
L C T B T O S C D A T E W I L V I I P R P A O B B
O J H W I T E E Y E J E G D S N F N D Q D M J A I
N V Q E T X R E P E A Y B R I T E S O L L K P C R
J Z Z J D P E R X T E N A R O M E N X R I Y V X X
Q X R Z S U D L H Q D C E J O U R N Q V H H V A L
S Z L J A C L E F J T H S R S J P U T H S Z C B O
B L A U S G R E A I C K J W X P Y Q U N V W X S X
I M A A J V C S V A T I Q S M A L L G R O U P S Z
Y U N E X K N E E D B K T Z K W D A M N M W S T O
J B E X M I L T R R O O D N I M G P X O X G D K Z
R B M C L B A L A N C E T J U Q G K Z M J B P Y B
E X I N D I V I D U A L C O U T D O O R D R V J
R G O T B I J Z W H N A P S N O I T N E T T A H S
B Y P P E B V C K U F D I I F T E C O X I P F O C
```

Find the words below and circle them in the grid above. They may read left to right, right to left, up and down, or diagonally in any direction. Two-word answers will have no space between the words and hyphens will be omitted.

ACTIVE	ACTIVITIES	AGES
ATTENTION SPAN	BALANCE	CHILD INITIATED
CONSISTENT	FLEXIBLE	INDIVIDUAL
INDOOR	MEALS	OUTDOOR
PREDICTABLE	QUIET	REST
ROUTINES	SCHEDULE	SMALL GROUPS
TEACHER INITIATED	TOILETING	TRANSITIONS
UNRUSHED	WEATHER	WHOLE GROUP

Answer Key
Equipment
for Toddlers

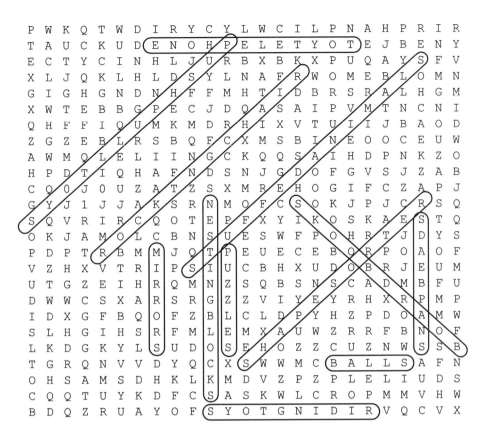

Answer Key
Scheduling
Considerations

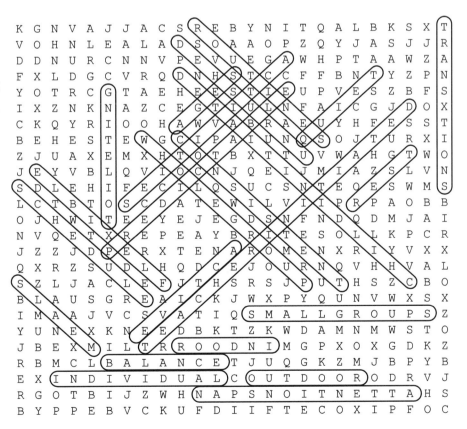

Index

O

Objectives
  defined, 257
Observation activities, 83–84
Occupational symbols, 154
Once a Mouse, by Marcia Brown, 120
Open questions, 168, 174–175
Openings, 26
  defined, 257
Ordering, 86
Ordinal numbers, 85
Organization, 91, 241–244, 260
  handouts, 243–244
Outdoor environment, 101–103
Outline of content, 257
Overhead transparencies, 40, 76–78, 84, 90,
  144–145, 157, 186, 220, 235, 252, 256
  accessories, 149
  creating, 144–145
  defined, 259
  storing, 244
  using, 145
Over-learning, 220–221
  defined, 257

P

Pace, 257
Padding, 162
Paddle balls, 42
Page protectors, 145
Pails, 85
Paints, 227
Panels
  defined, 257
  presentations, 63
Pans, 99
Paper bags, 36, 41
Paper clips, 60, 100–101, 152, 164
Paper plates, 52
Paper towels, 227
  tubes, 74
Paper, 74, 76
  airplanes, 219
  butcher, 172
  chains, 73
  colored, 37
  construction, 86, 89, 113, 121, 133, 172, 239
  heavy, 163–164, 166
  note, 36

shapes, 67
slips, 218
strips, 41, 73
Parachutes, 73
Paraphrasing, 177
Parents
  letters to, 229–230, 296
  meeting evaluation forms, 290
  questionnaires, 198
Parroting, 177
Participants' Bill of Rights, 187
Participation issues, 207–212, 238
  antagonistic participants, 210–211
  distractions, 209–210
  dominators, 211–212
  know-it-alls, 211–212
  latecomers, 209–210
  literacy issues, 209
  negative participants, 211
  reluctant participants, 207–209
  showoffs, 211–212
  side conversations, 209
Partner activities, 46–52
  choosing partners, 50–51
  defined, 258
  worksheets, 48–49
Patterning, 85
Patterns
  doll, 61, 275
  tent cards, 287
Pebbles, 72
Peer pressure, 191–192
Pegboards, 58, 85–86
Pencils, 60, 185, 217, 235
Pennies, 152, 212
Pens, 235
Peppers, 153
Performance
  changes, 195–196
  concerns, 191
Personality
  bags, 36
  clashes, 213–214
Peter Rabbit, by Beatrix Potter, 120
Petunia, by Roger Duvoisin, 120
Phobias, 186
Photographs, 40, 198, 219
Physical environment, 181–183
  assessing, 183